BEYOND HUMANISM

Essays in the Philosophy
of Nature

By
CHARLES HARTSHORNE

GLOUCESTER, MASS.

PETER SMITH

1975

Library of Congress Catalog Card Number 38–11150
Copyright © 1937 by Willett, Clark and Company

Reprinted, 1975, by Permission of
Charles Hartshorne

ISBN: 0-8446-5116-8

To

WILLIAM JAMES

who was equally unconvinced by the idealisms
and the materialisms of his day, and who more
than any other man startled and heartened men
to seek for a better philosophy

AND TO

CHARLES S. PEIRCE

James' friend, the philosopher-scientist, "scally-
wag," successless American and unpragmatic
pragmatist, whose brain conceived in the nineteenth century the logical principles by which
the twentieth century can live.

PREFACE TO THE BISON BOOK EDITION

In the thirty-two years since the writing of these essays, the philosophical scene has changed in many ways. Writings by Russell, Dewey, Santayana, Carnap, and Moore are less in the center of interest; while those by Wittgenstein, Ryle, Austin, Strawson, Heidegger, Peirce, and (in this country at least) Whitehead are nearer the center. The influence of formal logic is perhaps greater than it was, but what Ryle calls "informal logic," or some call "linguistic analysis," has become still more influential. Distrust of metaphysics, except in some very attenuated form, is probably stronger than it was. So far as metaphysics in anything like "the grand manner" is done at all, it seems due in large measure to the writings of Whitehead and Peirce and the writings and teaching of Weiss and myself. The effect of John Findlay's brilliant speculative mind is also beginning to be felt.

I hope that today I could be fairer to other points of view than my own, and more careful to avoid special pleading. Also I hope that today I have a clearer grasp of the logical structure of many of the problems. Nevertheless, I cannot find myself in sharp substantive disagreement with that former self of mine. I still view man, nature, and God in much the same way and for much the same reasons, although I think that the argument can be strengthened in certain ways. On the other hand, I am more aware of the diversity of philosophical attitudes which human life seems to make more or less inevitable. If there is such a thing as metaphysical insight, to have it is perhaps a privilege that is not extended to all. Still less can those who have it feel equally at home with any particular linguistic fashion of expressing the insight.

The chief retractions I am inclined to make are terminological. I have long ceased to call my position "pantheism," since I hold that classical theism, classical pantheism, and what I sometimes call "panentheism" form a triad, any two members of which are about as far apart as any other two. Classical theism and classical pantheism deny contingency, and the possibility of a real increase in content, to deity, whereas my panentheism asserts of God both necessity and contingency, both immutability and openness to novelty.

Also, long ago I decided to concede the term "naturalism" to those whose views are still farther from classical theism or pantheism than mine are. God is not "natural," if that means that he has had an origin, a beginning, or that his very existence is contingent. True, it may be held that nature as such is primordial and noncontingent, but it remains controversial what is left when we abstract from the idea of nature all those features which, in my view, have had an origin, including all empirically testable laws of nature. If supernaturalism is the view that reality has two levels—the level of contingent, generated entities and the level of whatever is necessary and ungenerated; or again the level of beings whose excellence can be exceeded by other beings and the level of the being whose excellence can be exceeded only by the being itself, and in some respects not even by itself—then I am an unabashed supernaturalist. My later writings make this clear.

There is also the methodological question. "Naturalism" means, to many, that all knowledge of reality is empirically testable. I hold that only the contingent aspects of reality are knowable in this way. In addition, while God, in my view, has contingent as well as necessary aspects, there is a radical limitation upon possible human understanding of the divine reality as contingent. God's awareness of contingent truth is itself (as the laws of modal logic require) contingent; so that we can take our own items of probable contingent truth and say that God must have contingent knowledge of them so far as true, but in what more comprehensive, distinct, and concrete way he knows them, along with unimaginably many other items, remains beyond us.

It seems probable that many more persons now think somewhat as I do about God and the world than in 1936. Also, while metaphysical speculation as such is not very popular among philosophers, the reasons advanced against it are, for the most part, only vaguely related to my "neoclassical" metaphysics. Some of the critical responses to certain of Whitehead's doctrines come close to constituting definite objections to that metaphysics. However, not only is Whitehead still widely ignored, but he is also only one extremely gifted and well equipped explorer of the general territory of "process philosophy." The possibilities of a constructive metaphysics of process are not exhausted by Bergson, James, Peirce, and Whitehead—not even if we add Husserl and Heidegger, or go back to Schelling and Hegel.

Much of the current criticism of theism as such is directed to supposed implications which logically follow only if neoclassical concepts are not adopted. According to those concepts, God is the eminent, but never the sole, agent in what happens, even in inanimate nature. His decisions literally take their chances with the more or less free creaturely responses to him and to other creatures. The only God I think

I can conceive is the one Einstein rejected, a "dice-throwing God." It is with no sorrow that I have observed the increasing tolerance for the idea of randomness (within limits, of course). The remark, often heard, "Quantum mechanics, as it stands, may be only temporary" is hardly relevant here, since there are any number of ways in which this mechanics may prove less than the whole and exact truth, without its turning out that the remedy lies in returning to classical determinism. I see nothing but prejudice to support that anticipation. And when it is said that at worst physics only shows that we cannot know an absolute causal order determining the details of process, I am content to add: then the only good, or apparently good, reason there ever was for a strictly deterministic metaphysics is done away with, since a suitably qualified determinism has all the *philosophical* merits of an unqualified one, without the disadvantages which Spinoza and Kant, in spite of themselves, and Bergson, James, Peirce, and Whitehead explicitly set forth.

Essentially we still face the same issues that we did three decades ago. That we must now be more careful about what we "do with words" should only mean that we can do a better job. We still have to deal with Marxism, psychoanalysis, emergent materialism, the dispute between metaphysicians and antimetaphysicians, theists and antitheists, the relations between minds (or experiences) and physical or extended reality, or between macroscopic and microscopic entities, or the logic of the causal principle. While we talk about words, these matters do not go away—though we may in a sense go away from them. And they are, in some respects at least, too general to be scientific or empirical problems. In a broad sense they are logical. In short, problems for philosophers.

CHARLES HARTSHORNE

The University of Texas

CONTENTS

Contents

PART ONE

HUMANISM and HUMAN NEEDS

THERE are few human beings, who, when they think of themselves in relation to the universe, are without a sense of curiosity, of wonder, and even of awe; and in so far as this leads them into speculation, they become philosophers. . . . And surely the questions that rise to the lips of every child should always be remembered — remembered if only as indications of the profoundest of all human needs. Overlook those needs, forget those questions, and you are likely to become satisfied with art that is petty, reasoning that is pedantic, and knowledge that is not bread but a stone.

—*L. H. Myers* [1]

I

GOD OR NATURE

IN THE best sense, " humanism " is simply the expression of an interest in man; in the worst sense, it is this interest become a monomania, excluding interest in anything else. In so far as it develops such exclusiveness, humanism contradicts its own intent, for interest in man implies interest in those things in which man is interested; and in what is man not interested? Darwin devoted himself to the study of earthworms; the astronomer gives heed to objects inconceivably remote in space-time. To indicate the scope of human interest we must speak with Plato of " all time and all existence." Hence when Terence made his famous assertion that nothing human was alien to him, he was saying by implication that nothing whatever was wholly alien and indifferent to him. To be a citizen of the entire human world is excellent; but the only way really to do so is to be a citizen of the universe — as the old Stoics, and in some degree even the Epicureans, recognized.

But superficially it appears simpler and safer to concentrate upon man, our " proper study." It is this specious simplification, of which there are all degrees, that constitutes humanism in the sense intended in this book. Humanist exclusiveness has two aspects: one, a narrowness of interest; the other, a doctrine which rationalizes, more or less unconsciously encourages, this narrowness. In effect, the doctrine is always a theory that the non-human portions of nature, and nature as a whole, need not interest us because they are not intrinsically interesting — however useful they may be as means to our ends. They are interesting as a bank check is, for consequences which human behavior can cause to flow from them. Calverton puts it with almost brutal clearness:

> . . . Man will find a new strength and a higher form of courage in viewing it [nature] as neither friend nor foe, but simply as an outer force or substance that he can convert into malleable forms which can be hammered and chiseled and cemented and harnessed in ways advantageous to his exploitation.[2]

Other humanists state the matter less harshly and negatively. Dewey, for instance, advocates a " pious " sense of our dependence upon the forces of nature and of nature as a whole inclusive of us and therefore not wholly alien to us in character. But this position is on the very edge of humanism as I have defined it. In general, humanists hold that, so far as we know, man is the highest type of individual in existence, and that therefore if there is any proper object of religious devotion, any real " God," it can only be humanity considered in its noblest aspirations and capacities, together with nature so far as expressed in and serviceable to humanity. Humanism is thus not so much atheism as a reinterpretation of God, not so much irreligion as an attempt to separate the sound human kernel of religion from its supernatural husks. It is the faith of humanists that the essential values of religion are independent of these husks. Thus Calverton speaks of " superior substitutes for religion and the gods."

Humanism, so conceived, amounts to two claims. First, it implies that, except for the animals and for the speculative possibility of inhabitants upon other heavenly bodies, man is evidently alone in the universe, dependent for friendship upon his own kind. Second, it maintains that the recognition of this loneliness will aid rather than hinder the good life here upon earth. In naturalism, as opposed to supernaturalism, the humanist finds not only truth, but the truth that makes us free and strengthens and enlightens us for the tasks of living.

The position which I wish to defend against humanism is not supernaturalism in any usual sense. If by " nature " we mean the average quality of things in our environment, or the mere collection of natural entities, then any God worthy of the name must be supernatural or transcendent. But nature as a whole may be an individual in a deeper sense than a collection can be, and with a very different quality from that of its parts; and this quality may be divine. Supernaturalism and humanism are, I hold, two aspects of the same error, the mistaken notion that nature, in her non-human portions and characters, is wholly subhuman. Not finding the superhuman in nature, the supernaturalist seeks it " beyond " nature; the humanist, in the unrealized potentialities of man. Could both perceive the living divinity which in a certain sense *is* nature, the one would cease to locate the object of his worship in a vacuum, and the other would cease to deify man and romantically to exaggerate the good and underestimate the evil in man. Theoretically and practically both would, I believe, have reached a superior position. But as long as nature is so conceived that its divinity is concealed, the choice is between two non-natural Gods (for it always turns out that the humanist sees in man something more than is actually there, even potentially), and neither of these Gods is satisfactory. The strength of each doctrine lies chiefly in the weakness of the other. Yet both agree that there is no third possibility. Thus these opposites, like so many others, unwittingly conspire to support each other.

The difficulty of the third position, that nature in her

highest non-human aspects is God, is that we have insufficient knowledge of these aspects clearly to see their divine character. Humanism can say that the highest human attributes constitute God, its advantage being that these human attributes are at any rate known with some definiteness. Supernaturalism can say that the beyond is God, its advantage being that the beyond is not definitely known to be other than divine — for it is not, in reality, known at all. Nature is neither so indefinite and passive a concept as the " transcendent," nor so definitely known to be admirable as " humanity." It follows that only an improved understanding of the higher aspects of nature can enable the doctrine of a natural but superhuman — and even, in a sense, perfect — God to take the place of the other two doctrines. In the meantime, those who require very definite knowledge of the object of worship will be humanists, and those who care more that God shall be really worshipful or divine than that he shall be really knowable will be transcendentalists. Yet man is not really worthy of our final devotion; and the transcendent, in the old sense, is nothing. That these things are so would, I believe, be generally admitted were it not that the failure to find God above man, and yet within nature, forces us to try to believe that we have found him either in the best that we know in ourselves, or in that which, since we do not know what it is, may be better than anything we know. The best clearly known reality, or the most ambiguous and empty unreality, are thus the easiest places to locate the supreme good.

It seems plain that the supernaturalist way is the greater obstacle to intellectual advance. It operates beyond the reach of evidence, whereas humanism pretends to deal with the known or knowable situation of man. In so far humanism is the first step toward a real solution. To progress beyond humanism it is only necessary to see that the human situation is other than as humanism supposes. In particular we may ask whether there is any defensible halfway house between the crass pragmatism of a Calverton — surely inadequate to human needs — and the intellectual, aesthetic, and moral love of nature as the body of God, in all parts having some degree, however slight, of kinship with ourselves, and as a whole immeasurably superior to us, and hence worthy of our highest reverence.

The great phrase of Spinoza, *deus sive natura,* " God or nature," expresses this conception of nature as worthy of unstinted admiration and boundless interest. It is also a key to tolerance in the modern world. For all men feel some of this appeal of nature, so that in so far as God is defined as the lovableness of nature, no man, not even Calverton, is an absolute atheist. Only the pure supernaturalist, who claims to distinguish utterly between God and God's creation, and the pure pragmatic humanist, who alleges that there is no hint of divinity in nature, appear to disagree in all their positive contentions (negatively they agree to a suspicious extent!). Yet that the creation is his implies that it resembles the Creator in some degree; and that nature can be rationally controlled implies that she has an intelligible order, and this is, for all theologians, part of nature's godlikeness. So there is really no one who cannot see some meaning in the phrase, " God or nature."

If we have the will to intellectual cooperation, we shall hesitate long before indulging in dogmatic proclamation of either the absolutely supernatural or the merely pragmatic natural. The difficulties which both naturalists and supernaturalists have felt with " pantheism " may be real but due to errors in our understanding of nature or in the logical or metaphysical categories — such as those of Spinoza — which have been applied to the problem.

Today, when both conceptions of nature and theories of logic are changing as rapidly as at any time since the ancient

Greeks, it is a revelation of intellectual incompetence to regard the question of the relations of the religious object to nature as having been settled by the older discussions. Theologians themselves have in the past few years been abandoning the old supernaturalism in greater numbers than ever before (in spite of the neosupernaturalism of German theology), and scientists have grown incomparably more critical of the traditional forms of naturalism. The only reasonable working hypothesis for our time is that the old questions are too badly formulated for any of the old answers to possess validity. For instance, I may be asked if I deny the transcendence of God. I should have to answer that I deny that any traditional definition of transcendence — or, for that matter, of immanence — is unambiguous. According to current metaphysics every individual is immanent in and transcends all others, and the transcendence and immanence of God is the supreme case of this double relation. I should reply also that I am very confident that God transcends " nature " as nature is conceived by supernaturalists. In short, only those capable of confronting the problem of God or of nature with fresh wonder, without arrogant confidence in their scientific or theological sophistication, only those who with the age can be intellectually born again, are likely to contribute to the discussion of this problem.

A few Barthians — and even they are chary of the term " supernaturalism," but are, I fear, nevertheless caught in the old categories — and a few atheist Marxians — and even they might remember that Marx himself was, by his own account, " not a Marxian " — may be useful as stimuli; but sanity and profitable discussion depend upon neither group's becoming too numerous. We should remember Spinoza and his view of the study of nature as " the intellectual love of God." Or the Stoics, from whom in part Spinoza learned this natural piety. Or — perhaps even my less pious readers will permit me to add — we should remember Jesus, whose love for man was compatible with his seeing the reflection of superhuman values in flowers, animals, sun, and rain, and whose preferred cathedrals were the mountains and the desert.

The heart of Christendom has been with Jesus — *deus est caritas* — but its intellect has been with Spinoza — *deus sive natura.* The medieval attempt to unite heart and intellect in supernaturalism did not succeed; and Spinozistic pantheism was too one-sided to satisfy men even as much as medievalism had done. Our good fortune is that we no longer have to choose between Spinoza and Jesus, for it can be proved that the reasons which prevented Spinoza from regarding nature not only as God but as the God of love are erroneous in the light of the new science and the new logic. Spinoza today would not be a Spinozist but a Whiteheadian. And I dare say that Jesus today would not be very tender toward a theology which has left mankind so confused and comfortless and unable to profit spiritually by the unselfish labors of the men of science If the man of today leaves humanism, it should be to go beyond and forward, not back to those things which the humanist has so acutely criticized and found wanting. If we can see nothing providential in the last three hundred years of earnest but increasingly destructive inquiry into the logic of traditional theology, can we reasonably assert a belief in Providence at all? And on the other hand, if we really love humanity can we be indifferent to the new possibility that the sympathetic, social nature of man, with its ideal of perfect love, can be made to interpret also the intellectual relation of man to nature upon which all his practical power depends? The man who will not try to give fair-minded attention to this possibility makes us wonder how it can be either man or God in whom he has faith.

In any case, I believe, there are enough open-minded scientists and theologians to insure that the discussion will go forward, perhaps to lay a foundation for future civilization as enduring as that effected by the church Fathers, who worked out the best available compromise between the only philosophy they had and their religious inspiration. But we work with far more freedom than they — provided political tyranny does not overtake us. Fortunately the outlines of the new view are almost finished. Religious metaphysics has just gone through one of the greatest transformations in its history, just as has natural science. The reconstruction is mostly accomplished; what is lacking is effective exposition, application, criticism, diffusion, defense. These require perhaps lesser talents, but in far greater number and variety. Sooner or later the new vision will receive the widespread attention which it deserves. Not much longer, we may hope, will the masses of men be required to choose between alternatives both of which, by modern criteria, are almost equally wrong.

Concerning revelation and popular fundamentalism, I would in some measure agree with the humanists. The more the rational elements of culture, that is, science and critical metaphysics, advance, the less need or excuse there will be, it seems to me, for authoritative revelation as a rival or supplement to knowledge. We need inspiration as well as proof; but infallible inspiration seems a meaningless idea. Even if God dictated the Bible, it would be of no help until he taught us how to translate it into modern language and thought and life, and if we were taught to do this infallibly, we should acquire a degree of insight clearly incompatible with human limitations.

Popular fundamentalism is either a negative evil, a callowness of culture which should be kindly assisted to cure itself; or a positive evil, an unloving and therefore unchristian dogmatism which is to be greeted, like every other form of arrogant power, with indignation and ridicule. An infallible dogma or book or church is a boast or a bludgeon, not a call to comradeship in human strength or human modesty and repentance. It may well be that in all of nature and history the Christian record is the chief single source of inspiration, the chief expression of Providence so far as man is concerned. But to say more than this for it is to contradict the spirit of the record itself, whatever justification from the letter there may be.

Christianity is not a code or a scientific metaphysics; it is, at its best, the sublimest inspirational source of true ideas and good acts that we have. To belittle this sublimity with literal-minded claims to finality is an old but tragic mistake. Call if you will, the Christian story the center or turning point in history, as Tillich does, but do not make Providence a pedant!

Nor are the utterances of reason in science or metaphysics to be regarded as iron-rigid against the pressure of inspiration. It will not do, for instance, to scoff at or overconfidently explain away men's feeling that they are genuine initiators of new causal series, even though the science, or the philosophy of science, of the moment has decided against this idea. Inspiration, intuition, on so fundamental a matter is not to be brushed aside so lightly. It now turns out that the spokesmen for science were in this matter not nearly so sure of their ground as they long seemed to be. But inspiration was flouted even longer by religious metaphysicians who claimed, by virtue of their Aristotle or Plotinus, to have discovered that God does not, except in a Pickwickian sense, have purposes, or sympathize with men in their joys and sorrows — because then he could not be immutable, or " pure actuality." Human beings do not slip into omniscience so easily that they can afford altogether to neglect any type of clue which may serve to check the method they may be primarily relying upon. We must revere nothing if reverence means rigidity, paralysis of inquiry. We must revere everything that sincere men revere, if reverence means respect made mobile by curiosity and flexible by modesty.

Another problem to be briefly mentioned here is the relation of theistic belief to ecclesiastical institutions. The question of God's existence seems too clearly distinct from the question whether or not we wish to have churches for any decision concerning the latter to play the crucial role in deciding the former. The question of group worship and its leaders, professional or otherwise, is a practical question at a considerable remove from the theoretical one of the basic nature of this great universe. The practical problem is a topic more for sociology than for philosophy. Although the chapters which follow discuss human needs, including social ones, it is a main conclusion of these discussions that man needs at times to forget himself and survey the whole of which he is a member, using his humanity as an observation platform, not as the scene to be observed.

Of course, too, there are those who will say that every effort to find a way of reconciling science and religion is treachery to science, since religion has always been the foe of science. And there are those who regard every encouragement to religion as an aid to social and political oppression. But here again the question for our day is not the traditional one. In actual fact, as even Russell concedes, the great foe of science in the present world is political tyranny; and this tyranny is also the greatest threat to religious liberty, and therefore to genuine religion. Against the menace of dictatorial nationalism science, and the Protestant religions at least, belong on the same side. In Germany it is not science that seems to have offered the greatest resistance! But it is also true that religion has too often hampered both intellectual and political freedom and development; and this is one reason why I have no desire to give aid to any merely traditional form of religious thought. Theological revival without reform, and just such reform as is required to render theology genuinely and unambiguously favorable to science and social justice, would be a misfortune. But there is no way to prove in advance that such reform is not possible, and consequently the new theism must be examined on its merits. To try to prove from the forms and uses of theistic religion in the past that such religion must be antiscientific and anti-social is like trying to prove from the early association of medicine with magic and priestly power that medicine is necessarily superstitious and socially invidious. The question is not what has been, but what can be. And neither scientists nor socialists ought to be the persons to refuse to recognize the distinction.

NOTES

1 L. H. Myers, *The Root and the Flower* (Harcourt, Brace & Co., Inc., 1934), p. 10.

2 V. F. Calverton, *The Passing of the Gods* (Charles Scribner's Sons, 1934), preface.

II

HUMANISM AS DISINTEGRATION

IF RELIGION, or any satisfactory philosophy of life, has as its goal the integration of the personality ("salvation"), then humanism is a very partial and inadequate religion. No matter from what angle the question is viewed, integration by humanism will show itself incomplete and unsatisfactory.

In terms of time and of our interest in the future the humanist confronts a dilemma. Either he has faith that the human race will last forever — in spite of astronomy, which predicts the eventual uninhabitability of the planet (to mention only one consideration) — or he looks forward to the ultimate extinction of mankind and the complete blotting out from the universe of all the values we have striven to realize. If the humanist adopts the first alternative, then I do not see how he can bring the charge of overcredulity against the believer in divine Providence. All the available evidence is against the immortality of the human race. At all times that race is exposed to some risk of extinction, and a risk, however small, when *endlessly repeated,* is virtual certainty of the threatened disaster. If the humanist does not believe in racial immortality, then he looks forward to a time when all our achievements will be exactly as if they had never been. And what will these achievements have mattered if the very memory of our joys and sorrows, and of all joys and sorrows — that is, of all values — will have vanished? The man who really adopts this conception of the future cannot be an integrated personality, and the more genuinely he grasps its meaning, the more must he fail to be so.

Of course we need not think often about the long-run future. If we were animals we should not think about it at all. And I grant that it is necessary and healthy that we should slip often and for long periods into animal innocence upon this matter. But what is neither animal nor worthily human is to fail to adjust ourselves to whatever the long-run future appears to be when we do look at it. What we then see will be there when we no longer see it, and its implications will not be nullified by inattention. Now what adjustment to the final destruction of all values is conceivable? The thought can inspire no useful action. There is literally nothing to be done about it. Some will say they see in the thought reason to value the hours of human life all the more, since there will not be an endless number of them. But this is confused thinking. For though each hour will be a more significant fraction of a finite whole than of an infinite whole, the difficulty is that there will be no whole whatever, since when the series is completed it will also be destroyed without a trace. The thought of the world's end cannot encourage the will to life, but only the will to death — if there could really be such a thing. The only rational effect of the thought would be to paralyze our entire being — and this is not a rational action, but simply a ceasing to be able to act. The fact thus seems to be that life and the thought of the absolute end of all life are altogether incompatible, and hence this thought is an impossibility, a thought that cannot really be borne. It is a pseudo-idea. If the eternity of life is a "vital lie," it is an inevitable one and in no vitally significant sense a lie. We adjust ourselves to life, not to its absence. The notion of a lifeless universe seems to have meaning at all only because any *particular* form of life in which we have an interest — except the eternal living source of life — might conceivably be or have been absent from the universe.

The matter can be approached otherwise. It is often said that though life may end it will be good while it lasts, and if it is good it is really good, and what comes after will not make it less or more so. With a certain qualification, this may be granted. The qualification is that when the good present becomes past, it still must be a good thing that when the past was present it was a good present. Otherwise it will be false that what has come after has not unmade the good in question. As the past event, real in the universe for all its pastness, its goodness must still be real. Even if you say it need not be good now that the past was good, still it must be *true* now, and what is the truth of a proposition about a value but the reality of the value asserted? In short, the past must be capable of containing value. How does it do so?

Consulting experience, which both humanists and theists often ignore, we find that the only ascertainable value of the past is in its preservation through memory in the present. In the recollective background of the personality something at least of the riches of the past exists still. But when all of life is in the past, what then? What will it mean then that "man had a good time in his day"? Nature will not know it, he will not know it; in what sense will it even be a fact? To say that such an eventuation may be ahead of us, that the very last moment of the future may after becoming present immediately pass into nothingness, and with it all the past moments of whose values it is the cumulative sum and depository, is to talk sheer nonsense. It means that something may become absolutely nothing. Humanistic naturalism thus can give no intelligible account of the relation of past values (or of the past generally) to time. This is true, though less glaringly so, even if we allow humanists to suppose that human life, or something else of the kind, will be perpetually produced in nature. For human memory is a very incomplete storehouse of past values, and cannot adequately explain what is meant by the belief that these values really were; i.e., though past, they are not now simply nothing but are somehow still contained in the universe of real facts. Divine memory explains this perfectly:

> God has said, " Ye shall fail and perish,
> But the joy ye have felt this night
> I shall keep in my heart and cherish
> When the worlds have passed in night." [1]

Then indeed is it true that no future can nullify the goodness of our living. The humanist may object that that assumption does not save the goodness for us but only for God. But if we can live for posterity, who are not real parts of us, nor even real existences now, how much more should it be possible to live for God, who is even now identical with the dim cosmic background of ourselves — dim to us, but in that other focus brilliantly lighted! Moreover, God is the guarantee that some posterity or other of finite creatures, not necessarily exactly human, but more like us than God is, will always be produced in a world in which life-creation is the basic process. In an infinity of conceivable ways our living may contribute to the living that comes after us, the whole always integrated and summated in the living of God. To this conception of the future one can adjust oneself by continuing to feel the worth of his life no matter what seems likely to happen to him or the human race. What other conception can pass logically as the conceptualization of this adjustment? And what other adjustments can there be which are not maladjustments, simply evils?

The habit of failing to distinguish between the finite and the ultimate — which is the essence of humanism — is shown in an extreme form in the almost childish notion that the thing to do about the distant doom of humanity, when we think about it at all, is simply to be brave about it. Plato would have smiled at this feeble reasoning — Plato who distinguished between courage and mere folly. For when the question is how life, on a certain assumption, can be intelligibly conceived to have any value whatever, it is no answer to talk about the particular value of courage. Yet this sophistical answer is all that there is to Russell's " Free Man's Worship " [2] conceived as bearing on the present question. And Russell is one of the rare humanists who have the candor to ask the question. The theist can indeed be brave about the human fate, not because he sees no tragedy in it, but because he does not see sheer tragedy, pure and unredeemed, but rather sees the same sort of mixture of evil and good which characterizes existence everywhere, and bravely forces himself to dwell upon the brighter possibilities sufficiently to endure the darker. In this he will show the only real courage, courage through understanding and expectation of some good, even if only the good of knowing afterward, or of others' knowing, that one has not failed to do one's best. In the face of *absolute* tragedy neither courage nor defiance nor even fear would have any significance, but only total paralysis of thought through absolute discouragement, and hence cessation, of all interests. Humanists are forever reasoning as if the ultimate background of value, within which relative matters of more and less value can be estimated, had been provided for by their hypothesis, and are forever translating questions about God, which are questions about this background, into relative terms of the foreground. But their hypothesis provides no background and cannot do so, for it is couched only in relative terms.

A beautiful expression of the problem is found in the letters of W. H. Hudson:

A sea . . . high, fine cliffs and a long stretch of yellow sand at low water with a thousand bare-legged children at the old everlasting game with the sea. *They*, the children, are beautiful and their old joy is beautiful to see and only the men with the mentally diseased liver, whom we call pessimists, would feel sad at the sight, sad because these are not the children of last year and of a thousand years past, but are new to the sands and in another year will be gone, to be succeeded by others and others till there is no more any sea or any child or even an earth.[3]

The " diseased liver " is not to be cured by a forgetting of our ultimate situation in the universe, and of our racial mortality. Hudson's is too candid a mind to slur over this difficulty.

Let anyone read Hudson's account of his mother in *Far Away and Long Ago,* and then think of all the mothers, perhaps not less wondrously lovable, whose sons had not the genius to immortalize them, and ask himself if the significance of these forgotten lives is not infinitely increased by the assumption that the universe does not forget but forever treasures them and whatever beautiful, and likewise ultimately perishable, human memories of them may have lingered after their death.

The personality, as finite, must be integrated with other aspects of the infinite than infinite future time. In many senses man is the finite-infinite being. His thoughts " wander through eternity," survey "all time and all existence," refer to the " universe," and thus far are equivalent to any god's. And more than that, man conceives the maximum instance of the idea of value, the " perfect." Yet this infinite scope of existence and value is not fully possessed, and never can be. This tantalizing discrepancy is the reason for the indefinite possibilities of discontent inherent in human life. Animals have finite wants. Satisfy these, and the animal is satisfied. But man is satisfied only if, in addition to favorable circumstances, he can adjust himself to the fact that he always knows a better than he either has or is, an infinitely better in fact. Only by virtue of this spark of divine power could Schopenhauer or any atheist pass judgment upon the world and find it abysmally bad.

If the infinite in man is not in any aspect a real superhuman being with which he can identify himself — though vaguely and inadequately — through sympathy (which because of its inadequacy must also be humility), then he is mightily tempted to persuade himself either that there is no infinite in him at all, or that this infinite can be effectively possessed by him. The two come to much the same thing, since a finite which is not contrasted with any absolute standard is not clearly seen in its finitude, and whatever finite thing happens to be of supreme interest at the moment will be quasi-infinite. Thus the alternative to religion in the true sense is megalomania in some form, the deifying of something human; or else it is the discouragement of man's vital impulses by the notion of an absolute so alien to man that he can derive no sympathetic satisfaction, no participating joy and fellowship from its existence, but must rather seek to annihilate himself as irrelevant to ultimate value. The Freudian " death instinct " may be significant in this connection. Only if the infinite is on one side actual as infinite love, though on another side (as we shall see), its value is indeed potential, not actual, can it be recognized as the spur to endless endeavor and creation, and at the same time as the key to contentment in the midst of more or less uncontrollable circumstances. No one is jealous of a superior with whom he really sympathizes, whose superiority he thoroughly understands. But the only intelligible superiority is itself superior understanding and love. Divine love is the only energizing and at the same time sobering answer to the paradox of man as the knower, and hence in some sense transcender, yet not transcender, of his own limitations!

A unified person is a synthesis of knowledge and love. This synthesis is inhibited by humanism. For only humanity can be deeply loved by a humanist, whereas the knowledge required for the realization of humanistic ends must embrace all nature. The humanist must *know* all the principal parts of nature, but he can literally *love* at most only his fellows and the animals, and the latter much less than humanity. Of course the humanist can feel the beauty of nature and experience curiosity concerning it, but there is nothing in his theory to exalt these experiences to love, properly so called; that is, sympathetic identification with, living the life of, another sentient or rational being. Yet this love has played an immense, and for all we know indispensable, role in stimulating that science whose products humanists are so desirous of multiplying. Scientists have generally loved nature in that explicit fashion which involves the imputation of feelings or thoughts to the object loved. Darwin loved animals as fellow creatures; the physicist likes to think he is reading the thoughts of a mathematically minded God. In this way the intellectual and the sympathetic-social natures of men of science have been integrated into the all-embracing attitude of religious love. To the extent that humanists approach this attitude, the only complete integration of thought and emotion, they will also approach theism. For God is, according to the new theism, simply nature as literally and profoundly lovable, and not merely as pleasant to our senses or interesting for us to think about. We have high authority for saying that something like this is the secret of science. Says Einstein:

The cosmic religious experience is the strongest and the noblest driving force behind scientific research. No one who does not appreciate the terrific exertions, . . . the devotion without which pioneer creations in scientific thought cannot come into being, can judge the strength of the feeling out of which alone such work, turned away as it is from immediate practical life, can grow. What a deep faith in the rationality of the structure of the world, what a longing to understand even a small glimpse of the reason revealed in the world, there must have been in Kepler and Newton.[4]

It is true that Einstein says his God is impersonal, but this does not greatly weaken the argument. For, apart from the fact that few of the greatest scientists have been so Spinozistic as Einstein on this point, it can be shown in Einstein's own words that the impersonality referred to is the most unhumanistic aspect of his religion — being one with his sense of " the vanity of human desires and aims." [5] Also we are entitled to infer an element of non-integration since, after all, Einstein does take human values seriously and gives himself to human causes. The only final integration here is in the realization of a Will which affirms human aims and also affirms the whole ordered cosmos as the fulfillment of larger aims.

A biographical historian of science declares, with excellent documentation:

Copernicus, Kepler, Galileo, Newton, Leibniz, and the rest did not merely believe in God in an orthodox sort of way, they believed that their work told humanity more about God than had been known before. If men had not wanted to know about God, it is highly doubtful if they would have worried to know about nature.[6]

The whole biography of science strongly suggests that knowledge is fundamentally love, and by no means love only of man, but love of nature: the animals, the subanimal particles, the eternal Creator more or less incompletely and subconsciously revealed to the scientist's delighted vision. And this thought throws light upon the discouraging slowness with which the spiritual vision of the scientist is assimilated by the ordinary man who, without the delight of extraordinary creative powers or experimental opportunities, is more in need than even the scientist of seeing *why* nature is worthy of rapt, disinterested (not merely pragmatic) attention. Will he ever see this if he is forever told that nature is merely a system of crinkles in space-time, and that all appearances in nature of free individuality, or of the deliberate production of beautiful forms — such as the marvelous wave pattern which is aesthetically so superior to the monotony of rigidly continuous action — is baseless fancy or " meaningless " nonsense? I do not believe it. Nor is this to the ordinary man's discredit. Naturally we cannot all be satisfied, as most scientists themselves are not, with the mere spatio-temporal outlines which are the official deliverances of physics. We wish to know how these are related to qualitative and meaningful properties, not primarily with a view to finding partiality to man, some promise that the course of events will be steered to suit his convenience, but in search of a satisfaction less stupidly unimaginative and more generous than that, the discovery of something worth while in the world apart from man.

Primitive man used animals to his own ends, but he did far more than that: he admired and loved them — in the somewhat fanciful form in which they existed in his mind — and derived from them much partly disinterested and adventurous joy. And more or less all things were animals for him, so that this more than pragmatic interest was a great factor in the life of the savage. Not allies merely in the struggle to live were the things of nature, but much of the color and stuff and romance of the living itself, by virtue of their own other than merely human aliveness. All this we are now to lose because, forsooth, engineering is a better way of controlling nature than are magic, the telling of fables, or prayer.

The fables and the prayer were much more than presumptive controls; they were in part also that for the sake of which it was worth while to control the course of events. Nor were they or can they ever be " mere poetry," enjoyed but not believed. They need not have been nor need they in future be believed to be the literal and precise truth; but if they are not thought to indicate in more or less free and extravagant and riotous fashion aspects of nature which at least *might be* really there no less than the bare outlines described by physics, their only remaining value will lie in the realization that men once did believe in them. We may perhaps enjoy nature poetry we think is wholly fanciful, but we shall hardly write it. In his *The Concept of Nature in Nineteenth Century Poetry,* Joseph Warren Beach furnishes evidence of the truth of this assertion. We of today are much more likely to write about the coming revolution in human affairs — for the time being perhaps a more suitable occupation.

It seems almost to justify the worst caricatures of pragmatism when a pragmatist judges the belief in the essential spirituality of nature merely by its tendency to promote or hinder technological advance, without even troubling to prove that it is *not* an aid to such advance, or even the chief condition of it. Religion, theistic religion, is more than a device for controlling nature or society; it is the great undertone and overtone of life itself, that with which alone the void of infinite time, the unknown parts of space, and the other supreme dimensions of existence disclosed to man by thought can express and confirm the values in the finite foreground of life instead of negating or endlessly dwarfing them. The *infinite* frame of the little picture is inescapably 'there. If it is empty of value, the picture is of vanishing beauty; if it is at best a mere question mark, the result for us is the same, since the picture also is then indeterminate to an indefinite extent. We escape this result only because we contrive to bury ourselves in " animal faith," that is, we almost succeed — through the suppression of thought — in taking the picture, as it were, out of the frame of infinity; or because what we really believe or fail to believe about the frame may not be that which we say to ourselves or others we believe or do not believe.

Humanism condemns us to a lack of integration within knowledge itself. For just as God is nature as infinitely lovable, so he is nature as infinitely intelligible. To say nature is godless is to say that it is not basically intelligible. The only thing that fully explains itself to a purposive rational mind is a purposive rational mind; everything else suggests the need for explanation. To ask, " Why is purpose? " is plainly absurd. Or again, we " understand " when we see the unity of the diverse. Now the more unified the world is conceived to be, the more it is conceived to approach the maximum case in which all diversity is embraced in a single experience integrated by a single purpose or value. No other form of unity approaches this in degree. All other conceivable forms are, as Kant pointed out, loose or chaotic by comparison. To say God is not, is to say that the intelligible unity of the world is slight, not simply for our understanding but in itself. This attitude discourages the attempt to enlarge our comprehension of nature, for it makes it always possible that our failures to do so are results of defects in nature as a whole, and not merely in ourselves as parts of nature. (The idea of this paragraph will be treated in detail in Part II and in *The Vision of God*.)

Apart from the relation of love to knowledge, humanism is unable to integrate love itself. It cannot really solve the ethical and social problem.

The old-fashioned view was that atheism and immorality were almost identical. We now rightly regard this view as naïve. But it is not necessarily wholly mistaken. A violent exaggeration or oversimplification it undoubtedly is.   But is there no germ of truth in it?

Humanists are likely nowadays to react to this question by proposing the counterquery: Has not theism been the real cause of immorality?   By directing attention away from the sure facts of human relationship to the doubtful and irrelevant idea of the will of God, theists have deprived men of the only morality which is beyond the reach of skepticism and adequate to human needs.   To the theist's accusation that atheism deprives men of the motives to virtue (as distinct from the merest prudence), atheists have learned to retort that theism provides only the spurious or ignoble motives of fear of God and desire for personal reward in heaven.   Atheism, for its part, points to the social nature of man, to the sympathy for one's fellows which is more or less spontaneous and which can be encouraged by education.   After all, says the atheist, whatever we can know of goodness and love must be first learned through relations with other human beings; hence the extension, by analogy, of these ideas to God is obviously a derivative from human goodness and not its basis.   If we do not know in ourselves what goodness is, then we cannot know what is meant by the goodness of God.   Nor can acts be regarded as right simply because God commands them. For it has first to be granted that his commands are just, and this assumes that " just" is more than a synonym for " divinely commanded."   The contrary notion encourages a vicious neglect of the real meaning of the ethical ideas.

But the theist may reply that the social nature of man, in so far as it is a *fact,* can be exploited by all theories.   Therefore it can be exploited by theism, and hence theism need not make morality dependent upon metaphysical beliefs except in so far as the mere sociality of man is in fact not a sufficient basis for morality.   There is consequently nothing which the humanist can say in defense of morality which the theist cannot also say. Hence a theist who loses his faith has lost nothing which the humanist possesses. He has exactly the resources which would have been his had he never been a theist. (This reasoning is of course based on the assumption that his theism is of the naturalistic kind, favorable to science, which I have in mind in this book.) And it is as much a libel on theism as on atheism to accuse it of necessarily turning generosity into prudence; and this may be said in spite of the prevalence of egoistic attitudes toward heaven and hell. Let it not be forgotten that Jewish theism reached an intense expression at a time when Jewish interest in immortality was slight. And if immortality does come in, it gives extension to sociability as well as to prudence to such a degree that many take no interest in a future life until they are faced with the death of a friend, child, or lover.

Having disposed of crude misunderstandings, we come to the subtler meaning of the question: What, if anything, does theistic morality add to humanistic? In a word, it adds infinity, the explicit recognition of the absolute in relation to which the relative is experienced as such, the whole of which all lesser values are parts. As Reinhold Niebuhr says, it adds " depth." To the social nature of man it adds, as complement and means of perspective, the social nature of existence in general; to the apparently temporary life of man it adds the eternal life which is eternally creative of lesser life. It is not true that the addition throws no light on human goodness, for in infinite extension all the categories meet and illuminate one another as they do not in the finite. Thus in man there is goodness and there is power, more or less casually interrelated. But when we try to conceive power on a cosmic scale we find that only love in the highest degree can fulfill the requirements. Similarly with cosmic knowledge; it can only be cosmic love.

The extent to which human power or knowledge is capable

of divorce from love measures the weakness and danger inherent in human nature, and to take this measure is a valuable means to humility and sanity in judging human affairs.
Again, a consistent theist could not make the error of trying
to force all goodness into the mold of " self-interest "; for in
theology love, as the relation of sympathy, cannot be derived
from anything else since, according to theism, it is the foundation of all other relations.   In Thomistic theology, which is
founded on imperfectly analyzed ideas of causality, matter,
and form, this does not come out clearly, and the cosmological and ethical results are unfortunate in almost equal
degree.   I say almost equal, for it would seem to me that
this error in ethics produced even more serious confusion
in cosmology.   Thus through the integration furnished by
religious metaphysics, ethical questions can be illuminated
and mistakes detected by the tracing of their consequences
in other branches of philosophy.   Again, the pernicious
ethics of absolute rules and iron codes, the ethics which makes
it virtuous to condemn people we do not understand because
they violate some precept — an ethics which has caused as
much suffering and real evil as most of the vices which it
condemns — is put into its proper place by the vision of a
Being whose judgment is not from without, by abstractions,
but from within, by sympathy — whose judgment indeed *is*
sympathy for all the individuals concerned, together with the
vision of the possibilities of beauty inherent in each situation.

The notion of a God externally issuing commands like any
benevolent tyrant may sometimes pass the ethical censor,
but it can hardly pass the cosmologist's logical tests, since
the notion explains nothing cosmologically.   On the other
hand, absolute pacifism, which thinks to settle all human
affairs by love, without resort to force, is also contrary to
theism, which shows that only God possesses the degree of
love which renders superfluous the non-sympathetic forms of

power (they are all forms of love, but in a sense not here relevant). Whether we will or no, we are bound to coerce one another more or less unsympathetically; and there are those who will do so in an egregious and intolerable fashion if they are not themselves coerced into moderation. The potential and actual tyrants feed upon the pacifist delusion (as they have in Europe since the World War) almost as much as they do upon the delusion that unsympathetic power is divine. It is a sentimental, not a rationally metaphysical, theism that leads to such confusions. The need for widespread scientific study of religious metaphysics is to be inferred from the fact that both pacifist and militarist heresies are found in secular as well as in religious circles. (The *New Republic* and the *Christian Century* come to mind as examples relative to the pacifism.) But the advantages of theistic ethics can be appreciated only on the basis of a careful exposition of the God-idea, which is here omitted.

One who supposes that our love of God derives everything from and can contribute nothing to our love of men forgets also that we have no knowledge of a state of human love which preceded man's love of gods. And if God is really the hidden but always more or less dimly felt life of nature, it cannot even be said that animals are without a sort of sense of him, and certainly not that men ever are. It is not a fact that men improve their ethical insight step by step and *afterward,* in each instance, improve their idea of God. The oldest high ethical insights are those of theists who were theists as soon as they were moralists. And when the Greek thinkers criticized the ethics of the Homeric gods, they were not so much arriving in this way at their own conception of God as using this conception as a standard. Zenophanes knew that Zeus would not do because the ultimate of nature could not be a mere finite thing among others. Plato shows higher ethical insight in explaining why God creates than in most

of the passages where he is simply considering human behavior. Socrates does not consider certain things shameful
in the gods merely because they would be shameful in men;
but rather they are wrong because when we consider what we
really mean by God, or what we feel God, or the voice of
God in us, to be, we see that such things are incompatible
with his nature.

Jesus saw that nature is tolerant and inferred that we
should be so. He saw that life had been made a matter of impulse as well as thought, and inferred that we
should live by trust and spontaneously, like children and
flowers, and not, like Santayana's "last Puritan," by anxiety and rules. The Stoics saw that nature is orderly
and thought human conduct should strive to be so. The
prophets knew that God was the God of all the universe,
hence that he could see beyond the Jews and judge them
in relation to other peoples. In the Stoics, in Jesus, and in
Paul, this thought was brought out more clearly and led to
the ethical conception of mankind as a whole. This summary account of the history of the relations between ethics
and theology is doubtless more or less inaccurate and one-
sided, and certainly more or less speculative. But it may
make clear that the merely derivative character of theological
ethics is far from evident historically.

The ethical weakness of humanism is seen both in personal
and in group relations. First of all, the relation of the mind
to the body loses its religious, its high ethical character. The
humanistic theory of value cannot adequately integrate spirit
and flesh. The mind becomes merely the functioning of a
certain system of particles of matter, the ultimate particles
being dead and soulless altogether. Enjoyment of physical
pleasure is then sheer egoism, having no element of love.
The new philosophy, on the contrary, sees the mind-body relation as essentially one of sympathy between the radically in-

ferior sentient cells and our human consciousness. Thus physical lust is not sheer egoism but a rudimentary form of sympathy to be subordinated to higher forms, but not to be dismissed as totally incomparable to spiritual love, and sensualism and prudery are both eliminated. This view admits that the soul is not complete in itself, apart from the body, and fully explains the dependence of thought upon brain states; and yet, while taking physiology seriously, it does not imply that dead matter is fundamental and mind and value inexplicable accidents.

If, on the other hand, most of the universe is a loveless machine and even our own bodies, in their automatic aspects of digestion, metabolism, etc., are driven by purely blind forces without the slightest spark of indwelling spirituality, then it is impossible that the conception of spirit or love should have more than a very fitful hold upon us. For in so far as we think about physics and most of biology — and much of economics and politics — we shall be thinking not about love, the sharing of emotional values, but about mere laws and mere bits of matter and mere " collisions " and " repulsions " and impersonal " forces." The self is a unity; and if to much of its activity the idea of love is irrelevant, then, in so far, this idea cannot be the supreme integrating principle of life. Philosophers may deny this, but I believe most people are well aware of it and act accordingly, as do some of the philosophers — Schopenhauer for example.

The Darwinian conception of animal life as primarily a ruthless struggle certainly did contaminate ethics extensively. Those who wished to resist this contamination did two things: they emphasized the distinctiveness of man (Huxley), and they pointed out that cooperation is as genuine an aspect of all animal life as conflict, even if the scope of the cooperation is usually very narrow (Kropotkin). This insistence that human love is not an utter stranger in the world was logically and psychologically imperative. We must somehow see the world as one, even in respect to ethical problems and to whatever relative dualisms may be inevitable and important. And the inorganic background counts as well as the biological foreground. It is true that if atoms are purely dead they are not egoistic or ruthless in the positive sense. But equally, dead atoms cannot, even remotely, faintly, or in any other fashion, be assimilated to the ideal of love by which we have to live.

What happens to persons who do not achieve this assimilation of all aspects of life to one ideal?

One of the most fearful signs of disintegration today is the revival of cruelty. Now without doubt the necessity, brought about by technology, of economic reforms which selfishness and inertia have dangerously delayed is a main cause of concentration camps and the like. But if we ask, who are the thinkers that have encouraged the tendency as such, can it be denied that they are such atheists as Nietzsche, Spengler, the Marxians, and the earlier, atheistic Wagner? " Man is a beast of prey! " shouts Spengler, and adds some choice corollaries! In the very Sunday schools no more shocking picture of atheism is presented; in fact, the pious have if anything underestimated the lengths of barbarity to which the impious may go — not to mention the lengths of careless, dogmatic, superstitious thinking.

Fascist brutalities have occurred chiefly in contexts partly Romanist and partly atheist, and have been greatly stimulated by the Russian example. These contexts agree in that in all of them power and necessity have been exalted above love and freedom as final explanatory concepts. It was the " pure actuality " of medieval theology which led to Spinoza's denial of freedom and divine love. The fact that much so-called theism is really a kind of perverse humanism which makes the supreme Being less than the soul of nature by pretending to make it more and which degrades the divine love by making it cater to the all too human preference for power over sympathy, renders the whole discussion of ethics and theology exceedingly awkward at the present time.

Let us return to the mind-body problem. To mention one example out of myriads — H. G. Wells, for a time a theist but now definitely a humanist, tells multitudes of people, in an autobiography which documents such pitiable misfortunes as could hardly fail to prevent their victim from ever understanding the best possibilities of sex life, that as soon as puberty is reached sex life should begin.[7] Yet Hornell Hart, an authority on the scientific study of the subject, holds that two conclusions are statistically established: (1) that marriage is unwise before the age of twenty-one, and (2) that premarital sex experience is unfavorable to a happy marriage.[8] Thus science and theistic ethics agree in condemning what an atheistic man of letters (and he is only one of many) feels perfectly free to recommend, largely on the basis of an obviously eccentric life history. Is it or is it not a sign of cultural disintegration that recommendations of this importance are so casually offered by writers of the widest reputation? Incidentally, Hart makes whatever legitimate criticism is to be made of *traditional Christian* sex ethics, and shows how little such criticism has logically to do with atheism, and — by implication at least — how much it has to do with the difference between true and consistent theism, and degenerate, illogical pseudo-theism.

Particularly common among humanists is the view that premarital intercourse is favorable to if not almost a necessary condition of happiness in marriage. This is an essentially materialistic view of the matter, and there seems to be no strong factual evidence to support it. Moreover, it is mere fallacy to argue from the results of Victorian stupidity, the failure to furnish sane instruction about sex, to the necessity for personal experimentation. Many people are misinformed about sex hygiene and sex art, but the intelligent cure is to consult experts and the best available knowledge, to learn by the mistakes of the race as much as possible rather than by one's own.

In the present state of society the important point is that the human individual and the human group require a third term to mediate between them, as well as between different groups of individuals. The individual is embraced in his group, club, church, or nation. But what is so embraced is not the individual in his completeness, the whole man. No human associates can be fully sensitive to all that passes in any one person; and no human laws or institutions can be perfectly adjusted to any individual, to say nothing of all individuals. Human privacy transcends human publicity. The consequence is that the individual is bound to claim rights against society as well as through it. He cannot admit that its will is *ipso facto* right. This suggests that the real unity of man is in some superhuman organism. Failure to grasp this fact leads to falsification of human relations. The falsification is either toward a vicious individualism, an ethics of enlightened self-interest, or toward a vicious state-worship, class-ism, or mob-ism.

Enlightened self-interest would eliminate most crude forms of wickedness but not all socially injurious modes of behavior; and besides, it is a fact that man has always some genuine sympathy for others, so that if he pretends to make self the absolute end and criterion he is as much self-deceived as if he pretends to live wholly for others. What, then, is to arbitrate between self and others? There seem to be two possibilities only: the good of the greatest number, self included, or some superindividual unity. Now the good of the greatest number is an abstraction. Is it really *one* good? Can there be value in a sum of values unless there is a valuation which summates them, which embraces them together in a single good? And what unites anyone to so vast a group as all mankind? We have a profound intuition that the good is individual, unitary, personal; and if the group is for us the supreme good we shall tend to see the group as a personality, a real unitary being. This leads in practice to state-worship, for mankind is too vast and formless to attract effective loyalty.

But we must not exaggerate. Love of mankind is a real though a weak force; and nationalism is opposed by still another and stronger force upon which humanism might rely, the tendency of nationalism to defeat its own aim of collective aggrandizement and power. A revulsion against patriotism may in this way arise and the strife of nations diminish as the revulsion increases. But there are still two serious difficulties. One is that the probable result of this negative conquest over collective egoism is not the achievement of the peaceful and healthy world state, but a lapse back toward the war of each against all (where " each " stands rather for families or classes or other non-national groups than for mere individuals) ; that is, back toward anarchy, with a counter-tendency toward some towering supernational dictatorship. For the only healthy conquest over a narrow love is the achievement of a greater love.

The second difficulty is that, supposing the world state a reality, there will arise a new and more appalling form of the tragic problem of the rights of the individual in relation to the state. If the national state is nearly God, the world state will be God indeed in the imaginations of men. What then? Why then the fact that the individual is much more than a citizen, or much less than a man, will result in such a tyranny of the state-God over the private creative aspects of the individual as to constitute a major catastrophe. For the state will impose itself on the individual not, as the true God does, by secret understanding and all-embracing love, but chiefly by technological instruments of power. Whatever the world state may be, it seems certain, in an uncertain world, that it will be relatively abstract and brutal and blind in relation to the intimate life of the personality, and that its indirect sources of power over persons (guns, radio stations, fixing of salaries, hiring and firing) will be on a much more godlike scale than its direct power to move the individual through understanding and love. It follows that the world state may become the final and most colossal of false gods.

The real solution is to see the cosmic group, the universal community, as the body of God, the integrating spirit of the world members. For nature is closer to us than are the Chinese; and nature is palpably a unity, with its continuous forms of space, time, gravitation, and the like. Refuse to men the worship of God, and they fall back upon egoism or state-worship.

It may be objected that state-olatry arose in religious countries. However, it arose chiefly in countries where Roman Catholicism is well represented; in the first instance, a country almost entirely Roman Catholic. Nor should we forget Hitler's Catholic origin. Now is Romanism really free from humanistic taint? I do not think so. What is the real God of Romanism? On the one side there is the human divinity of Jesus, reflected in the Virgin Mary as the sun's light in the moon, and incorporated in the church as the mystical body of Jesus. On the other side there is, not nature, but the absolutely supernatural and really inconceivable *actus purus* of Aquinas. The non-human parts of nature are mere machinery for the drama of human salvation. When astronomy began to reveal how non-central is man in the gigantic scheme of things, the church was shocked, shocked because of its humanistic bias! The betraying symptom is the absolute authority, the unqualified divinity claimed for certain aspects of the church. As with the Hegelians, human institutions, instead of the eternal living framework of nature, become the real absolute. And all too similar is the Lutheran attitude toward the Bible, toward Luther, and toward doctrine. A real reformation never came in Germany. German Christianity fell apart into the supernaturalistic and the naturalistic branches of humanism. The basis of liberty is in neither.

The Russians also absolutize something human, the party. It is true that this action is described as a temporary expedient. But this is only because behind it lies another human absolute, the dreamed-of equality and harmony of the classless society. Thus, when Marx turned Hegelian idealism into dialectical materialism he did not overcome its humanistic limitation. Matter is held to be independent of man; but the dialectical movement is essentially human or pseudo-human, even though economic interests are held to be the determining forces of history. It was from the study of human history above all that Hegel derived the dialectic; and whether in Hegel or in Marx or in Lenin, it is in man and not in nature that the workings of the dialectic appear with any clarity or reach any high development.

The Anglo-American tradition has its own weaknesses, which are also related to humanism. The doctrine that social cooperation results almost exclusively from the pursuit of selfish individual ends is an extreme opposite of the Hegelian view of national solidarity; but the extremes meet in this, that both conflict with the theistic view of nature as a *superhuman but man-including* organic whole. The Hegelian view admits solidarity but makes this essentially a relation among human beings; English individualism has no principle of solidarity which could make any kind of superior whole conceivable.

In economic relations individualism leads to the evils of monopoly, for egoism must be profoundly modified if competition is to be preserved against the tendency of " using power to get more power." [9] And of course competition is out of the question in some industries under modern conditions. The worship of the group leads to the evils of a purely bureaucratic industrial system, with a centralized and irresistible political power, which, having all industry in its hands, will not in practice be democratic whatever it may be in theory. A third term is needed, a mighty mediator, which can equally sanction the delegation of vast powers to the state and the withholding of vast powers, to be divided among private individuals or groups, including groups of cooperating consumers. In this way a healthy balance will be possible between the highly imperfect private citizen and the highly imperfect public official. Each will have enough power to " stand up " to the other. The proportions of the various elements — competition, state socialism, consumer cooperation — will and should vary widely in different countries according to local conditions and sentiments; but in principle this is the only ideal.[10] It involves the transfer of the present fanatical hatred of socialism (balanced by an equally fanatical hatred of competition) to the one object deserving of hatred — private monopoly, which is neither free enterprise nor group activity but the monstrosity of a private individual in his capacity as private individual exercising public functions, a monstrosity we try to conceal by setting another individual to watch what the first is doing (" regulation ") .

Where is the mighty mediator by which the requisite division of powers is to be given the religious appeal without which it will not be effected? It cannot be mankind. At least it must be mankind with its face turned upward toward what is greater than men and greater than human groups, toward some abiding Truth which cannot be coerced by state-suborned scientists, some lasting Good which can com-

mand innermost loyalty while measuring by its own transcendence the relativity of all human achievements, purposes,
and powers. Insist upon reducing this transcendence to the
mere ideal potentialities of man himself, and you throw
everything into doubt, vagueness, and confusion: doubt,
for man appears ultimately doomed upon this planet, so
that, if he is the ultimate value, the ultimate value is apparently the value of doom; vagueness, for only by thinking
of God as the maximal value of all variables can we see
clearly the direction in which man must move to reach higher
values of these variables; confusion, for if man is the measure
of value, then the line between opinion and verity, preference and right, becomes too subtle for ordinary people to see,
whatever philosophers may think they still see.

I shall be accused of contradicting myself. First I have
shown that without the idea of God unfortunate attitudes
cannot be controlled. But I have also claimed that without
the idea of God there can be no clear criterion of good and
bad, fortunate or unfortunate. So how can the argument
reach one who lacks the idea of God? The answer is that the
possession or non-possession of belief in God is a matter of
degree. According to the theist, all men know, and at some
point betray that they know, that the object of our total
allegiance is God. To argue that the totalitarian state is
an abomination because it places unlimited power where
there cannot be anything like unlimited understanding and
love, or because its pretended inclusiveness is really exclusive
of the most valuable things, is to point to the idea of a power
which *is* the power of love and a unity which really does unite
the highest in men.

The whole of nature as carrying in itself all truth about the
past and present and all purposes for things to come as parts
of a single Life whose integrating principle is sensitiveness
seeking harmony, and which is progressively revealed to man

by rationally clarified religious inspiration, whose two great expressions today are ethical and scientific ideas — this is the superhuman being with reference to which all human power and valuation can be seen in perspective. Old supernaturalism possessed only a distorted and meager vision of this being; new humanism is not necessarily blinder, or as blind. But the question is, can we not do better than either?

NOTES

1 From "At the End of Day," by Richard Hovey, in Richard Hovey and Bliss Carman, *More Songs from Vagabondia* (Dodd, Mead & Co.), p. 72.

2 *Mysticism and Logic, and Other Essays* (Longmans, Green & Co., 1921), pp. 46–57.

3 *Letters from W. H. Hudson, 1901–1922*, edited by Edward Garnett (E. P. Dutton & Co., Inc., 1923), p. 140.

4 Quoted in *Has Science Discovered God?* edited by E. H. Cotton (Thomas Y. Crowell Co., 1931), pp. 101f.

5 *Ibid.*, pp. 99–100.

6 John Langdon-Davies, *Man and His Universe* (Harper & Bros., 1930), p. 11.

7 H. G. Wells, *Experiment in Autobiography: Discoveries and Conclusion of a Very Ordinary Mind* (The Macmillan Co., 1934), pp. 350 ff., 399.

8 "Christian Ideals and Sex Problems," *Christendom*, I (1936), pp. 647–60.

9 Frank H. Knight, *The Ethics of Competition* (Harper & Bros., 1935), p. 309.

10 See Henry C. Simons' brilliant pamphlet, *A Positive Program for Laissez-Faire: Some Proposals for a Liberal Economic Policy* (University of Chicago Press, 1934, 25c).

III

DEWEY'S PHILOSOPHY OF RELIGION

RELIGION, according to a dangerously abstract but suggestive definition, is man's consciousness of his paradoxical infinity. Man is finite, imperfect; but, according to religion, there is in him that which is more than finite, which is in some sense perfect — his consciousness of which is the essential factor in his humanity. It is this consciousness which humbles his pride while at the same time it exalts his ambitions immeasurably above the desires of other animals.

Because of the paradoxical character of the religious consciousness — the tension which it involves between the finite and the infinite — there is a natural tendency for men to seek to escape from religion. They do this in two opposite ways: by trying to escape from their human sense of finitude through mystical illusions of absolute oneness with God, or by trying to obliterate their no less human consciousness of the infinite. One of the best statements that has yet been made of the second mode of escape is found in John Dewey's *A Common Faith*.[1]

According to Dewey, we should indeed be religious, but we should distinguish between the "ideal factors in experience that may be called religious," and the various *religions* as involving "beliefs and practices that are irrelevant" to the ideal factors. Being religious means being adjusted to life as a whole both in its actualities and in its possibilities.

39

Adjustment to life as a whole implies reference to " that imaginative totality we call the universe." The universe, so far as it is relevant to the realization of human ideals, may even, Dewey suggests, be called God, provided it be borne in mind that the word signifies only whatever in the universe is amenable to human purposes, and hence does not designate a single individual, but simply all the forces the existence of which constitutes our human opportunity. Crudely, God is simply nature as serviceable to man.

So far, there is nothing but choice of words to distinguish Dewey's position from ordinary atheism. But Dewey feels there is a difference. Atheism, like traditional theology, is, he feels, lacking in appreciation of the fact that without nature we could do nothing. The atheist lacks " natural piety," the sense that all we do to nature is done — as Shakespeare said — by means that nature furnishes. Moreover, this sense of our debt to nature must not be weakened by a dichotomy between human and non-human nature. It was, according to Dewey, precisely this dichotomy which favored supernaturalism; for if the rest of nature is in any respect totally different from man, then in that respect the origin of man is incapable of natural explanation and a supernatural one is suggested. In short, if man is natural, then nature is manlike. (For obvious reasons Dewey does not put it quite this way!)

What does this belief in the kinship of man and nature imply? For one thing it means for Dewey that the Newtonian science, with its dogmatic assertion that purposes have no real part in natural process, at least below the human level, was from a religious standpoint unfortunate; and Dewey hails the newer tendencies in science as favorable to the recognition of the naturalness of purposive action. Consistently carried out, his attitude here must, if I am not deceived, carry him all the way to a radical panpsychism, according to which all process has a psychic character. For if the psychic emerged from a non-psychic world, no matter at what level — say that of the protozoa — then the dichotomy Dewey objects to seems in principle unavoidable.

If natural piety means panpsychism, then there is a fairly obvious reason for suspecting that it also means a kind of theism, though not the kind Dewey is explicitly opposing. For if every individual is psychic, is not nature herself as a whole an individual and thus psychic — and what would this be but a kind of God? To be sure Dewey's reference to the universe as an "imaginative totality" suggests the idea of an aggregate rather than an individual. But there is reason for doubting that this is a logically sufficient conception of the world-whole.

Whether individual or mere aggregate, the world-whole referred to by the religious attitude contains two relatively distinguishable factors: existences and possibilities. The latter are for religion no less vital than the former. If we asked Dewey, is there nothing "above" nature, full of flaws as she is, he might reply, "Yes, above the actualities of nature there are the unrealized but realizable possibilities of nature." There is a better world than the one that exists; but this better world is simply the one which might exist and would exist if the forces of the existent world were rightly used. It is Dewey's pregnant thesis that this potential better world has been misconstrued by supernaturalism as a world actually existing, though outside or above or beyond "this" world. God as an actual individual endowed with perfection is, for Dewey, simply the vicious identification of the possible and the actual. The result, he believes, is to destroy the very meaning of the ideal factor in experience, the religious factor. For moral and religious faith are not so much in what is, as in what, through our action, might be. To destroy this "might be" character of the ideal is to cut the nerve of action. The idea of a God so perfect that he eternally realizes all possible values is fatal to religion, for it makes human choice of no significance whatever. Infinite value will exist no matter what we do. "Serving" such a God really means only serving oneself by securing his favor. But even this self-service cannot make any difference to the totality of values, since this totality is always an absolute maximum.

In my opinion Dewey gives here an unanswerable objection to the theism of Augustine and Aquinas. However, I cannot regard this theism as having much to do with that of the Bible![2] And certainly the conception of nature as the supreme individual does not conflict with Dewey's rightful insistence that ideals should refer to unrealized possibilities. For there is no reason to think that everything man *may* some time do is for nature already, and actually, done. Even the theory of relativity does not, in spite of some assertions to the contrary, force us to deny the reality of time or the difference between past and future. A naturalistic theism, therefore, may be temporalistic and admit open possibilities for the future. Human choice may then make a difference to God as the actions of a man's cells make a difference to the man. If we injure ourselves or others, God, as the unity of the world, will include that injury as an aspect of his own quality. If we make one another happy, that happiness will flavor his own. His future enjoyment will thus be partially contingent upon our actions.

Naturalistic theism will not deny that existence is through and through, even for God, a mixture of good and evil. In this way theology will clear itself of the charge of wishfully thinking away evil. But not only can naturalistic theism meet Dewey's challenge; it can also challenge him. Life as involving both good and evil is, it is true, by no means intolerable. Animal life consists in such toleration. Nor does the human need for God arise merely because human beings anticipate future evils. For aside from the fact that animals also do this to some extent, there is the obvious objection that human beings anticipate good as well as ill fortune and that much of their happiness is due to this optimistic anticipation, so that they ought to be able to enjoy a balance of good over evil quite as well as the animals. But the real problem arises from the fact that man's anticipation is in a sense *infinite*. By seeing himself as others might see him he can form the idea of his own death, which animals can scarcely do, and, most fateful of all, he can form the idea of the destruction of his entire species. There seems, in fact, even less likelihood that the human race will be able to propagate itself forever, on this planet or elsewhere, than that human individuals will enjoy some kind of personal survival after death. Man alone of the animals has the sense of a threat to all values whatsoever, the possible destruction of life on this planet, and the apparent possibility that there is no life elsewhere. This threat is not a finite affair to be balanced against the finite goods of this planetary existence, but an infinite one, since it concerns the *endless* future. Russell's " Free Man's Worship " is an attempt to face the difficulty; but the attempt is patently unsuccessful. Defiance, courage — these virtues are irrelevant when the question is, What will it matter in the long run whether we were virtuous or not? And the standpoint of the long run is the standpoint of man as man, that is, so far as he is endowed with the power to generalize with intelligence. Dewey calls for intelligence in action, but intelligence is essentially the power to generalize beyond the merely finite (as, for example, in mathematics), so that it can hardly make a satisfactory religion to conceive of human ideals as referring to a merely finite future. Yet what other future can Dewey derive from his form of natural piety?

The human need is not for the exorcising of all evils, but for *extending to the infinite horizon of the future* that balance of good over evil which makes life tolerable. This extension theistic naturalism effects, as explained in the preceding chapter.

Dewey is a shrewd critic of the human lust for absolute knowledge. But the " quest for certainty," as the cowardly search for a life without risk, is one thing; while the quest for assurance that there is a minimal significance to the brave facing of risk — and to all life when well lived — is another thing. The one is cowardice or madness, as you choose. The other is merely rationality, the intelligent understanding of the implications of courage.

In its early stages religion means certainty about many things. But we now see that he is most religious who is certain of but one thing, the world-embracing love of God. Everything else we can take our chance on; everything else, including man's relative significance in the world, is mere probability.

In one passage Dewey seems for a moment to face the infinite aspect of existence. Significantly, he states his position by quoting a rather evasive, ambiguous passage from the not very precise though mellow and charming philosopher, the late Justice Holmes. Here are a few phrases from this quotation: " If a man sees no reason for believing that significance, consciousness and ideals, are more than marks of the human . . . the conclusion is that the part cannot swallow the whole. . . . We do not know what we are talking about when we speak of brute matter [matter without consciousness or significance?]. . . . The universe has in it more than we understand, . . . the private soldiers have not been told the plan of the campaign, or even that there is one. If we think of our existence not as that of a little god outside, but as that of a ganglion within, we have the infinite behind us. It gives us our only but our adequate significance . . . the chord of a harmony that breathes from the unknown." [3]

Dewey's comment here is that men move between the two extremes of conceiving themselves to be gods or " feigning a powerful and cunning god who bends the world to do their bidding and meet their wishes." But what we should do, he says, is to see that while our wishes " are not final measures of the universe " they do " imply a unity with the universe that is to be preserved. The belief and the effort of thought and struggle which it inspires are also the doing of the universe; and they in some way, however slight, carry the universe forward. A chastened sense of our importance, apprehension that it is not a yardstick by which to measure the whole, is consistent with the belief that we and our endeavors are significant not only for themselves but in the whole." [4]

Now the question is how a universe devoid as a whole of consciousness or significance can be " carried forward" by the consciousness of some of its parts, or how, being as a whole without value, it can gain value from the parts, or how the universe, as it is not a volitional being, can " do " anything in the sense here relevant. And if we are ganglia within the whole, I should think that implies the organic conception of the world to which the question of theism ultimately refers. It may also be asked *how permanently* the unity of man with the universe can be preserved. The infinite long run is not mentioned. As for the " two extremes " Dewey describes, I should hate to accept either of them as stated. The function of the " powerful god " is not primarily to bend the world to our wishes but to provide a larger and more permanent system of wishes and their satisfactions than the merely human, so that our satisfactions can form part of a cosmic good that is lasting. Not as a mere means to our life is the divine life to be thought of, but as a superior life to which we can also be in the relation of means. All life is in some measure means to other life, and in some measure end to which other life contributes. But lower life is primarily in the relation of service to higher; it is more because he wishes himself to enjoy the value that comes through functioning as an ally of the god than because he wishes the god to function as his ally that a man on a high cultural plane values religious belief. It is true that the early stages of religion exhibit a relatively opposite emphasis; but if the argument is about the validity of the higher stage, in which it has been realized that the nobler conception is also the more reasonable, then the argument is about that. I fear that advanced theism cannot be refuted by people who prefer to talk about something else!

But Professor Dewey and Justice Holmes seem to admit it is necessary to feel that we are significantly related to the " infinite " or the " whole " — even though these be incommensurable with " significance." Now the inalienable infinity of human aspirations has other aspects than that of the infinity of the future. The central values are social, values of love, of participation. Participation has degrees of completeness, implying in the ideal case full realization by one individual of the joys and sorrows of another. But this ideal case can never be actualized in purely human experience. No man can be fully understood by another. We cannot even say that all aspects of a man may be understood by all of his friends taken together. The very real human desire of being completely understood has not as its correlate the ideal of *oneself's* completely understanding, if by ideal we mean, as Dewey does, a possible human achievement. Indeed, complete understanding represents an ideal which cannot be identified with any mere possibility. For no being which lacked complete understanding could subsequently attain to it. Either complete understanding is impossible, or an all-understanding being is eternally actual. Thus not all ideals can be reduced to the Deweyan formula: potential human achievements. It cannot be the goal of human endeavor to attain complete sympathy and appreciation of others, because such attainment would contradict the conditions of human life as such. But it is a very deep aspiration of men and women to be able to feel that they are *now* completely understood, not necessarily, indeed not possibly, by other human beings, but by someone. To hold that this ideal is based upon the actuality of a perfect understanding is not at all to fall into the error, so properly condemned by Dewey, of destroying the meaning of the ideal as that which we *might* accomplish. For here is one ideal that could never correspond to actuality — unless there exists a God.

Yet it might be said that perfect understanding does derive all its meaning from human potentialities, since it is merely the mathematical limit which the latter may approximate but never actually reach. Furthermore, Dewey might say, to hold this limit to correspond to an actuality has after all the vicious effect of implying the unimportance of human potentialities. For if the unattainable limit of human sympathy already exists in non-human form, what difference does it make how far human approximations to that limit are carried? If perfection exists, why concern ourselves with multiplying imperfections? The answer is that the perfection of God naturalistically conceived is an absolute only in terms of one dimension of value, and that there is another dimension in terms of which there is no absolute maximum, but only an inexhaustible opportunity of improvement. The value of the world does not reside merely in there being a single perfect understanding of the individuals in that world, but also in the aesthetic richness arising from the variety and intensity of the experiences of those individuals. The perfect sympathy of God is his ethical goodness; but sympathy means sharing in negative as well as positive values, so that ethical goodness alone does not guarantee supreme value. Not unless men are worth sympathizing with, and only in proportion as they are, will the divine sympathy constitute divine happiness. If all men were bad and miserable, perfect sympathy with men would be the unrelieved crucifixion of deity. Christianity, of course, teaches that the crucifixion is real but not unrelieved.

Suppose the belief in an actual perfect love is given up. What follows? There are two opposite dangers. If the conception of the ideal remains vivid, then its unattainability is a ground for sadness or cynicism. The essential loneliness of the human individual in spite of all friendships is an ancient theme, just as is the mutability of human existence, and neither the one nor the other can be banished by any social reform. He who is keenly aware of the depths and complexities of the mind will have to admit that in " earthly love " is no complete fulfillment of our social aspirations. Besides, earthly love at its best cannot be realized by everyone nor by anyone all the time. Unrequited love, rivalries, separations, death will persist under any social forms, so that he who remains sensitive to the ideal must be more or less discontented with the actuality. To escape this discontent seems possible in but two ways: by stifling in ourselves the consciousness of the ideal, desensitizing ourselves to its attraction; or by accepting the religious faith that ideal understanding of every human soul is a constant actuality in the universe. The first or non-religious escape means the avoidance of cynicism about life's actualities at the cost of cynicism about life's ideal. One of its practical consequences is the blurring of the distinction between the highest and the second best or mediocre in social relations. Bertrand Russell's depreciation of loyalty in the sex relation is a typical and ominous example;

another is the brutality in certain aspects of atheistic communism. A further result of the denial of theism is that the individual tends to identify himself with the understanding which others have of him in order to avoid the painful feeling that he is not understood. The secret springs of confident originality, which are religious in a more than humanistic sense, tend to dry up, and the originality of other people and their need for understanding beyond definite limits tend to be overlooked.

The sum of the matter is that human life is in fact not merely finite, and yet, if humanists are right, is not genuinely super-finite. It is not merely finite, for each particular limit is provisional only, and progress a perpetual human obligation; yet without God the thought of the infinite ideal, by which alone this perpetual progress can be inspired, is intolerable, since its actualization is both desirable and impossible. Only in the aesthetic aspect is a divorce between the ideal and the real free from this contradiction. For the aesthetic ideal refers not to any definite maximum or completion but to an inexhaustible series of possible worlds, each richer than its predecessors in value. To deny that the aesthetically potential is already actual is not to tantalize desire but to inspire hope. For here is no definite perfection that can never be realized, but only an inexhaustible opportunity to realize new values. "Perfect love" is a phrase with a meaning; "perfect beauty" is not. An ideal friend may be conceivable, but an ideal poem or symphony?

It is noteworthy that knowledge is to be classed with love, not with beauty. We seek the truth about the actual world; and the ideal here is the whole truth about it. But how can such a truth-whole be conceived except in terms of a perfect mind and its omniscience? However, this omniscience is of the actual world, not of all possible worlds as though they were actualized.

Of course, too, there is aesthetic value in the notion of the world-whole as the most beautiful actuality embracing all real beauties in itself. But only all real, not all possible beauties! Thus science, ethics, and aesthetics call for a relative or moving absolute, a supreme synthesis of actuality and un-actualized possibility.

Dewey is greatly, and justifiably, concerned about the fail-ure of traditional religion to enter whole-heartedly upon the task of social amelioration. He believes that supernaturalism turns attention away from the " values that inhere in the actual connections of human beings with one another," or from " the sweep and depth of the implications of natural human relations."

Of course my own response to this charge is to admit that it is largely true — of supernatural but not of natural theism. The divorce of God from nature, of spirituality from ma-teriality, found in some forms of theism has undoubtedly worked havoc with orthodox ethics, as no less a theist and moralist than Reinhold Niebuhr admits. But it is precisely this divorce that the new theism rejects. It is also debatable whether or not there is much or any of it in the Gospels (Paul's Epistles are of course somewhat different). Dewey himself seems, however, to believe that dualism is the false premise upon which all theism essentially depends. This seems to me profoundly wrong, in spite of the fact that medieval theology appears to justify it. According to Dewey, God is brought in to explain man as a being so different from the rest of nature that only a supernatural explanation of him is possible. But not only is this not the mode of argu-ment of the new theism; it is not, I believe, the original conception which is presupposed by theology, but a radical corruption of this conception. The argument is rather, as al-ready suggested, that the principle of continuity, the supreme law of rationality, implies that every individual in nature is in some degree akin to man, either as inferior or as superior to him, and that nature as a whole, as the inclusive individual, can only be conceived as superior, and this in a *maximal* way so far as, or in whatever sense or senses, value admits a maximum. At no point does this argument depend upon denying the " naturalness " of man.

To return to the question of religion and social amelioration, has not religion been almost synonymous with conservatism and with oppression? Suppose we grant this (allowing for some exaggeration), does the admission favor humanism? Not altogether. Supernaturalism certainly did tend to make reform of " this " world appear a secondary matter; indeed, as we have seen, the whole time-process had for it no rational significance. And the arbitrary power of kings or economic overlords certainly showed a sinister analogy to the arbitrary power of the transcendent God over nature. Nevertheless, the mere humanist rejection of supernaturalism leaves the basic requirements for social action still unsatisfied. The lust for arbitrary power is not something baseless in human nature, so that the removal of a theological foundation will banish that lust. What is needed is a strong curb upon this dangerous desire.

Whence is the curb to come? From pure reason and humanitarian sentiment? From education? This notion might be plausible but for one circumstance. Emotions are conquered, as Spinoza taught us, by other emotions; and it cannot be that any group of intellectuals can impose humanitarian ideals upon average egoistic mankind unless it can point to an object of admiration and devotion emotionally more stirring, not merely than each man is to himself, but also more moving than are the objects of devotion furnished to most men by the groups to which they belong, such as family or nation. Without God as a real individual above man, what can each of us concretely realize as so great and definite that his individual and collective egoisms are humbled in its presence? Humanity? Surely this is too abstract and formless an object to perform any such function. And surely there are none so blind as they who will not see that in fact it does not perform it! And what have recent times shown if not that humanism is a feeble bulwark against the collective egoism of state- and race-worship?

It is generally agreed that the liberalism of earlier decades was dangerously optimistic, blind to what might be termed the tragic strength of human weaknesses. Professor Dewey says the trouble is cultural lag in the social sciences, chiefly due to supernaturalism. He holds also that our difficulty is much more lack of knowledge as to what is good than lack of willingness to act on our knowledge. In a fashion I agree. Wicked men are not clear-headed men in a deep sense. Virtue is " knowledge " if the word be used in its fullest, most concrete meaning. But why do not men see things as they are, especially in the moment of making important decisions? Surely not chiefly because sociology is backward or priests have inculcated piety! Is it not rather because certain very deep as well as many superficial desires natural to man are satisfied by such self-deception, and by inducing others to share in it? The will to power, to make oneself or one's group pseudo-divine, does not thrive on the truth, but it can very well make use of the results of science, including social science, given ingenuity to turn truths into lying half- or three-quarter truths. Social science is nothing if not a perpetual temptation to just such falsification — as even Marx did not sufficiently see. And the fearful resources of advertising and propaganda are not the only gifts of science to the will to lie and to spread the disease of lying which is close to the root of what theologians have called original sin. The real root, of course, is itself the basic lie, the demonic lie that the only God I need to recognize is not the universal God who sees all individuals in the perspective afforded by the adequate understanding of the merits and needs of all, but some lesser reality, greater indeed than I but still not so completely humbling to my pretensions. The false God may be a philosophical system, science, humanity, or any other system or concept or abstraction. But the essence of the matter is that something which participates in the partiality of my ego is held — without full recognition of the fact — to be the only standard by which that partiality may be judged. This is original sin, and it is original enough so that the minimal defense against it which sanity can accept is at least full and fair warning that the danger confronts all men, whether they are scientists or not. Can one imagine a less effective preparation for the tragic spectacle of demonic sinfulness in the world and in oneself than a reading of the writings of liberal humanist philosophers! (I except Marx, whose dialectic is the ghost of the true prophetic God, but whose vision of original sin narrows it to certain aspects of economic life.)

One argument against theism which, according to Dewey, theologians have never even attempted to face is based on the evil in the world. But this argument seems to depend upon the assumption that God's "omnipotence" means complete responsibility for all that happens. "All-powerful" is taken to mean possessing all the power there is, so that there can be no power not the power of God. If this is true, if power is not *divided* between God and other beings, then responsibility can certainly not be divided either. But the division of power, and hence of responsibility, is an analytic truth since, evil or no evil, power must be employed upon something, and that upon which it is employed must also possess some power, for the completely powerless or passive is nothing. Hence "all-powerful" can only mean possessing all *possible* power over all other things, that is, all the power there is except that which is inherent in those other things by their very existence.

To maintain this conception of omnipotence consistently we have to renounce the standard theological doctrine of the " purely active " character of God; but naturalistic theism is in any case prevented by all its major principles from accepting that doctrine. Thus it is free from any motive for asserting the responsibility of God for evil merely on the ground that evil exists. Since God must be partly passive to the actions of the creatures, of whom men are only an almost infinitesimal proportion, we cannot hold that he could coerce complete harmony or goodness in these actions. It might be held that the amount of evil is too great to be explained in this way; but that is at least not self-evident. It might also be held that omnipotence so defined is really the renunciation of the idea of a being perfect in power; but by what logic is it an imperfection to possess no more power than is possible to any one individual? God's power is not " finite," in the sense of being less than an individual power might be, but on the contrary is the fullest possible extent of individual power. I think we may safely deny that practical religion ever intended anything else by the perfection of God. But I agree with Dewey that traditional theology, with its notion of God as sheer power without passivity and without change, certainly did make the temporal struggle of men with evil unintelligible altogether.

Dewey has expressed the fear that the concentrating of all values in a supreme value, in God, must lead to the neglect of ordinary values in their rich diversity. Once more, as against Aristotelian or medieval theology with its notion of God as the pure thinking of thinking, as absolutely simple, disembodied, and so on, I would heartily agree with Dewey. But the new theism makes a clean sweep of this conception of the supreme good. For exclusive simplicity it substitutes inclusive integration of the diverse; for thinking of thinking, the thinking and feeling of things and persons; for impassivity, supreme sensitiveness to all that happens; for disembodied spirit, the soul of the world-body. To be interested in God is accordingly to be interested in the supreme interest in men and women; it is to be sympathetic toward all lives under inspiration from the supreme participating sympathy. In this context, Dewey's fear is as though an electron in the human body, in the interest of itself and its neighbor electrons, should begrudge the admission that it and they are members of the total organism and contributors to the human mind.

It is really society which is likely to do what Dewey fears God will do, namely, simplify and impoverish in order to reduce multiplicity to unity. The state, or public opinion, is always more coercive than sensitive or understanding; only a world-soul could really include all by treasuring and tolerating all. Flee the divine tyranny, and you may be appalled by the group tyranny which will take its place.

One of Dewey's strongest points is the colossal waste of religious apologetics, a literature almost inconceivably vast and still rapidly growing. Why, asks Dewey, could not this energy and ingenuity be applied to solving practical or scientific problems? Now it is not so clear as Dewey seems to think that science and art have had nothing to gain from theology. We do not know that Kepler and Newton and Maxwell would have been so interested in nature if they had not been interested in the only idea of God that Greek theology made possible. And the weaknesses of this idea were such as to call for apology. But granting Dewey's point that men ought to turn from God to nature, how, as a practical matter, are they to be induced to do so? Must it not be by showing them in nature values something like or even superior to those they formerly found in the abstractions of supernatural theology?

Perhaps, you may reply, nature is not susceptible of being so highly regarded. In that case, Dewey's project seems unlikely to succeed. To be frank, I find in Dewey a mild sense of the grandeur and fascination of nature, but no eager delight and no burning passion to penetrate her secrets. This seems to me generally true of non-theistic writers. And I suggest that when Dewey says that nature as a whole need not be supposed conscious, he ought to ask himself whether this does not imply that nature need not be supposed worthy of the love of an ethical and intellectual being like man. Perhaps, when the truth is out, nature must appear ultimately baffling, repellent, and even dull. But, you say, if this be indeed the truth, must we not accept it? Still, I answer, the truth is lovable only if it is worthy to be loved, and those who out of loyalty to the truth are compelled to confess truth not to be worthy of loyalty are in strange case. Moreover, if we are to be pragmatic let us be so. Let us ask: Will men give up God for nature unless they can find nature to be divine?

Great men, it seems, do modify the course of history, but it is well said that they seldom do so in just the direction they intend. Professor Dewey has sought to lead men from supernaturalism to a not too egregiously atheistic naturalism. It is possible that, somewhat indirectly at least, he may prove a principal creator of what may appear as the twentieth century's supreme theoretical discovery — theistic naturalism.

To conclude, we may say that Dewey's religious doctrine is convincing in its opposition to old supernaturalism, but that it is unconvincing in what is really a point of agreement with supernaturalism. This is its treatment of the ideal *en bloc* and without any regard to the distinction between those aspects which refer to a final or eternal maximum, and those which refer only to a *de facto* or *pro tempore* maximum. Also, Dewey and traditionalists agree in giving pantheism short shrift. Either God alone or nature alone appears to be the choice. Again, there is a third position. We may agree with Dewey that there need be no extra-natural being, and yet hold that there must be in nature a being not only higher than others, but in some aspects the highest possible, the supreme or maximal being — supreme in temporal endurance and in power to embrace within itself the content and value of other beings. This supreme natural being is nature herself, taken not distributively, but as an integrated individual. The ideal is truly the potential, but there may exist nevertheless a being who, as a worthy object of devotion, as an ethical and intellectual companion, and as a preserver of values once realized, is without blemish. There is, one may believe, a Cause infinitely worthy of service, even from the standpoint of all the future and of all ideal demands.

NOTES

1 Yale University Press, 1934.

2 Cf. Duncan Black Macdonald, *The Hebrew Philosophical Genius* (Princeton University Press, 1936) .

3 John Dewey, *Experience and Nature* (Open Court Publishing Co., 1925) , pp. 418–19.

4 *Ibid.*, pp. 419–20.

IV

OTHER HUMANIST PHILOSOPHIES

An exceedingly influential writer of humanistic persuasion is George Santayana. In what follows I am concerned chiefly with that brilliant production of his, *The Last Puritan*. Here is a picture of life as seen by an intellectual without the conviction of God. Still, perhaps it is not quite correct to describe Santayana as a humanist or an atheist. He has a feeling of the sublimity of nature and of its creativity which suggests at times a pantheistic interpretation. Thus he seems never to suppose, like some atheists, that life on this planet may exhaust the life of the cosmos, but suggests rather that the potentiality of life is inherent in matter, ready to actualize itself under favorable circumstances, which presumably will never wholly cease to exist in the universe. But, assuming Santayana's philosophy, this can be only a matter of guesswork, since astronomy is not as yet of much help in determining the prevalence in space-time of conditions favoring animal organisms. And the main consequence of atheism is not in this way escaped, for the other life in the universe has no intelligible connection with ours, such that our achievements could enrich its values.

Is Santayana's novel, scintillating as it is, expressive of a basically creative and integrated human will? We must, to be fair, remember that Santayana's purpose in the novel is to depict the disintegration of Puritanism. Yet, allowing for this, is there not something distinctly " poisonous," a not quite concealed treachery to life, in its atmosphere? No simple statement can reach so subtle a matter. But there is in the book a haunting feeling that no value can be quite affirmed, since it is beyond human power to believe without illusion. To be safe from illusion — the great ideal which Anatole France has done so much to popularize — we must mingle a little mockery with all appreciations and loyalties. This is highly defensible; but a more religious person would think that it is not quite so necessary to be safe from all danger of illusion, and more necessary to act upon the most reasonable beliefs we are able to form. The potential ferocity and intolerance of belief would then be mitigated not by mockery but by sympathy and humility, by the realization that none *can* be wholly free of illusion but God and that absolutes, even absolute caution or safety, are not for man; also that it is not error but only carelessness, or stubborn disregard of evidence and the opinion of others who are in a position to judge, of which we need be ashamed. In other words, skepticism is easily exaggerated into a negative form of the megalomania, the wishing to be God, which is the specific disease of humanism.

More precisely, we find in Santayana's novel a fourfold decadence. There is the decay of Puritanism, that is, of the worship of the all too human schoolmaster God of moral rules, whose service is far from perfect freedom. This is, in Santayana's phrase, the decay of a Protestant Christianity which had " retained its illusions but lost its poetry." Then there is the decay of the Church of England, which had abandoned the illusory beliefs while retaining the poetry of religion. The cynicism of the Darnley children is the result. Then there is Roman Catholicism, which had kept both the illusions and the poetry — Mario and Uncle Caleb. Santayana has admiration for the values inherent in this rich and ancient synthesis, but sees that it is intellectually and ethically somewhat irresponsible. Where then is there hope? It seems — and this is the fourth form of decadence — that there is no hope. Oliver, having seen through Puritanism theoretically, has also, unfortunately, seen through almost everything else. He is haunted by the impossibility of being human and a finite individual while at the same time preserving philosophic impartiality and comprehensiveness of vision.

This tantalizing ideal of superhuman fairness and all-sidedness becomes in a religious person the fruitful source of creative endeavor, solaced against despair by the sense that the perfect vision of the truth, while beyond us, is not merely alien, nor yet a dream only, but is the indwelling love of God in whose perfection we can vicariously glory and in which we can ever more largely participate or aid others to do so. Religious humility makes joyous and inspiring, humbling not humiliating, what Santayana pictures as either a sterile torment, in Oliver, or a responsibility to be shirked — light-heartedly in Jim or Mario, grimly in Uncle Caleb or Rose.

Thus the loss or lack of an intellectually honest theistic belief does disintegrate character and sanity, even though Santayana by his exquisite genius achieves a poignant beauty in the midst of the decay he describes in part wittingly and in part unwittingly.

For the disintegrating effect of atheism, particularly upon the will to know, we can see evidence in the career of a great scientific mind of our age. It is always precarious to judge in such complicated matters — indeed we can do little more than guess — but have not the writings of Bertrand Russell shown a marked and almost tragic decline in intellectual strenuousness and vital curiosity since his great early works on mathematics and logic? There was some such change in the later years of Hume. After disposing of the religious question in a relatively negative manner, he turned from philosophy to history, and his history became more and more partisan. Russell long ago came to an even more negative position, and his attitude toward philosophical and scientific problems has since become a curious mixture of boyish pleasure in aiming darts at the pious, anxiety to justify his own practice, some very real longing to help suffering humanity, an all too moderated though still marked and admirable curiosity, and finally a very keen interest in clarity, style, and wit.

It is true that the decline in Russell's intellectuality still leaves a magnificent residuum. And, as already remarked, nothing of a conclusive nature can be made out in such matters. We have to remember also that mathematical genius commonly matures young; and other explanations of Russell's history, equally independent of the effects of humanistic tenets, are not hard to imagine. Only a scientific development of comparative biography, that scarcely existent study, could enable us to give such questions the treatment they deserve.

The value of the essays in popular ethics and theory of education, not to mention history and economics, for which Russell has almost abandoned technical philosophy and mathematics is of course a matter of opinion. It might be interesting to compare them to Hume's *History*. But it is clear enough that in certain respects these essays are exceedingly vulnerable. Russell tries persistently to convince his reader — and indeed there is truth enough in it — that religious thought has inculcated a morality of restriction upon self-enjoyment and even more of interference with the enjoyment of others. Encourage the will to enjoy and discourage the will to persecute, and all will be well, he seems to be forever saying. If there is evidence against this simple solution, Russell systematically ignores it. And there is evidence. Does any anthropologist believe that asceticism is merely evil or foolish? To believe so is to ignore the fact that there is a real choice between strenuous effort toward worth-while goals and what Whitehead refers to as " obvious enjoyments." The Freudian theory, which is sometimes held to imply the superiority of the uninhibited life, seems logically to do nothing of the sort. For if all culture is produced through sublimation of primitive impulse which is partly denied direct expression, then it follows inexorably that such denial within limits is immensely valuable — even though dangerous. Russell ignores all this, and in so far shows the weakness which distresses him in religious apologists, the weakness of unfair selection of evidence.

Russell's widely influential view of marriage involves the belief that the sex relation is profoundly serious when children result, but otherwise is only a pleasant way of being friendly. At least, it should be so, and would be so, if people only realized that jealousy is a mean possessiveness which a right education can reduce to a minimum.[1] H. G. Wells knows better than this, knows that some individuals at least can become so attached to others that it is most disadvantageous for them, to put it mildly, to suffer separation or the parceling out of the loved one's affections.[2] But the deeper aesthetics of sexual love is largely missed by both writers. The beauty of this relation is so supreme in human life that one does not know whether to laugh or mourn when one finds Russell praising it in terms which would not be extravagant applied to any delicacy of the table.

Russell's denial that scientific philosophy has anything to do with values is no doubt partly responsible for the crudity of his ethics and sexual aesthetics. But it would be a poor theism which could have failed to furnish the clue to a sounder view. (Yet one cannot, alas, deny the prevalence of poor theisms!) Love has in it, as theology shows, a principle of infinity such that one cannot do justice to love among human beings, especially the most intimate and many-sided instance of this love, except by seeing in it a partial realization of what, in its fullness, would be divine. Those who take love as merely finite end by making human love even more finite than it need or should be.

Another indication of the weakness of a purely finite theory of values, that is to say, a humanistic theory, is afforded by G. E. Moore. This writer shows that none of the usual humanistic definitions of value are satisfactory.[3] Granting that this or that is preferred or enjoyed by this or that person or group of persons, we can still ask meaningfully, Moore argues, whether or not it is good that it should be so enjoyed. But this observation only shows that imperfect human enjoyment or love is not its own complete excuse for being; it does not refute the idea of a final evaluation which is its own criterion. As Plato said, the perfect is the measure of itself and of the imperfect. Moore, thinking of finite human enjoyments and loves, reaches the conclusion that value is irreducible to them and hence is utterly indefinable, a simple ineffable quality like yellow. From this it follows that the relations of value to other things are wholly inexplicable. There is nothing about the nature of "the good" which explains why enjoyment is better than suffering, or why enjoyment plus intelligence is better than simple enjoyment, or why it is better to be aware than not to be aware. We can only say that more of the simple quality of goodness occurs in the one state than in the other. Here is humanism unwittingly confessing its helplessness in theory of value. Good is indeed not satisfactorily analyzable except in theistic terms. Only the divine love and enjoyment can be finally good without the implication of an ulterior standard. But Moore does not consider the theistic analysis in his proofs of the indefinableness of good.

There is one humanist who has wrestled with most of the difficulties I have pointed out in the non-theistic position, the Rumanian writer Draghicesco. Perhaps the most thoroughgoing attempt ever made to find in humanism the veritable values of religion is his *Vérité et révélation*,[4] especially volume two, entitled *Vers une nouvelle idée de Dieu*. Apparently it really is, in some degree, " a new idea of God " which is set forth. This idea is that the attributes of God posited by traditional theology can be applied with almost complete literalness to man considered in his ultimate potentialities and his long-run destiny. To be sure, man is not now omnipotent, omniscient, and completely benevolent. But as science and technology develop, man's power and understanding increase, and the limit of this increase is nothing less than omnipotence and omniscience. The limit will never be absolutely reached; but any definite point short of it may, for all we can tell, be surpassed. Thus, man can be defined only as " the being the limit of whose development is divinity." The perfect goodness of God is the unreachable but indefinitely approachable goal of ethical progress. Even the eternity of God is not without human meaning; for the advance of technology has as its maximal achievement nothing less than the conquest of death. (This, of course, would mean immortality, not eternity.) Thus Draghicesco's proposal is that humanism should not neglect or reject theology, but that it should translate theological concepts into dynamic and anthropomorphic terms. If I am not mistaken, this is the most completely positive attitude toward theism ever expressed by a non-theistic writer — admitting that it might be regarded as an attempt to bring Comte's humanistic theology up to date.

One thing, at least, seems clear to me. If humanism cannot

frankly confess faith in the infinite perfectibility of man and especially in his immortality as a race, it cannot honestly claim to have preserved the essential values of religion. For the question of infinity, including infinity in terms of time, i.e., eternity, is precisely the question that the high religions have raised; and it is, I repeat, not a candid answer to that question to prattle about any merely finite human goods, however attractive. In this respect much American humanism is infected with scandalous ambiguity. On the other hand, there are some objections to the doctrine of human infinity. Given infinite time, it is perhaps defensible to set up divinity as the limit of human progress. But the omnipotence which is held to be the goal of this endless development cannot be used to guarantee that the development will, in fact, be endless. At any finite time in the future human power will not be absolute. This means that human security will not be absolute, that there always will be a finite risk of the ending of the human adventure through disease, race suicide, stellar collision, or what not. A finite risk, endured for infinite time, looks like an infinite probability of destruction. This is only one way in which the finitude of man appears to be more decisive than our author allows.

Draghicesco mentions two alternatives to humanism. These are traditional theism and pantheism. The former is criticized on the ground that it reduces human progress to the idle task of " re-editing deity." If the limiting value which human achievement approaches is eternally achieved in God, why the approach? This objection, however, would not hold against a form of theism which (1) regarded the perfection of God as a matter of righteousness, power, and knowledge rather than of the completed actualization of all possible enjoyment and beauty; and which consequently (2) admitted a real growth in time of the aesthetic value possessed by deity, to which value human progress could make real contributions. Draghicesco, like so many humanists, ignores this possibility.

The other alternative to humanism is pantheism, the view that the whole of nature is related to a divine mind as a man's body is related to the man's mind. Draghicesco says this hypothesis is "unverifiable and chimerical," but he cleverly translates it into humanistic terms as the infinite goal of technical-scientific progress. The further man develops, the more nearly it will be true that mankind through social unification will constitute a single supermind which will be aware of and control changes throughout nature as a single man is aware of and controls changes in his body. Here, again, there is more distortion than is quite admitted in the humanistic translation. For a mind is related to its body by immediate intuitive rapport, and it does not seem that the advances of science have so far increased the scope of such rapport by any degree. Only if scientific knowledge were to issue in telepathy and the kind of non-instrumental control of material things claimed by some spiritualists or magicians, could the goal of science be described through a humanized pantheism.

On the other hand, objective pantheism has more evidences in its favor than Draghicesco allows. It offers the only hope of construing the world as a genuine and orderly whole, the only hope of intelligibly relating together mind, matter, and law. For instance, Draghicesco's own faith in natural law as real *now* is the basis of his faith in the scientific achievements which man is to enjoy in the future; and the former faith is exactly as unverifiable as pantheism. The logical positivists admit this in insisting that the foundation of induction is purely pragmatic. But there have been and are great and informed intellects (in Orient and Occident) who hold that the divine orderliness of the world is capable of metaphysical verification. With much of the best work in recent metaphysics, e.g., that of Peirce and Whitehead, Draghicesco seems not to be familiar.

If I were convinced with this author that there is no hope for a revised theistic pantheism, I should see nothing better to do than to try to adopt his entire position — or else give up the attempt to deal with the great problems of religion and philosophy. Humanism regards itself as an appeal to intelligence against superstition; but the problem of infinity (and eternity) is of all problems that which is most purely due to intelligence. At any rate, it is the problem of philosophy.

NOTES

[1] Bertrand Russell, *Education and the Good Life* (Boni & Liveright, 1926), pp. 220–22.

[2] An anthropologist's view of Russell's dogmas concerning sex jealousy and possessiveness will be found in Edward Sapir's contribution to *Twenty-Four Views of Marriage* (The Macmillan Co., 1930), pp. 343–61.

[3] *Principia Ethica* (The Macmillan Co., 1903).

[4] Much of the material below is taken from the author's review of Draghicesco's *Vérité et révélation* in the *International Journal of Ethics*, vol. 47, pp. 133–35.

V

RUSSIA AND MARXIAN HUMANISM

THERE ARE some who will reply to all arguments against the practicality of atheistic philosophy by pointing to Russia. Does not the Russian experiment demonstrate the practical superiority of this philosophy to all forms of theology? I confess that I think this contention is plausible. But there are some objections to it the force of which only special students of Russia, and with any finality only posterity, will be able to judge. To embark upon a discussion of this matter is in some measure to leave the role of philosopher and usurp that of historian, economist, or sociologist. Nevertheless, a philosopher may be permitted to express a frankly amateurish opinion.

The fact that the Russian masses have made great advances and now face the future confidently and patriotically, while religious beliefs have reached a low ebb, does not prove that irreligion is a cause of this happy state. Before the revolution Russia lacked both of the two great merits of Western civilization, liberty and a widely diffused prosperity. Undoubtedly the Russian Church was an obstacle to the attainment of either. But the Russian Church is not theism; and the features of that church which made it a barrier to progress cannot be deduced from (naturalistic) theism. When the clerical and political barriers were swept away, an enormous improvement in economic productiveness could be achieved. A wave of optimism, like that of frontier America, was the natural accompaniment of this advance. Moreover, in spite of dictatorship, there were great gains in liberty as compared to the old Russia. We need not stop there. Even as compared to the West generally, there were some gains in freedom for the working class. Russians had known the most extreme modern form of subordination of worker and peasant. When they revolted they went far. And there was no great middle class to overcome, but only a minority class of economic, political, and ecclesiastical rulers.

It is true that, *in the situation,* the only feasible way to oppose the church, which supported the old regime, was to attack the idea of God. What chance had the Russian peasant or artisan to understand the possibilities of a new theology, compatible with science and genuine democracy, which are inherent in the modern climate of opinion? Even less chance than the frontiersman of America had to cultivate philosophy or pure science. The Russians *had* to take a short cut in philosophy if they were to devote themselves to the transition from economic medievalism to the machine age. They left theology behind as Daniel Boone and the prairie schooner left libraries, picture galleries, and pianos. The Russians have not neglected books or the arts, since these are essential to the social unison required for rapid industrialization. Nor have they abandoned all philosophy, for that is impossible. But like the Americans they took just enough philosophy to enable them to concentrate on the practical task, and they took — in an uncritical, evangelical spirit — the kind of philosophy which was available at the time and which suited their practical needs. The Americans took the Protestant sectarian dogmas, founded some new sects, mostly with even more unsophisticated tenets, and thereafter left philosophical subtleties to look after themselves. In this way — and what other was then possible? — they guaranteed the individualism and regionalism necessary to pre-industrial frontier life. The Russians took Marx's inverted Hegelianism, the materialistic dialectic, because it alone expressed the absorption in industrialization and proletarian uplift which was the task of the hour. In both cases the makeshift, short-cut manner of philosophizing is obtrusive. In the eyes of most philosophers Lenin and Stalin as metaphysicians are not much above the level of Mrs. Eddy or Joseph Smith, and Marx himself was no Plato or Leibniz.

An important fact about the Russian situation is that Russian theology failed, if I am not mistaken, to develop any such hearty recognition of the role of mechanism, any such sharply formulated conception of God as supermechanic, as enabled European theologians from Leibniz down to sanction the scientific-technological attitude. Veblen, to be sure, has argued that the religious attitude inevitably encourages an animistic conception of nature which is irreconcilable with mechanism and discourages efficient understanding of technical processes. But with subtle sophistries Leibniz evaded this difficulty. And the new statistical mechanics shows definitely that there is no contradiction whatever between mechanism in all practical matters and animism, or panpsychism, with regard to the ultimate individuals of nature. The reconciliation depends upon the gigantic numbers of individuals and the insignificance of the eccentricities of any one. But we need waste no words to show that it was natural for the scientifically backward Russians to shelve the whole problem by denying the religious concept.

It may be said that nothing of all this can refute the fact that without God the Russians do well. There are here two questions: how far are they " without God," and how far is it " well " with them?

It is important first of all to remember that belief, in its full sense, is more subconscious than conscious, more a matter of behavior and feeling than of words. From this point of view, to what extent do the Russians really believe there is no God? The Russian lives by faith, faith that he can persevere in his constructive efforts, that a sufficient number of his fellows will also persevere, that other nations will not fatally interfere, that the order of nature will not lapse into chaos, that something at least of the significance which his acts, with his limited knowledge of the world in space and time, appear to him to have, they really do have, even considering the most distant objects and events. All these things the Russian might believe if he believed in God; some of them he would then have to believe, and to this extent he virtually does so believe now.

But it will be said that the Russian faith is in man, not in God. The matter is not so simple. Faith in man is absurd without faith in nature as an enduring, and for man tolerably convenient, system of activities. It is also absurd without an implicit trust, which need not be verbalized, that the future, however remote, will leave intact something of the value of our hour of achievement. This is part at least of what is meant by Providence. It is quite naïve to suppose that men who "rely on their own efforts" are therefore not relying upon God. The old principle, God helps those who help themselves, is not a cynical paradox but the only tenable notion of Providence. The essence of human values, as Aristotle long ago said, lies in the exercise of human powers, so that to sit with folded hands while asking God for blessings is to reject in advance the gift asked for. Providence means, among other things, that the world is so arranged as to provide ample scope for the exercise of human powers. But among these powers the greatest of all is the power of dramatizing to ourselves, and in this way participating in, the larger activities around us — those of our fellow men, and at the

limit those of all nature. The power of living consciously
as a citizen of the cosmos is the basic human prerogative, and
the more fully this power is realized, the more clearly it reveals itself as the vision of God.

The Russians do not wholly believe in this aspect of
Providence. In so far as they see the dialectical conflict in
all nature as well as in human history, they are living as world
citizens. But nowhere are the dialectical thesis and antithesis and synthesis more tenuous or artificial than in application to physics. Only a people overwhelmed with economic
concerns could for a time be satisfied with such a crude theological minimum. Since man lives by symbols as well as by
animal impulse and habit, it is not a matter of indifference if
his verbal beliefs are inadequate to express his behavior.
Sooner or later he must improve his symbols or his behavior
will degenerate.

Genuine belief in a God of love means a disposition to love
those whom God loves: all men. However, the saying, "Inasmuch as ye have done it unto the least of these, ye have done
it unto me," indicates that we are to love God's friends not
merely because they are such, but for the very reasons for
which God loves them, their actual and potential values, their
merits and their needs. *In so far as* we do this, we are putting
ourselves in the position of God and are even identical with
him. Now the Russians are succoring the unfortunate and
seeking to minister to human needs on a grand scale. To
this extent they have the substance of the love of God. But
the reason they cannot in the fullest sense be said to love God
is that they do not value sufficiently the whole man, nor see
him as an integral part of the whole of nature which, as really
an organized whole, *is* God. To love this man plus that man
plus a third man is different from loving God and these men
as beloved of God. Also, to love the social whole as an abstraction is different from this; but to love all men in their

individualities and their social solidarity, and to love the other parts of nature, and to bind all these lines of sympathy into a living unity in oneself, is to imitate in the small way possible to man the divine love. The more conscious we are that it is our purpose so to love men and nature, the more conscious we must become of the ideal criterion by which this purpose is inspired and its success estimated; and this ideal is God. We must agree that the Russian purpose has not reached this degree of clarity.

How far, then, is it really well with the Russians? Their material instrumentalities have been enormously increased. Literacy has been diffused with wonderful rapidity. A vast army of scientific investigators has sprung up, though it is too soon to say how much they will accomplish. But the romance of love has been injured by a crass casualness — admitting that there have been gains in equality for women. Economic competition being largely set aside, the will to power is concentrated in the struggle for party control. If the struggle is not yet bitter, that is because attention is absorbed by the rapid industrial progress and the new privileges in education and the arts. Satisfied by these, as the mujiks formerly were by religion and folk art, the great mass of Russians accept their rulers and their own humble position. But as the novelty wears off and confidence in individual capacity increases, the gigantic power of the party and its heads will be differently evaluated. The promises of real democracy will then fall due, and a ruling class more powerful than that in almost any other country will be asked to submit to the radical diminution of its powers. If the will to power is inherent in man, there will be trouble. (Since these sentences were written an incipient rebellion has occurred, resulting in the execution of over a dozen prominent party leaders.)

The will to power is inherent in man. For on the one hand

man is conscious of an infinite ideal, and on the other hand it is always easier for him to conceive of the good in terms of his own than of others' realization. And besides, the inability of men to understand one another except very partially and abstractly makes the necessity of entrusting our affairs largely to a few executives (a condition of efficiency) a bitter necessity. And stung by the sense of the unlimited possibilities of existence, in contrast to the always narrow limits of their own actual achievements, men will always be tempted to excessive ambition. It is a perfect example of wishful oversimplification and fancy to indulge in the dream of the fading away of the struggle for power simply because ordinary competition for " profit " has been done away with. Prestige, direct political power made to include also economic power — and salaries and other material advantages of party officials are not and certainly will not be negligible — will quite obviously invite competition for the largest share of this power.

Meanwhile the highest of all liberties, liberty in the search for truth, is crippled in Russia. Science is held to be essentially pragmatic. Truth is to be valued if its industrial utility can be seen. And the philosophical short cut of the dialectic is sacrosanct. Physics may not accept doctrines which offer difficulties to the belief in blind material forces. Metaphysics can only repeat Marx, as in the Roman Church it does little but repunctuate Aquinas. The question is not if this sketch is precisely just to the actual situation in Russia; it is enough that there are strong tendencies in the indicated directions. A mature and healthy culture will have largely eliminated such insults to the intellectual life.

The Marxian critique of religion affirms that religion is historically an illusory technique for controlling nature, and an all too successful technique for exalting one class over another — and of consoling the exploited class with the

" opium " of otherworldly hopes. These charges are force-fully expounded in Calverton's *Passing of the Gods*.

Taking the second charge first, it seems that a naturalistic theism provides no ground whatever for exploitation or tyranny and every ground for opposing them. God is not a super-king, on the side of lesser kings, but the sympathetic unity of the world on the side of whatever makes for such unity. Kingly power may, at a given time, be a necessary means to such unity; but the power is godlike only in so far as it directly depends upon sympathetic identification with the subjects. The fact that kings, and priests wishing for kinglike prerogatives, have presented the matter otherwise is no reason for accepting their authority in questions theological, but only shows that the will to blind power, and the inability to imagine power that is not blind and that understands and is sensitive to what it influences, are prominent characteristics of human beings.

As for the " opiate " function of religion, it has been real enough; but part of this function is necessary to any society, and part of it is not necessary to theistic religion and might occur without it. Sacrifices will always be required of individuals and groups. The Russians gave up wheat to buy machinery; some of them were dead of starvation before the machinery could provide consumable goods. There will never be unlimited abundance of all luxuries and all enjoyments for everyone, and with the best efforts at just distribution there will still be injustice. Whoever can believe otherwise can believe anything. The remedy cannot lie exclusively in rebellion against injustice; and the hungry Russians did not rebel. But they did console themselves with hopes, including some that were illusory, such as the hope of a world rapidly converted to communism. The ideal is that there should be resentment strong enough to check injustice, but patience and good humor sufficient to make cooperation and happiness possible in spite of ordinary miscarriages of justice.

The trouble with organized religion has been that the conceptions of heaven and hell were such as to imply the insignificance even of major wrongs in society. A man needed only to preserve his piety to win an infinity of blessedness in return for a handful of terrestrial joys. But the theistic doctrine does not of itself imply any such heaven or the corresponding idea of hell. Oriental theism took a different tack, and naturalistic theism may take still another. It is debatable whether theism logically implies any personal immortality at all, and quite clear that it does not imply a miraculously untroubled heaven to be gained by a few years of goodness. If God is the Life of Nature, then piety means love of that life, and people whose children cannot see anything of nature except what can be seen in dirty streets filled with work-weary or drunken men and women cannot suppose that it will make no difference " in heaven " that these children saw so little to love around them. And whatever the future of personality may be, the conviction that God lives nowhere if not in nature, which is his body, means that the natural values of human life — the most godlike part of nature known to us — must be given high religious significance.

On the other hand, the thought of the sublime total of values in God brings a legitimate solace in misfortune. The Marxian says that the fear of death or individual loss is to be overcome by stress upon the group. But the group may itself be in danger from other groups, and no human group, not the race itself, can be known to be immortal. Moreover, as we have seen, the group is essentially an imperfect integration of the values of individuals; hence extreme collectivism passes either into the myth of the group personality, imaged by the quasi-divine leader or hero, or relapses into egoistic separatism. Only a real person who really embraces persons in his own life can enable us to escape both selfishness and an ignoble submergence in the mob. The many must also be the one, and both the unity and plurality must be genuine and adequate. A disciplined theism puts the emphasis here, not upon personal immortality into the thought of which egoism so easily creeps. (Even so orthodox a Christian as Berdyaev says that the doctrine of eternal punishment is a piece of sadism.)

The charge that religion is essentially the attempt to move mountains by prayer and faith when they should be moved by steam shovels is, to my mind, the most cogent of all criticisms of religion. It may be answered as follows: In so far as men find in nature minds somewhat like their own to deal with, the method of emotional appeal does work — as with dogs and horses. A dog will sometimes execute our wishes, our "prayers," when he apprehends them. And he certainly appreciates the "sacrifices" of food and drink we put upon his plate. The savage could not be expected to know that only an insignificant portion of the world consists of high-grade individuals open to such treatment, for he could not have guessed that the senses are far too gross to reveal the minute and low-grade individuals which mostly constitute the universe in its present form. Nor could he have appreciated the "law of high numbers" according to which it is a matter of indifference to us what individual units may do, so long as certain average effects obtain. These average effects cannot be produced by individual or collective appeals to the low-grade units themselves, for we have no means of signaling to them nor they the capacity to read such signals, being too elementary for that. But the units are sensitive to their neighbor units, and in this way they are united indirectly with our own bodies, and upon the units of these bodies we can and do act by a relation of direct rapport which, as we shall see, is very well interpretable as one of sympathy, but so immediate and so little conscious is this rapport that it does not take the form of verbal appeal. It is this *unnoticed* sympathetic action which alone enables us to control the non-animal parts of nature. Thus the savage was not necessarily wrong in principle in imputing power to social rapport, but he was almost entirely wrong in his conception of the grades of such rapport and their distribution in nature.

But there is the question of nature herself, the inclusive individuality. We can manipulate nature in detail; the large features, or at least the *largest* features, we must submit to. If we believe that these features express a cosmic life whose value transcends the value of man, we can cheerfully accept the restrictions which it imposes upon us. Prayer is in that case our attempt to participate imaginatively in the larger process, to enjoy a sort of social relation with its principal personality. Moreover, since "love" implies the will to understand, love of God means the desire to know the laws of nature which are his ways; and hence there is no concession to irreligion in preferring scientific control to blind petitioning of deity.

But control is not the only important aspect of our relation to nature. No one who has ever seen a playing kitten or a singing bird can think so. What is enjoyable about the bird is not anything we can do with it, but our intuitive and, if we are ornithologists in any degree, our intellectual understanding of its life, its enjoyments, desires, and fears, to which our own human existence is merely incidental. The supreme form of this participating relation is enshrined in religion. That religion has often appeared as merely a spurious form of pragmatic activity only shows how hard pressed man has been, but does not determine how religion should develop in the more leisurely future. Science can be an improved substitute for religion, or, if you like, a better religion, only if science does well not only what old-fashioned religion did so ill — control nature — but also what that religion did at least moderately well and merely pragmatic science does not do at all, namely, enable us to enrich our own life by seeing in nature everywhere life more or less radically different from our own. The fact that primitive man saw in the gods mainly allies or foes should not prevent us, who have more secure power over nature, from developing a more detached enjoyment of natural activities. The Marxian apparently wants us to be as narrowly pragmatic as the primitives, or as the less enlightened of the privileged classes, although he wants our pragmatism to be more efficient. Sydney Hook's contention that Marx was a pragmatist in his theory of knowledge is, I fear, all too true. But Marx's pragmatism is, in emphasis at least, opposite to that of Peirce. Peirce held that in order to define our ideas we must consider how they would affect action. But this did not mean that the essential purpose of ideas is to affect action. On the contrary, the chief value of action is that it enables us to define our ideas and to think the thoughts of nature after her. No man valued knowledge for its own sake more than Peirce. For him the love of nature was religious, a means of appreciation, not primarily of utilitarian control. Who disagrees with Peirce here cannot, it seems, have watched animals or ever have given his heart to scientific inquiry into the nature of things.

A final Marxian argument is that just as in Russia ecclesiastical barriers to advance could be swept away only by complete no-godliness, so in America the churches, as allies of the wealthy, will have to be discredited by atheistic propaganda before effective social reform — that is, revolution — will be possible. This is an intelligible position. But three remarks are in order: The temporary utility of atheism would not demonstrate its truth; the relation of religion to reform is not the same in America as in Russia; and the case for revolution as the method of reform is on a very different footing in the two countries.

On the first point, the Marxian cannot have it both ways. If he admits, and I think he must, that religion was necessary to man at a certain stage of his development, yet holds that religion is not a true account of the universe, then he must also admit that the present necessity for atheism, if there is such necessity, does not establish its truth. To be sure, Marxists usually claim that atheism will be a permanent necessity to human welfare through all the future. But I think we may safely defy them to prove this. All such arguments turn out, upon analysis, to concern not theism as such, but certain special historical forms of it, or even more, certain historical forms of ecclesiastical organization. And obviously, if there is ever a classless society the emergence of religion in that society could not embody class tyranny. It would be a classless religion; and if that is a contradiction in terms the reason escapes me — except in so far as all organized human activity, whether scientific, religious, or artistic, implies a division of labor and some delegation of defined responsibilities to certain individuals in accordance with their capacity. But what has the vision of nature as a unity through love to do with class?

On the difference between religion and its relations to reform in Russia and America there is much to say. Russian religion was a static orthodoxy, relatively autocratic in organization. American churches are more familiar with the inevitability of change (most of them are relatively young, and many have no formal creeds) ; and their very variety compels the more intelligent of their members to suspect the relativity of the doctrines which divide them. The American churches are mostly rather democratic in government. Russian religion was the antithesis of a scientific-technological philosophy of life; American Protestantism has inspired industrialization, talked incessantly of progress, and displayed great zeal in the promotion of education. Protestant preachers who submit current economic methods to drastic criticism are fairly numerous, and some have wide influence. In the seminaries there are many young men who are eager to join this group if they can find sufficiently tolerant congregations. Whether they can do so or not depends partly upon the failure or success of Marxian propaganda in driving liberals and radicals out of the churches. If reform insists upon alienating itself from religion, the attempts of religion to go reformist may fail partly through that very insistence. This is the kind of divisiveness which communists have too successfully practiced in countries where their own ends are not unambiguously advanced in this way.

Between the hostility of radicals and the dependence (not so great as is often supposed, however) of church plants and salaries on men of wealth, it cannot be doubted that there is hard sledding ahead for Christian radicals. But it may not be to the interest of radicalism in general to make the sledding harder than it need be. Even the autocratic Roman Church has in America one asset it lacks elsewhere, association primarily with the underprivileged, which should make it easier for it to side with justice here than anywhere else.

But the significance of these facts depends on our third point, the peculiar status of the revolutionary method in America as compared to Russia. It was one thing to " take over power " from a ruling class in a non-industrialized society in order to industrialize that society. The overthrown rulers were *not themselves industrialists;* hence their loss was unimportant, and this was so obvious that no mass support could be found for them. But in a country with a large class of persons both influential and industrially trained, the situation is as nearly opposite as could be, and can hardly call for

anything like the same method.   This is a big-industry and
middle-class and white-collar-employee country; and in all
such countries anything remotely analogous to the Russian
move has been shown to be out of the question.   Accordingly,
the unlikelihood that American religion will go revolutionary
in a Marxian sense is not necessarily to be deplored.   A child-
ishly inapplicable idea of reform ought to be opposed.   And
certainly we should be only grateful to the churches for defending, in so far as they have defended and will defend, the
ideal of freedom of conscience against totalitarian tendencies.
This ideal the Russians knew almost nothing about a century
and a half after America was founded upon it.[1]

It is not the elimination of freedom or privacy of enterprise
which we Americans can envy in the Russian scheme; for too
much other freedom and privacy appear to be eliminated
with the economic.   But the absence of privately owned mo-
nopolies, trusts, cartels — monstrous bastard forms of private-
public business run for profit but with virtually political
powers — that is the marvelous and far too little noticed
blessing which the revolutionary method has brought the
Russians.   If in Russia free enterprise should spring up in
spheres in which there is no necessity to permit monopoly
privileges, it would not be a loss but a gain; for a state which
runs everything must boss everything and produce mob-
minded individuals not worthy of human potentialities.

I am tempted to give the last word to the Marxians.   It is
a sorry enough record, that of religious connivance with industrial cruelty and religious blindness to the needs of a
changing social order.   But one really must add that out of
religion has also come the demand for justice which Marxism embodies.   Tillich has shown how far there is correspond-
ence between the Hebrew prophets and the Marxian critics
of modern society.[2]   Who can doubt the immense debt of

Marxism to Jewish and Christian theism?[3]   And one must also add that the religion of the future is not obliged to repeat all the mistakes of the religions of the past.

NOTES

[1] For an illuminating comparison of communistic and Anglo-American ideals see T. V. Smith, *The Promise of American Politics* (University of Chicago Press, 1936).

[2] Paul Tillich, "Marx and the Prophetic Tradition," *Radical Religion*, vol. 1, no. 1, pp. 21–29.

[3] That these religious elements of Marxism do not remotely exhaust the aid to economic reform derivable from religion will be evident to most readers of Kagawa's *Brotherhood Economics* (Harper & Brothers, 1936, pp. 99–196). The development of credit, insurance, medical, consumer, and producer cooperatives on a community, national, and international scale is the most hopeful plan of reform today. But if a generalized cooperative movement is the best hope of the world, there is evidence that religion is the best hope of the cooperative movement. Secular economists and atheistic radicals tend to neglect its possibilities, or to deny them, and in America retailing is too efficient to make the hope of immediate material gain to consumers an adequate motive for cooperatives. On the other hand, economic cooperation agrees with religious ethics in a clear, direct manner, as competition, monopoly, dictatorship, or state socialism do not. Doubtless there will be some who will dare to say that brotherhood economics is irreligious; but the hypocrisy will be too transparent to escape detection. Religious idealism may well find here its chief escape from the terrible dilemma: predatory capitalism or dictatorship. If I have made concessions to competitive capitalism or to state socialism which appear to conflict with the program of the great leaders of cooperatism, I hope that these concessions will be viewed with suspicion. (Kagawa, it is true, favors a minor element of private capitalism even from a long-run point of view, but is not hopeful about state or municipal ownership so long as the money must come from ordinary banks rather than from funds accumulated and owned by cooperatives.)

VI

FREUD'S VIEW OF RELIGION

PROBABLY no man of genius has influenced our time more than has Sigmund Freud. Freud's humanism is indicated in the title of his little book on religion, *The Future of an Illusion*.[1] When we remember that the two predecessors of Freud in the theory of unconscious motivation were the atheists, Schopenhauer and Von Hartmann, we have at least one clue to Freud's position. The fact is that theism had in German culture reached what might be called an " all-time low " in prestige and intellectual quality at the time Freud was working out his doctrine. Nietzsche's brilliant repudiation of Christianity was almost forced upon him by the Christianity which he found, when judged by the standards of reasoning which science was suggesting. Thus it would have been strange if Freud had not been atheistic, if he had not taken atheism almost for granted.

Turning to Freud's *The Future of an Illusion*, we find such expectations fulfilled. In this powerful little book the question of the truth of religious ideas is hardly a live issue at all. Freud does indeed say that we are equally unable to prove or disprove most religious doctrines.[2] Yet he also says that the contradiction religion offers to reason and experience is " only too palpable," and he insists that the only way to save religious belief from ultimate destruction by science is to empty it of all religious content "by calling ' God ' some vague abstraction " invented by philosophers, some " higher spiritual being whose qualities are indefinable and whose intentions cannot be discerned," [3] instead of " the mighty personality of religious doctrine." [4]   Freud does not think there is any need of psychoanalysis to establish atheism, for he holds that the essential considerations have long been well known. [5]   All the evidence is opposed to the notion that man is " the center of creation, . . . the object of the tender care of a benevolent providence." [6]

But psychoanalysis does strengthen the case against theism by showing how the assumption of a Father-God can be explained as the extension of the childhood attitude toward the father as the overawing protector and guide.   The adult sees that in the face of the forces of nature he is permanently in a position of childish dependence; and this realization is made tolerable by the conception of a fatherly power behind nature.   Religious ideas fit our wishes so exactly and correspond to other forms of wishful thinking, such as dreams, so beautifully that it would be " very odd " if they were also true. [7]   Still odder would it be " if our poor, ignorant, enslaved ancestors had succeeded in solving all these riddles of the universe."   Finally, religion shows many traits parallel to the neuroses which are the more or less normal accompaniments of leaving childhood.   This is shown too by the therapeutic value of religion for the believer: " By accepting the universal neurosis he is spared the task of forming a personal neurosis."

Freud's argument seems to me a supreme example of intelligent, honest atheism.   One can see how truly inevitable the rejection of religion is for him.   Nevertheless his reasoning suffers from too many oversights and ambiguities to settle the question.   He does not really define the issue.

First, take his contention that it is only by emptying religious doctrines of religious meaning that philosophers have made them more or less defensible against scientific criticism. This is also Santayana's point when he says that though " much philosophy " leads a man back to God, it is not the same God as that from which " a little philosophy " had alienated him. Now my belief is that this observation is true of traditional theology. But the most recent changes in theistic doctrine are a *reversal* of theological procedure in this respect; and this change is not at all a mere matter of deciding once more to defy science and logic in order to defend genuinely religious ideas, but rather of perceiving that, up to a certain point at least, the present state of science and logic supports religion in its preference of the more humanly meaningful conceptions over the vague abstractions of the older theology. If asked for evidence for this statement I have to point to this whole book and the one which is to follow it, or to the works of Whitehead, Bishop Tennant, and other writers who are dealing with this remarkable change in the relations of theology, religion, and science.

In the argument from the " fatal resemblance " of modern religious ideas to those of our benighted ancestors, there is a similar ambiguity. If it were a question of agreement with these ancestors without essential improvement upon their beliefs, then doubtless it would be a suspicious circumstance. But theism — as those not trained in metaphysics are continually overlooking — is a question of first principles, not of details. If God is, he is the center and unity of all our basic meanings. It is then impossible for a reflective person not to be conscious of him in some degree. Our ancestors were incapable of scientific accuracy, or perhaps of logical precision in analysis, but some more or less concrete feeling of God they must have had, or they would not on theistic premises have been able to generalize, to philosophize, at all. The case for theism, if there is a case, is that all philosophizing is clear and consistent only in so far as it is explicitly and persistently theistic. But ideas begin in a sort of intuitive form. Why should not men long ago have reached the basic outlines of a sound though relatively unanalytic theistic philosophy? The fact that they were full of radically erroneous ideas concerning details and ideas of less generality than first principles is no proof to the contrary. But in any case it begs the whole question to assert that the development of theology has brought no radical improvement. Primitive theism had no real analysis to offer of the relation of God to the world, of mind to matter, of change to eternity. Aristotelian theology sought for such an analysis without very striking success. But there is now a radically different approach which utilizes what the modern age has learned about logic and other branches of philosophy, and many suggestions from natural science as well.

The wishfulness of religion is of course Freud's primary point. Now, once more, it is not a question of religion or no religion. There are at least degrees of wishfulness, as involved in different kinds of religion, to consider. The ideas of heaven as a place where there is no labor and no suffering and no uncertainty, or where there are many beautiful and complaisant women or "happy hunting grounds" are plainly enough dreams in which men compensate for the trials of this life. (The notion of a state of existence above time and change I should regard as another such genuine illusion, whether this state is ascribed to deity only or also to the saved in paradise.) All such details of religious doctrine can have no rational philosophic ground; for philosophy has no concern with details, and it is natural that wishes should have played a decisive role in determining them.

For instance, the notion of God as "moral governor" of the universe is subject to wishful distortions. If it means that the moral code of the given society is enforced by the deity upon the cosmos, then it is illusion. There is no such thing as a cosmic code or an eternal code, but only the cosmic eternal ideal of love, of the social enjoyment of aesthetic feeling, including that aspect of such enjoyment which is found in the intellectual life. Manners and customs and rules of conduct embodying this ideal are relative to time and place and local history. Naturally societies have tried narcissistically to get cosmic sanction for these manners and customs, not only as best for them then and there, but also as better than all others universally. This attitude was wishful and is eliminated from philosophical theism.

Again, the notion that man is the center of the universe is one thing, and the notion that there is a benevolent Providence is quite another. The former idea is not yet completely shattered by astronomy, since we still do not know that we are *not* the highest of the creatures; but it certainly has no positive support from reason — to say the least. Its wishfulness is patent. But the fact that men have valued the idea of Providence chiefly as a guarantor of human benefits should not be allowed to obscure the logic of the idea. This logic has nothing whatever to do with the centrality of man. Universal love in God means regard for the values which the creatures embody; and there is no logic whatever in the notion that such love must be bound by our own tendency to think primarily of human values. Even we can love animals; and if Providence has guided the world into the production, at some point, of beings who are more intelligent or more richly sensitive than we are, we could not possibly make rational protest because Providence recognized this superiority and gave it its due significance in the course of events. How can the ideal of perfect love be identified with the belief that the imperfections of human love are cosmically binding?

But, Freud would perhaps say, by eliminating the human partiality and selfishness from the religious idea you deprive it of its power to console and interest ordinary men and women, that is, of its specifically religious content. Perhaps so, but admission that a sane theism is not in this sense a " religious " doctrine and that it will never be popular leaves untouched the question of its " reality value," and of its inspirational value for sufficiently generous souls. Maybe the word " religion " ought to be reserved for the wishful perversions of the theistic ideal. That ideal is the notion that the most perfect example of social sharing is also the supreme power, that there is a knowledge which is adequate to all facts and to all values by virtue of supreme sensitiveness to all feelings — which, as the new philosophy holds, are the stuff of existence — and finally, that there is a purpose which envisages the fulfillment of lesser purposes, so far as they are compatible with one another, and in accordance with their aesthetic-social value. Now this ideal is not wishful in an ordinary sense. It does not flatter our individual or human self-esteem any more than it flatters all creatures of value. The standpoint of God is the standpoint we seek to occupy when we try to see our limitations and the values of other creatures as they are.

Is this ideal too high, too austere to yield religious inspiration? I am sure that it is at least closer than medieval theology, with its denial of divine sensitivity and change, to the ideal that actually did inspire Jesus and Isaiah and Confucius.

But it may be held that the idea is still a wishful one. Nature seems to have no particular tenderness for *any* of her creatures. How, except on the basis of desire, can it be held that she has such tenderness for all of them, us included? Yet if an inclination to this contention be called wishful, it must at least be admitted that it is in a class by itself among wishful thoughts. For it is the wish of a rational being as such that each member of the universe should count for what it is worth, that each of us human beings, for example, should have not only a private value for ourselves alone, but also a public value, a value for the whole. Even Dewey, as I have pointed out, feels that we must affirm so much. For Freud it is thoroughly irreligious — but yet the only sane and mature attitude — for men " humbly to acquiesce in their insignificance in the universe," [8] but if " insignificance " means of no significance whatever, cosmically speaking, then the reply is that even a worm should think better of itself than that.

Thus the issue is subtler and more complex than Freud sees. Much that he says we should renounce ought to be renounced — as wishful illusions or neuroses if you will — but why should we give up the only rational conception possible of the relation of values to the universe?

Freud argues cogently that the religious way has been tried long enough to show what it can do. Yes, many wishful specializations of religion have been tried, and so has Aristotelian or Neoplatonic theology, but not the theistic kernel of religion conceived in terms worthy of modern knowledge. For less than two decades has such a theism been tried, even on a small scale. The preaching of God which sees natural science as the most authentic revelation of the beauty of the divine body, and past or present social systems as but a few of the inexhaustible ways of achieving on the human plane the beauty-in-sympathy, and sympathy-in-beauty, which is the divine principle, has only begun to affect education, popular literature, religion, and art.

Not a word does Freud say about the religious spirit of most natural scientists. Like many social scientists he scarcely sees the problem of scientific motivation, probably because lively curiosity about ourselves and our fellow men is intelligible enough on any doctrine. He hopes for a state of human life to be enjoyed by remote posterity in which existence will be tolerable for all without illusory compensations; and, reasonably enough, contrasts this objective with the more "selfish" and impatient aspiration to personal bliss immediately after death. But he says nothing about the probable destruction of the human race either before or after it has reached such a state.

As for the father complex, man must stumble upon ideas as best he can, as chemistry grew out of alchemy, and this in part out of greed, or astronomy out of astrology, and this in part out of a desire to cheat time and see our human future before it is made. And since in trying to interpret the universe man has to conceive how he is related to that which is greater than he, and since only as a child dealing with adults has the human being relations to that which is essentially and unambiguously superior to himself, it is not illogical to use this relation as an analogy, the only one we have — apart from science, with its revelation of the structure of reality as one of organisms within organisms — of the more obscure relation of man to the universe. Of course much is misleading or open to wishful development in the analogy, and it is to make the needed corrections that theology exists.

The Freudian emphasis upon sex, and the idea that our motivations are much deeper and darker than they seem, need not disturb the theist. Both features of Freudianism are religious rather than the reverse. Religion, which actually compares marriage to the relation of Christ to the church, to mention but one instance, has always known that sex was the great example, on the plane of instinct, of the union of beings which is the divine principle of the world; and religion has certainly always known that human nature is full of obscure possibilities of evil almost entirely concealed from casual introspection. The doctrine of original sin has more in common with Freud's doctrine of the libido than with Russell's damning of sex with faint praise as " decent, healthy, and delightful." But — deeply indebted though we are to it — there are some inadequacies in Freudianism if it be taken as a theory of values. Freud shows that life is never really as tame and harmless as it sometimes seems on the surface; that some expression of physical and emotional desire there must be, since passion cannot simply vanish at the behest of some moralist — even if the passion is jealousy, and the moralist Bertrand Russell! Passionate love for a person (in some cases oneself), or sublimated passion for an idea, or something from the human standpoint impersonal or superpersonal — between these we must choose. Passion, as Spinoza said, is overcome by another passion, not by mere emotionless thought or a fiat of will. But there is a wide range of choice among passions. How far shall we sublimate physical passion into intellectual or religious or humanitarian passion? How far can the cultural devotions be made exciting enough to hold their own, retain their due place? To this question theistic religion has a clearer answer than any Freudian humanist. Even Spinoza's attenuated theism illustrates this advantage.

The mere therapeutic question is not really solved by the Freudians. For apart from the fact, if it is a fact, that they sometimes fail, and that their successes leave something to be wished, the crucial objection remains that the method is vastly too complicated and expensive to meet the needs of more than an infinitesimal portion of mankind. This has been admitted by at least one foremost practitioner. Surely religious inspiration can sometimes do even better, and with far less strain on the community's economic resources, what the analyst effects so painfully and slowly and with such risks of inducing new morbidities. An able psychiatrist, a student of Freud, told me that in his opinion a strong force on the side of normality was the belief in God — which, interestingly enough, meant for him the conception of ourselves as something like cells in the divine organism. A non-Freudian psychiatrist also expressed the belief that agnosticism was a disintegrating tendency. In fact all three of the competent persons with whom I happen to have discussed the question agreed in this conclusion. Jung appears to be of the same mind, and likewise many other trained writers. And surely the position makes sense. A supreme and indestructible object of devotion — why should that not be the ideal way to overcome lack of perspective in other devotions, to atone for necessary renunciations which no social arrangement or code can entirely eliminate, to counteract narcissism, make compensatory roles superfluous, balance the powerful tendencies toward sadism and 'masochism? The case seems too clear for elaborate argument. Nor does it prove anything against it to call religion itself a compensatory phenomenon.

Freud remarks that human culture tends toward narcissistic nationalism. But the need for an object of reverence above the nation, yet concrete and real and unified, and such that to it the values of individuals are even more intimately relevant than to the organized nation, seems to escape him. Only nature is concrete and real and unified and supernatural, and only nature includes the whole man with all his values. To try to understand this inclusion is our supreme problem, as Dewey says. Freud insists that it is from science that the answers to all questions must be derived. But he sees no distinction between special science and general science, science of the relative generalities and science of first principles. The latter is philosophy, whose supreme achievement is the theistic concept. In considering this concept no man can fail to undergo temptations to give way to illusions. At the least, we all " wish " — and mightily, if we are thinkers — for a clear, decisive disposal of the question, as clear and seemingly decisive as that presented by Freud. But the case against theism is really not so conveniently and flatteringly simple. Even had we never had fathers, there would be no other equally applicable hypothesis of world unity than the binding power of love, the only mode of unity we know from within in *any* of our relations.

The theoretical first principle of Freudianism, the principle of subconscious memory as the background of action, points toward religion. For the new theism, at any rate, views memory as an attribute of God, and the imperfect degree of consciousness of human memory as that which distinguishes it from, while yet in a dim way uniting it with, the divine. If to know that one's past is participated in by another, the analyst, has a therapeutic value, why not also the realization that God at all times vividly remembers all that we remember, however dimly? Not that he simply " knows " our past in a colorless, timeless omnipotence, which is totally lacking in the drama of before and after, but that he literally remembers it. And with an incomparably more sympathetic and balanced understanding than any psychiatric practitioner.

NOTES

[1] Sigmund Freud, *The Future of an Illusion* (Horace Liveright and the Institute of Psycho-Analysis, 1928).

[2] *Ibid.*, p. 55.   [3] *Ibid.*, p. 94.   [4] *Ibid.*, p. 57.

[5] *Ibid.*, p. 65.   [6] *Ibid.*, p. 85.   [7] *Ibid.*, p. 58.

[8] *Ibid.*, p. 57.

VII

HISTORIC FORMS OF HUMANISM

It is interesting to consider the results of humanism as tested in the laboratory of history. Unfortunately — or fortunately — no important culture of the past was founded upon humanism in anything like a pure form.

Perhaps the greatest men of all time who have been claimed for humanism are Buddha and Confucius. Of them we have two questions: Were they humanists; were their views of life adequate to human needs?

The puzzling doctrine of nirvana, absolute deliverance from the pain of desire and the restrictions of individuality, is not easy to interpret in humanistic fashion. Historically it is plainly an echo of the Hindu vision of union with the Absolute. Certainly it is not the ideal of present-day humanism. Despite all its agnosticism concerning God, the soul, and immortality, Buddhism is as open to the charge of wishful thinking as is any theism. How delightful to escape the evils accompanying desire and yet somehow achieve all the real value of existence! Yet what grounds are there for believing that the conditions of evil — such as individuality — are not also the conditions of good? And does not Buddhism make for the ascetic neglect of human potentialities, just as did the early Christian belief in an imminent end of the world? Buddhists have, if I am not mistaken, contributed next to nothing to the development of natural science. The Indian Absolute is in general not positive enough, not sufficiently analogous to man as a rational being, to stimulate inquiry into the ways of nature; nor is it clearly enough related to man as a social being to stimulate to the uttermost man's sense of responsibility to his fellows. And Buddhism aggravated this weakness by placing a veto upon speculations whose utility for the ethics of personal salvation was not manifest. In this sense Buddha was the first great pragmatist.

If Buddhism is the only great near-humanistic religion of the past — and it seems to be so — its fate is suggestive. First, it failed in the country of its birth. Second, it is a minor religion even in China and Japan. Third, in all popular forms it deifies Buddha and makes other concessions to theism. Certainly, then, the history of Buddhism furnishes little support for the belief that humanism can provide a substitute for theistic religion.

It has been maintained that Confucius was a humanist. This seems to have been a mistake. Confucius makes a number of references to the will of " Heaven," to its interest in his life-work, and to its understanding — superior to that of men — of his purposes. And Confucian commentators took these passages at face value for at least fifteen hundred years.[1] Only in the last few centuries has agnosticism crept into some Confucian circles. The great religion of China, then, really was a religion, and not, as is so often asserted, a mere ethics. It did not take man to be the highest being in the universe. It would not have been content with the modern view of man and the higher animals as the sole bearers of value in a fundamentally indifferent, insentient cosmos. Confucius seems rather to have thought that values, particularly ethical values, are pervasive in nature. And how strange to deny theistic implications to the religion of a country whose basic political concept was the Decree of Heaven![2]

On the other hand, Confucius does not seem to have reached a philosophical conception capable of clarifying the relations between the king of heaven as an ethical will, and nature. The deity was too naïvely ethical, in an anthropomorphic fashion, to provide adequate inspiration for intellectual and aesthetic needs; indeed, to furnish a sufficiently exalted standard even for all ethical needs. God was the sanctioner of human standards, rather than the sole unconditionally valid standard by comparison with which all human customs and codes are of only limited validity. And in particular Confucius did not tell men to forget humanity and its ethical problems in order to appreciate the nonhuman manifestations of God. He too was something of a pragmatist concerning speculation without immediate human import. He seems also to have felt a reverential reluctance to indulge curiosity about superhuman things, a reluctance which is one of the reasons for his being called a humanist. Perhaps this pious inhibition is also one of the reasons why the country which he dominated did not venture far in the investigation of nature, though naturally enough it made remarkable discoveries in the useful arts.

The development of nature painting and poetry in China may be due in no small measure to the doctrine of Lao Tze, the second in influence of China's intellectual leaders. Lao Tze was of course not a humanist or a pragmatist but a mystical absolutist. Unfortunately, his doctrine of the Absolute was too paradoxical or negative to furnish positive guidance, and this may have been one reason for the degeneration of the Taoist cult into magic and demon-worship. Lao Tze failed to show the connection between his infinite and the finite problems of life and the universe. Confucius held fast to the finite, with only some vague hints as to its connection with any infinite. The first discouraged any clear grasp of the structure of things; the second led to an overfixation upon the particular (social) structures at hand, and caused or helped to cause stagnation. These are perhaps the two chief dangers connected with religious metaphysics.

Common to all three Chinese religions was the absence of an intense sense of the divine as love, such as the Hindus, and even more the early Christians, possessed. This defect may be one cause of what Lin Yu-t'ang calls the " old roguery " of the Chinese: their somewhat cynical, disillusioned attitude toward social evils and their tendency to sensuality.[3] Worldly knowledge and cultural sophistication without belief in an infinite love will always tend to such quietistic acceptance of social evils, or such preference of enjoyments which do not depend upon the capacity for devotion.

The Jews were like the Confucians in being absorbed in human ethical problems. But in Jewish monotheism the supreme majesty of God is more clearly conceived and more definitely suggests the contemplation of nature as an important approach to the Most High. Nevertheless, only the fusion of Jewish theism with Greek aestheticism and intellectualism produced a conception of the universal mind capable of inspiring widespread zeal in scientific study; and only very recently has it really been possible to unite the ethical and the cosmological aspects of theism or to define the relationship between the finite and the infinite without self-contradiction. By virtue of this last achievement the whole future of man presents new possibilities.

Greek thought was in a sense predominantly humanistic. For the Greek gods were immortalized men and women, little more. One result was that Greek religion was almost as great a hindrance as a help to ethical development, and consequently was viewed very critically by the great moralists of Greece. Aesthetically this religion had great charm and is one of the chief factors in the beauty of Greek art. But its gods were finite, all too finite. It was partly saved from this limitation by the notion of cosmic "justice" as superior even to the gods. Here was, in germ, the theistic principle of perfect righteousness, embracing whatever sense of natural law and of the ethical ideal the Greeks attained to.

The most literally humanistic thinkers of Greece were perhaps the atomists, the relativists (like Protagoras, who said that man is the measure of all things), the Skeptics, and the Cynics.

It is true that some of the atomists asserted the existence of superhuman beings, but they avoided the notion of a supreme God. On the whole, Greek Epicureanism is probably the nearest thing in history, before recent times, to a popular humanism on a high cultural level. The social and political world being in decay, the individual rather than the group becomes the human substitute for God. No unpleasant duties are admitted; social claims are recognized chiefly in the milder forms in which no one but a fool would quarrel with them. The movement possessed the greatest scientific theory of antiquity (atomism), but it used this theory not as a means of wrestling with nature to extract her secrets (as Aristotle used his concepts of form and matter) but rather to the merely pragmatic and negative end of delivering men from fear of death and of the gods. Knowledge, like other pursuits, was to be a mild and agreeable pastime, not a strenuous and consuming passion.

As for Protagoras and the Cynics and Skeptics, they contributed valuable ideas to logic and ethics, but few would see in their views examples of adequate philosophies of life such as could furnish support to a belief in the viability of humanism.

Surely Stoicism was the nearest to a philosophy adequate to ordinary human needs which the Greco-Roman world produced. By it men could live sanely and generously, not only in private but in public life, in prosperity as well as in adversity. Stoicism was saturated with a crude form of naturalistic theism — almost the first form of this doctrine as a technical philosophy. This theism was somewhat vitiated by determinism, and by intellectualism and voluntarism — that is, overemphasis upon intellect and will and underemphasis upon feeling — but it was of great value nonetheless.

Hobbes, the modern successor of the Greek atomists, exhibits partly the same and partly the extreme opposite tendency in ethics. He carries the individualistic account of motivation, that is, egoism, to an even more sharply formulated extreme, but combines this with an overexaltation of the state, an absolute political authoritarianism. Hobbes is the man who succeeded in making at once both of the two great and opposed mistakes to which humanism is driven by its lack of a third term between individual and social group. True, Hobbes was a theist, but his definition of God as absolute first cause was too empty and remote to effect the relativizing of those pseudo-absolutes, the individual and the sovereign. Only an unambiguous conception — such as medieval theology lacked — of the divine supremacy as immanent love can adequately perform this function.

Until the nineteenth century, modern heretics were deists rather than atheists — Thomas Paine for example. But Schopenhauer and Nietzsche and Marx and Comte are definitely atheistic. Nietzsche's doctrine is a valuable tonic in a world which tends to sentimentalize its religion. And Nietzsche was well justified in rejecting German idealism, the only approach to theism with much standing at the time. In his early days Nietzsche worshiped science with fervor; but in the end he repudiates the scientist as a man who subordinates life to a transcendent Truth, the ghost of God as it were, and his later philosophy involves the rather fantastic metaphysical hypothesis of the eternal recurrence. Schopenhauer's life was not exactly inspiring — think, for instance, of his willful insistence upon lecturing at the same hour as Hegel, thus determining his whole career by an act of petulant arrogance! For he thus was unable to secure a sufficient number of students, and in two different terms excluded himself, the second time forever, from university teaching. Comte was an unimaginative, humorless pedant, who allowed himself to be almost deified by his followers. Marx was possibly the greatest of the atheists of the last century, but that his character was blighted by hatred and quarrelsomeness is admitted, and these qualities have persisted in his followers — being somewhat mitigated just recently by the realization of the absolute necessity for a " united front " of radicals if they are to accomplish anything at all.

Only in the present century do we seem to find humanist thinkers in whom both greatness of mind and mellowness of character are manifest. But these are men preoccupied with ethics and the social sciences who profit from the results of the great theistic moralists and the example of the innumerable theistic good men and women past and present. Only after generations of humanism could we tell how independent of theism such men really are. On the other hand, it is only fair to remark that the defects of character and sanity found in atheists of earlier generations may have been due in no small measure to the intolerance and unkindness with which they were treated by religious bigots.

It is relevant to our purpose to consider the expressions of non-theistic philosophy in poetry and the novel. Until recent times humanism was a minor factor, in Occidental literature at least. Lucretius, Nietzsche, George Eliot, Turgeniev, Thomas Hardy, Mark Twain — a few names occur to one out of the multitude of poets and novelists before our day. Of course one may speculate about the humanistic inclinations of Shakespeare or any other writer whose private convictions are not apparent in his productions, but that would be guesswork.

Of the twentieth century, on the contrary, it could perhaps be said that most of its great writers are humanists — Proust, Joyce, Anatole France (if he is a great writer), Dreiser, Sinclair Lewis, H. G. Wells, Santayana. This is without doubt a startlingly new phenomenon. But it affords an argument for humanism only if it is possible to explain away the sense of cultural disintegration or decadence which haunts us when we read these authors. Of course the disintegration has economic aspects — we all know the Marxian cues here — but the point is that humanism has yet to show its compatibility with cultural integration on a high level. When the new Russian integration deserves to be so described, who knows if it will still be atheistic?

We must not overlook the distinguished authors of today who are not humanists. Shaw, with his religion of the life force, is perhaps not quite an atheist. There is Chesterton, one of the few great poets of our time, as well as a great wit. There is E. A. Robinson, with his annoyingly abstruse religious metaphysics and his delicate poetry not lacking in vigor. There is T. S. Eliot, great poet — and now, I fear, great obscurantist. There is Heinrich Federer, the gifted Swiss novelist, a Roman Catholic. And so on; one cannot pretend to complete the list.

Still, literature does seem on the whole to have "gone" humanistic. And not always with any clearly unfortunate consequences. There is at least one literary representative of humanism with whom it is hard to find fault — W. H. Hudson, a great writer, a splendid naturalist, a rare spirit — who gave up religious beliefs as a young man. It is true that as naturalist Hudson is not in the first rank. He lacks the burning passion to get at the plan, the order of nature, which marks the man who is all scientist. Nor is he primarily philosophical, being interested in relatively particular questions rather than in the highest generalities, so that it is not easy to be sure of his exact attitude toward religious ideas. In *Far Away and Long Ago* he speaks of a "mystical faculty" by which he explains his exceptional interest in nature; and Morley Roberts describes him, in vague terms, as a "pantheist." [4] There was little enough, one fears, in the theology or philosophy which Hudson is likely to have encountered to tempt him to reach for a more explicit view. As Roberts says, Hudson found that preachers were not much interested in kindness to animals. And the pantheisms of the time were not inspired by any great love of nature.

But when we find Hudson shocked by ill treatment of animals while he views war, past or prospective, with calmness, even with enthusiasm,[5] we see that his failure to find a supreme love in nature was accompanied, as it logically should be, by a tendency to see the values of man and animals out of due perspective. Nature as below man is a dangerous object of concentrated sympathy unless it is balanced by the vision of the superhuman in nature which man should aspire to imitate and with reference to which he should criticize all ideals.

In one respect Hudson might have been inclined to naturalistic theism. He did not, like Wells, regard the life of animals as primarily wretched, but, quite on the contrary, as on the whole abundantly happy. Of course Hudson was in a good position to judge, since it is the life of animals that he knew; whereas Wells is the typical city man, with a dash of laboratory science, who sees animals either as alien beings over whom hovers an anthropomorphic pathos, or as meaningless machines.

If we attempt to draw up a balance — obviously a highly perilous proceeding, promising largely subjective results — of humanism in literature, we might say something like this:

The denial of God has been accompanied by disintegrative tendencies or by literary values of less than the highest order. George Eliot and Mark Twain (who was not radically humanistic, as his *Diary* shows) ,[6] Hardy and Turgeniev are no match for Dickens, Thackeray, Shelley, Wordsworth, Tolstoy, Dostoyevsky, Balzac, Melville. Hardy's *Dynasts* or Mark Twain's *The Mysterious Stranger* are wooden, childish things compared to the richness and flexibility of thought shown in Melville's *Mardi*. Indeed, I wonder if there will ever be a humanist writer as grandly human as Herman Melville, who in *Whitejacket, Mardi, Moby Dick, Typee,* and *Pierre* showed a range of sensibility, philosophic depth and agility, respect for reality, ethical idealism, and intellectual tolerance and freedom not yet remotely approached, so far as I know, by any writer who disbelieves in God. Melville was no easy believer; he explored all the doubts (see *Mardi*) ; but, as Hume seems to have done, he concluded that atheism was even more likely to be an illusion than theism. I cannot forbear to quote a passage from this neglected philosopher:

"Is not Oro [God] omnipresent — absolutely everywhere? "
"So you mortals teach, Babbalanja. . . . Well, Oro is everywhere. What now? "
"Then, if that be absolutely so, Oro is not merely a universal onlooker, but occupies and fills all space; and no vacancy is left for any being, or anything but Oro. Hence, Oro is in all things, and himself is all things — the time-old creed. But since evil abounds, and Oro is all things, then he cannot be perfectly good; wherefore, Oro's omnipresence and moral perfection seem incompatible. Furthermore, my lord, those orthodox systems which ascribe to Oro almighty and universal attributes every way, those systems I say, destroy all intellectual individualities but Oro, and resolve the universe into him. But this is a heresy; wherefore, orthodoxy and heresy are one. And thus is it, my lord, that upon these matters we Mardians all agree and disagree together, and kill each other with weapons that burst in our hands. Ah, my

lord, with what mind must blessed Oro look down upon this scene! Think you he discriminates between the deist and atheist? Nay; for the Searcher of the cores of all hearts well knoweth that atheists there are none. For in things abstract, men but differ in the sounds that come from their mouths, and not in the wordless thoughts lying at the bottom of their beings. The universe is all of one mind. Though my twin brother sware to me, by the blazing sun in heaven at noonday, that Oro is not; yet would he belie the thing he intended to express. And who lives that blasphemes? What jargon of human sounds so puissant as to insult the unutterable majesty divine? . . . Where our warrant, with Oro's sign-manual, to justify the killing, burning, and destroying, or far worse, the social persecutions we institute in his behalf? . . . Ah! let us Mardians quit this insanity. Let us be content with the theology in the grass and the flower, in seed-time and harvest. Be it enough for us to know that Oro indubitably is. My lord! my lord! sick with the spectacle of the madness of men, and broken with spontaneous doubts, I sometimes see but two things in all Mardi to believe: that I myself exist, and that I can most happily, or least miserably, exist by the practice of righteousness. All else is in the clouds; and naught else may I learn, till the firmament be split from horizon to horizon. Yet, alas! too often do I swing from these moorings." [7]

The theological traditionalist will of course say that Melville's concepts, as of omnipresence, are insufficiently subtle or accurate. But my deliberate opinion is that in this passage, and in the paragraphs which immediately precede it, Melville gives a substantially fair summary of the theology available at his time and of its intellectual bankruptcy. The retreat toward humanism of the concluding sentences is Melville's response to the failure of the theologians; but the affirmation that " Oro indubitably is " is his response to the universe. Melville could not know that the time would come when theologians would abandon the concepts of " foreknowledge," " immutability," and " almighty and universal attributes every way " — the unfortunate results of which he points out — and adopt a conception of an ethically absolute but aesthetically relative and temporal being. But Melville expresses as well as any man up to his time the considerations which make such a change desirable. And he shows as few have done the grandeur of a view of life which is open toward " Oro," in spite of the difficulties of conceiving of him. The interested reader who is not familiar with it can turn to *Mardi* itself (especially from chap. 57 to the end) to see the basis for my claims for the author.

Passing to a less sublime but justly valued author, I find it of interest that Clarence Day, our most beloved modern satirist, says of himself: " Like many a modern . . . I've no creed; but I don't feel quite positive that this army of planets just happened, and that man's evolution from blindness to thought was an accident, and that nowhere is any intelligence vaster than mine. So I am always hoping to win some real spiritual insight." [8]

When this hope dies, men are likely to grow bitter, or depressed and fearful, or genially cynical and selfish, or mad with megalomaniac ambition, or slavishly worshipful of power or wealth — or just dull and apathetic and unimaginative, like a number of agnostics I have known. And if they avoid all these fates, it can only be, I am persuaded, because they nourish themselves upon the sane idealism stemming from the great theists Socrates, Plato, Spinoza, Locke, Kant, William James, Tolstoy. Such a treasure house of theistic idealism exists, and men — even philosophers — are so little logical that it is possible to be to a great extent a theist in practical attitude while professing a metaphysics or theory of knowledge incompatible with this attitude. Only by surveying the long-run and average effects of doctrines can one with any confidence pronounce upon their practical bearings. In such terms the case against humanism is serious enough to deserve more attention than humanists ordinarily give to it.

NOTES

[1] Cf. H. G. Creel, " Was Confucius Agnostic? " *T'Oung Pao*, 1931, pp. 55–99.

[2] Cf. H. G. Creel, *The Birth of China* (London, Jonathan Cape, 1936), chap. 28.

[3] Lin Yu-t'ang, *My Country and My People* (John Day, 1935).

[4] Morley Roberts, *W. H. Hudson, A Portrait* (E. P. Dutton & Co., 1924), pp. 195, 290–91.

[5] *Ibid.*, pp. 292–93.

[6] *Mark Twain's Notebook*, edited by Albert B. Paine (Harper & Bros., 1935), pp. 301, 379, 394.

[7] *The Romances of Herman Melville* (Tudor Publishing Co., 1931), pp. 611–12.

[8] Clarence Day, *After All* (Alfred A. Knopf, authorized publisher, 1936), pp. 110–11.

PART TWO

NATURE

MAN is but the place where I stand, and the prospect hence is infinite. . . . The universe is larger than enough for man's abode. Some rarely go outdoors, most are always at home at night, very few indeed have stayed out all night once in their lives, fewer still have gone behind the world of humanity, seen its institutions like toadstools by the wayside.

My profession is to be always on the alert, to find God in nature, to know his lurking places, to attend all the oratorios, the operas, in nature.

— Henry David Thoreau [1]

VIII

THE COSMIC VARIABLES

As MAN looks out upon the world, he sees entities which he regards as " below " but akin to himself — the animals; other entities still farther below, yet remotely akin to him — the plants; and finally, two kinds of entity apparently so different from human beings that they seem not relatively but absolutely non-human — inorganic objects on the one hand, and the universe as a whole on the other. The inorganic objects we can hardly think of as equal to ourselves in importance, but they seem more alien than inferior. The status of the universe is even more ambiguous. As composed mostly of the inorganic, it seems either alien or else utterly inferior; but it includes organic parts as well and is, in size and variety of parts, the greatest of all the realities manifest to us. On the other hand, it may be questioned whether the universe is to be regarded primarily as the sum of all individuals or as itself an individual or superindividual.

Thus there seem to be two great classes of existents: organisms, which form a scale from " low " to " high "; and " inorganisms " (if one may coin the word), which cannot readily be put upon this scale. There are good reasons, however, for thinking that the inorganisms are simply aggregates of parts which are themselves organisms. Molecules, atoms, and electrons all show more analogy of behavior to animals than do sticks and stones, liquids, or gases. The constituents of inorganic masses may then after all belong on the scale of organic being, but they come below what are ordinarily described as organisms. And though it is difficult to locate plants on the scale, this difficulty can be mitigated by considering the typical plant as rather a colony of cells than as a single organic individual. As for the universe, it cannot be held obvious that it is not an organism, since the universal laws of nature are its modes of organization. It is indeed arguable that the universe is incomparably the most organized of all things.

Thus it is a reasonable view that all things, so far as they are individuals rather than aggregates, fall upon a single scale (allowing for parallel branches, such as the races of man), running from the least particle of inorganic matter to the great universe itself. Now the questions for philosophy — which in this chapter can be discussed only in outline — are these: What are the *variables* of this scale; that is, the properties which entities higher in the scale possess in greater degree than those lower in it? In what sense are there "local" variables, that is, variables in terms of which entities in one section of the scale can be compared, but not entities from other sections? For instance, ability to speak English varies from one human being to another, but no difference between frogs and worms can be stated in this way. In what sense are there cosmic variables applying to all members of the scale, and how are these related to the local variables?

Several considerations limit the assumption of local variables. First, even for the lowest members of the scale a logically complete description must be possible. For instance, we must not say of even the lowest entities that they have relations but no qualities; for relations must relate something, and this something must have a nature, must have a quality. Quality is accordingly a category with universal range. Thus a minimal set of categories or variables must be cosmic. This minimal set will apply also to the universe as a whole in so far as this is one entity. Second, though this point will seem highly debatable to some, the local variables must somehow be expressible in terms of wider variables. Ability to speak English is clearly a special case of ability to communicate through signs, and this latter ability is in some slight degree common to the higher animals at least. Moreover, whatever local variables appear in the evolution of species, the "potentiality" of these variables must have pre-existed in cosmic variables which did not emerge. Or, if this potentiality seems verbal only, there is still another argument. The emergent local variable differs from other local variables, and not anyhow but in a determinate way. Now something must *measure* the difference between the new local variable and other variables, must indicate the *extent* of the likeness and difference involved. Only a more inclusive, ultimately a cosmic, variable can furnish such a measure. Some of those who talk of "emergent evolution" forget this comparative meaning of variables. They think that the qualities of things need not themselves have quality. But in fact, red differs from orange or gray from black to a determinate extent. (In the latter case the common variable is brightness.) The idea that quality need not be comparative is really the idea that it may be an absolutely private, local affair. But the fact that in a given locale of the cosmos there is a given quality is a public and cosmic fact, not a merely private one. Fact is by definition public, hence whatever can be a fact is comparative, and the cosmic variables are the measures of all fact, the definition of "being." What, then, are these variables?

One thing is clear: they must be variables with an extraordinary range of "values." In fact, this range must be strictly infinite, in whatever sense or senses this word has a meaning. For the differences among all possible things must be statable as differences among values of the cosmic variables. Thus the breadth of the variables is that of the whole universe of what is and what might be. Surely this universe is not finite, since by finitude we can only mean a restriction upon its universal scope. So we conclude that every cosmic variable is one which has an infinite range.[2]

Is the converse equally true, that every variable with an infinite range is cosmic? It might seem that even a local variable could be infinite in some sense. The possibilities of variation in human nature are infinite in number; no finite number of persons could exhaust these possibilities. But this infinitude is one of subdivision of a range of values, not of the extent of the range. There are upper and lower limits of human nature on each of the cosmic variables. No man can live without breathing (I do not stop to try to state this in cosmic terms), nor can any man directly intuit wireless waves. Thus variables infinite in the number of their possible values may still be quite finite in scope. But a variable infinite in scope could only, so far as I can see, be a cosmic variable. If you will, it is tautology to say so. " Cosmic " and " infinite " mean the same thing. Nevertheless, each term makes more explicit a part of the meaning which we intuitively intend by both words.

Before we come to our question — What variables are cosmic, absolutely infinite in range? — we must face the objection that such a range would imply emptiness of all definite meaning. Do we not define a thing by contrast with something else, and must not all-inclusive variables, since all contrast is within them, be absolutely neutral and colorless, equivalent to bare " being "? If this be so, philosophy is indeed a waste of time, for concepts are philosophical only if they are universal, cosmic. But the truth is that a variable is not a mere common element among all its values, to be conceived by abstracting from them. To understand what sensation is, we should not try to abstract from all particular sensations and see what is left. Nothing would be left. What we should do is to look for the continuity (which is not bare identity) among sensations by which we can pass insensibly from one to another, as from red to yellow through orange — in fact from any color sensation to any other. It may appear that we could not in this way get from color sensations to those of taste or smell. But, as I have shown elsewhere, this is because there are gaps in our human sensory experience, not because there are gaps in the possibilities of sense experience as such. Again, to see how all memories are alike, we should not try to cease imagining particular memories; rather we should imagine how our human memories could continuously expand or contract in various directions, or could have been greater or less in various continuous respects. "Being" is the total system of all cosmic dimensions of continuous variation. It is not the abstraction from these dimensions, nor even in every sense from all particular values among them. To be aware of the dimension of brightness from black to white we need some values, a fairly "pure" black, a good white, a few grays, but it does not matter just *which* grays, and certainly we cannot possibly have all the infinitude of possible grays before us as definite items. Thus to be aware of a variable involves neither complete omniscience of its concrete values nor absolute abstraction from the concrete. As for contrast, there can be plenty of it — contrast between the dimensions, between cosmic and local variables, between variables and sample values, between all these and "being" as their mode of integration.

I come, at last, to our query: What variables are cosmic in range, applicable to the whole scale of beings?

The most obvious feature of the scale is increasing complexity of spatio-temporal structure. But over at least a part of the scale there is also an increase in psychological complexity — complexity of feeling, volition, and thought. For human beings, at least, differ among themselves in these respects, as well as from animals. Moreover, the "physical" complexity is, in this animal portion of the scale, regarded as the sign of the "psychical" complexity. The question is natural: Can the psychical variables be conceived as extending to the simpler or subanimal segments, and to the superhuman segments, if there are any such? Can psychology be so generalized as to apply to all individuals, or must we generalize beyond psychology?

There are two steps in reaching the answer. First, it is demonstrable that psychological concepts are capable of the required generality. Second, it is demonstrable that to fail to give them this generality merely means that we leave certain aspects of certain portions of the scale of beings impenetrable mysteries.

The psychological concepts are in essence variables with an *infinite* range of values. Thus the psychological category of cognition has a number of dimensions which admit, in principle, of variations infinitely greater than the variations among known animals. One such dimension is memory span. Man remembers vividly even after one hundred years. No animal is known to remember much longer. Indeed, the effective memory of even the longest-lived animals is doubtless vastly more restricted in time span. But the idea of remembering after 100^{100} years makes as much sense as the idea of remembering after one hundred seconds. There is in the idea of memory not a suggestion of any finite time as the upper limit beyond which memory would have to be regarded as something else. Nor is there any lower limit. All animals who remember at all must remember not vastly less than a second; for greatly shorter intervals are insignificant in terms of the tempo of zoological response.

But the idea of memory of a millionth of a second, and of correspondingly rapid response, makes sense none the less. There may be creatures with "specious presents" of one millionth of a second, and others for whom time intervals of less than a century are inappreciable. Again, the complexity of what is held together in attention or memory can, so far as the idea of knowing is concerned, vary much more widely than the nervous systems of vertebrates. Human perception can include in its sensory aspect thousands of different patches of color simultaneously; but the conception of an awareness limited by the nature of its possessor to a very few distinguishable portions of space at a time introduces no contradiction. Nor does one involving millions of such portions. Yet no animal is known that is likely to enjoy the latter. Moreover, the awareness of what is really in the spaces perceived can vary enormously in distinctness. In each least distinguishable part of the visual field the real object in nature involves millions of parts. Why do we not perceive these parts as such? There is no answer from the mere notion of perceiving. Nor is there anything in the mere idea of reasoning as a certain use of signs to explain why human mathematicians find the three-body problem too complicated for direct solution.

The category of feeling also involves dimensions which have infinite range. For instance, consider intensity — how great might the intensity of joy or suffering be? There is no finite answer. The related category of sensation is similarly infinite. The dimension of brightness in color sensations has no maximal limit which is set by the idea of sensation. Again, the dimension of saturation, say the series of more and more red colors, comes to no theoretical limit. There is no color so red that a redder must be impossible. To speak of "pure" red is to employ a language of mixture which is manifestly metaphorical and irrelevant in this connection. There is no sensation of sweetness than which a sweeter would be logically impossible. Or take vagueness — how vague may feeling or sensation be? Surely as vague or distinct as you like between the absolute absence of distinctness and the perfect distinctness which is beyond human experience. These dimensions of infinite variation cannot be exhausted by the sensations or feelings of the animals, for the range of terrestrial animality is clearly finite.

Of course one may object that there are physiological or physical limits to the variability of sensation or feeling. This objection will be met more fully later (chap. 12). Here I remark only that nothing in the ideas of these variables as derived from direct experience justifies the objection, which is based on a questionable theory of the mind-body relation. There is nothing in our direct experience of the qualitative difference between gray and red to give any meaning to the idea of a red separated from gray by a finite interval of just noticeable differences, yet so red that a redder red is a contradiction in terms. Or again, there is no necessity in the number (a few score) of noticeably different shades between the gray and the red which we actually experience. Any particular number of divisions of a continuum *must* be arbitrary so far as the continuum is concerned. The color pyramid is a continuum and as such makes manifest the infinite variability of feeling. But its boundaries are as arbitrary as its divisions.

It is to be observed that physiology can as yet furnish no reason for denying feeling even to so complex an object as the world-whole, for we understand too little how feeling is possible to an animal organism to be able to infer that it is impossible that a different type of whole, even one so vast as the world, should feel. Of course world-feelings would be very different from ours, and probably at least as much more complex as is the world than the human body.

But the intuition of a small number of color tones which constitutes ordinary human vision might, so far as the idea of qualitative intuition is concerned, be complicated beyond any particular number of qualities. In the idea of qualities, or of feeling them together, no reason for a maximal number can be found, though for *human* feeling a rough limit of the kind could assuredly be derived from a sufficiently advanced physiology. Thus nothing can be denied feeling on the ground of its complexity.

It is also to be observed that no proof for the non-psychic character of individuals is to be derived from their simplicity. For, taking the simplest known entity, the electron, we see that the environment to which it reacts and the reactions themselves are not so simple that there is any absurdity in thinking that these reactions are sentient, or that the electron has a brief after-feeling, a germinal memory, of them. The argument that feeling, memory, and the like could exist only in a nervous system is, I believe — for reasons to be discussed later — wholly fallacious. Here I will merely suggest that the argument is on a par with that which holds that it could not be true that paramecia swim, since they have neither motor nerves nor muscle cells. One could so define swimming that the contention would be just, but a broader definition is not excluded. The same is true of feeling and of the nervous system.

That volition has an unlimited range of conceivable values is obvious enough from its connections with knowledge and feeling. Thus the main variables of psychology are of unlimited breadth or flexibility. Hence it is bluff and not argument to reject the psychic interpretation of the scale of beings on the ground that this interpretation is " anthropomorphic," for it is precisely in its psychic makeup that a being can be *infinitely* other than man. The values of psychic variables which are used by panpsychism to interpret the subanimal and the superhuman are values for which otherwise there would be no embodiment and not at all the values realized in man. Those who say psychic concepts are too narrow to apply to all the universe are not thinking of these concepts in their full range. They betray themselves by their reiterated charge that to psychologize everything is to humanize everything — as if an animal caught in a trap must become a man to suffer. It is easy to show that we must generalize beyond psychology — if an arbitrarily restricted psychology is in question. But the only sound approach is first to generalize our psychology.

Of course there are very serious problems in a generalized comparative psychology. Just how much does the "suffering" of a trapped animal resemble that of a man caught in a bear trap? The difficulties of answering this question scientifically are immense. But the truth is not less true because it is less easily accessible to man. Psychological understanding, which according to panpsychism is the only complete understanding, is vicarious experience, and there are of course limits to man's capacity for that. But it is obvious that it is to his interest to utilize such capacity to the uttermost, since by just so much he increases the richness of his own experience and his knowledge of the ways in which it can be varied and extended. And to deny that we have any evidence by which to determine how animals or even electrons feel is to assert that the relation between "physical" (space-time) pattern and psychical nature is subject to no law, and if we are skeptical to that extent we should face the fact that any faith in natural law — or in the possibility of scientific induction — is for most philosophies except panpsychism only a necessary postulate. Even if we define the psychic behavioristically it will still be true that the idea of behavior is subject to continuous variables of infinite range. Thus even the contention of positivists that the physical language is the only scientific one does not dispose of the argument for panpsychism.

The second ground for using the psychological variables over the whole scale of beings is that there are no other variables. The variables of physics are not a different set but the same set with certain aspects altered, not into other positive aspects, but into — question marks (see chap. 11). For the space-time structures dealt with by physics, being the dynamic patterns of the world, do not of themselves answer the question, Patterns of what? A world of interacting minds must have a dynamic space-time structure. To say that a part of the world does not contain interacting minds because it is physical is to say that it contains no minds related in a pattern because it is patterned. It is also to say that our "knowledge" that the patterns will endure is a pure act of faith. For only the psychic or at least a quasi-psychic interpretation of nature throws any light upon the reality of patterns or laws (Plato, Aristotle, Kant, Peirce, Whitehead). This point will be discussed in the six following chapters.

The "psychic" variables, in short, are simply all the variables with unlimited range, the concepts with supreme flexibility or breadth. To call them psychic is justified, not because the associations of the word are pleasant or exciting, but because it may help us to remember the following truths. All variables, whatever *else* they may be, must be variables of human experience, must have more than one value satisfied by that experience. We cannot conceive any mode of difference *from* our experiences which is not in some degree also a mode of difference *between* these experiences. We can generalize beyond human experience only by generalizing "experience" itself beyond the human variety. For there can be no experiential meaning to a distinction between what is experienced and what is simply not experienced, but only to the distinction between what is experienced *by a given in-*

dividual or species of individual and what is not so experienced; and this distinction has a meaning because the *ways* in which one experience of an individual differs from another experience of that individual involve an infinite range of values in principle, but a finite range in fact. If it be asked how the individual can be aware of this infinite range if his experience is finite, the answer is that it is only the distinct or fully conscious aspect of human experience which is finite; while the faint, slightly conscious background embraces all past time (else this phrase has no meaning), all the future, all space, and all possibility. And thanks to this dim consciousness of infinity, we can conceive in principle an indefinite extension of the distinct consciousness which in us is finite. For the theist, the infinite we dimly feel is God, in whom are distinct all the values that are distinct anywhere, and whose experience is the measure of the infinite variables as such, as well as the integration of all the finite values which happen to be anywhere actualized. The infinite possibilities of experience are derived from the infinite power of God, in whom are realized the supreme values of the cosmic variables.

The notion that God must be even higher than the maximal case of known variables is simply a set of words without meaning. For " higher " is defined by these variables, or it is merely a veil for intellectual sabotage.

But there appear to be two rival claimants for maximal predicates, God and the Universe. Modern philosophy since Spinoza has wrestled with this apparent duality of supreme beings. Only in our generation has an at least plausible solution been found. This solution will be presented in *The Vision of God*. The key to it is the recognition that superiority in the scale of beings implies inclusiveness, not exclusiveness, of individuals of lower levels, *the latter not sacrificing all of their independence* in being so included (e.g., electrons in a cell, cells in a vertebrate). The higher include lower individuals *as such* — i.e., without reducing them to the role of mere " matter " for the higher " form," as Aristotle would have thought, though modern philosophy, even without the testimony of modern science (atomic theory, cell theory), shows that his conception is an error in principle. Modern thought has even tended to the opposite mistake, that of treating atoms (it is now electrons) as the sole form-giving or determining factor, while the higher individuality, say the human mind, becomes the helpless material molded by the omnipotent atom. These opposite extremes are both superseded in the balanced view which grants relative truth to both. This balanced view is also good common sense; for if it seems evident to the plain man that his mind and its purposes can act upon parts of his body, causing them to move, it seems no less evident to him that parts of his body can act upon his mind, causing it to undergo various sensations. Only the theory of the " compound individual," the individual consisting of individuals which to some extent, but not absolutely, are subordinated to the whole, can satisfactorily interpret the facts of modern science or satisfactorily solve the old philosophical problems of the one and the many, or of the mind and the body, or of the universe (or God) and its constituents.[3] The psychic or infinite variables and the compound individual — which is only the infinite psychic variable referred to by St. Paul when he said, " We are members one of another " — are the keys to the scale of beings.

NOTES

[1] *From The Heart of Thoreau's Journals*, edited by Odell Shepard (Used by permission of, and by arrangement with, Houghton Mifflin Co.) , pp. 125, 87.

[2] On the infinite variables see:

The Collected Papers of Charles Sanders Peirce, edited by Charles Hartshorne and Paul Weiss (Harvard University Press, 1931–35) , Vols. I and VI,

Book I B, especially VI. 169 (paragraph 169 of Vol. VI) –73, VI. 190–200, VI. 203–6.

Charles Hartshorne, *The Philosophy and Psychology of Sensation* (University of Chicago Press, 1934), secs. 2, 5, 6, 26–36, 39–40.

W. P. Montague, "Confessions of an Animistic Materialist," in *Contemporary American Philosophy,* edited by G. P. Adams and W. P. Montague (The Macmillan Co., 1930), Vol. II.

[3] On the compound individual see:

A. N. Whitehead, *Adventures of Ideas* (The Macmillan Co., 1933), Chap. VIII, sec. 7, pp. 197, 216; Chap. XI, secs. 5, 20; Chap. VIII.

Charles Hartshorne, "The Compound Individual," in *Philosophical Essays for Alfred North Whitehead* (Longmans, Green & Co., 1936).

William Stern, in *The History of Psychology in Autobiography,* edited by C. A. Murchison (Clark University Press, 1930). Also, Stern, "The Metaphysical Foundations of Critical Personalism," *Personalist,* 1936.

IX

ORDER IN A CREATIVE UNIVERSE

ONE OF the most difficult of the cosmic variables has been the idea of law or order. The question is whether this order is absolute, or whether it admits of a measure of disorder, of unpredictable novelty and irregularity. Descartes treated absolute order as a local variable applying to non-human nature, and (partial) freedom from order he regarded as another local variable, applying to man. God he apparently thought of as wholly free. This made it difficult if not impossible to find any cosmic variable applicable to the causal problem. Spinoza sought to solve this difficulty by denying freedom, except in the sense of internal necessity ("self-determination"), some degree of which he granted to all things, and a supreme degree to God. Modern philosophy generally followed him until about 1875. But since that time a very different conception has become more and more prevalent. This is the conception — for which Peirce proposed the term "Tychism" (from the Greek $\tau \chi \eta$, "chance") — of freedom as a cosmic variable.[1]

Humanists look upon the issue between theology and atheism as primarily one between the primitive-magical and the modern-scientific points of view. The distinctive trait of the former is the notion that personal wishes or purposes control reality; of the latter, the idea of impersonal law. Yet there is a defect in this formulation of the problem. For impersonal law applies either to non-human objects only, or it applies also to human bodies. If it does not apply also to human bodies, then man is not explained by " nature " as science conceives it. If it does apply to human bodies, then " impersonal " law and personal volition and desire may both be concerned in the same processes. It follows that there can be nothing in the mere " reign of law " to prove that most of nature is impersonal. The fact that nature is orderly does not conflict with the hypothesis that natural events express God's will, unless it is supposed either that human actions themselves are not orderly, or that they are not voluntary. From this dilemma humanists have been trying for centuries to escape, but in vain. The truth is that the reality of law constitutes no evidence of the non-existence of God.

Nevertheless, humanists have been strongly attached to the doctrine that natural laws are real and absolute. And undoubtedly it was the rise of this doctrine which weakened the primitive religiosity of man until in eighteenth century deism religious belief had been reduced to the empty idea of a divine manufacturer of a " world machine " whose operations, once started, were automatic, lifeless, blind. All this was plausible enough, except when one considered the small circumstance that not all natural processes are lifeless or blind. Human life, purpose, understanding — these exist and are parts of the world machine. We must either agree that laws are set aside for human life or give up the notion that laws imply lifelessness and the absence of purpose. Which shall it be? If we take the first way, then we can consistently regard the rest of nature as lifeless — but we must renounce the idea of understanding nature as a whole which includes and explains man; and then prescientific attitudes can hardly be prevented from deriving encouragement from this renunciation. If we take the second way, we are admitting that, in principle, the primitive-religious standpoint is compatible with scientific ideas.   Everywhere there is life and volition, said primitive man.   Everywhere there is law, says the scientist.   Both these statements may be true if man himself is an example of the coexistence of life and law in the same object.

Yet it is a historical fact that the idea of God which conforms to this interpretation of the relations of life and law has been felt to be pale and ineffective, an attenuation to the vanishing point of the original intuition of the divine will. This fact has been the real secret of humanism's fondness for the doctrine of "absolute and inviolable" laws.   It is a discreditable secret, however; for the sense of unreality infecting the deistic idea of the absolute lawgiver is due to the falsity of the assumption that life and absolute law are *anywhere* compatible, even in the human organism.   A cosmic "machine" would indeed be dead and unable to express the life of God because (we know this intuitively) *any* machine would be dead.   But the conclusion is that we, who are alive, are not machines!   Humanism must cease to rely upon an intuition of the spontaneity, the law-transcending character of life, in order to discredit deism; unless it is willing — upon the basis of the same intuition — to assert the spontaneity and partial lawlessness of human behavior.

Suppose humanism makes this assertion.   Then it must either accept — as at least conceivable — the same view of spontaneity (if not aliveness) for all nature, thereby giving up the strongest scientific bulwark of humanism; or it must divide nature into two parts quite different in principle, the one thoroughly law-abiding and thoroughly dead, the other more or less spontaneous and alive.   Dewey elects the first solution, apparently without reflecting upon the extent to which the humanist position is thereby exposed to pantheistic temptations.   Most humanists evade the issue.   Scarcely any have the hardihood to affirm the second position.   Yet it is the only one which can consistently affirm that scientific law, as such, has discredited the religious world view. Not only is this position distasteful to humanists, but its assumption that law is to be presumed absolute for the inanimate parts of nature is regarded with skepticism by most of the younger physicists.

There has been much discussion of the new conceptions of law suggested by current physics. But this discussion has not led to much agreement concerning the basic question: Is determinism, or the doctrine that there are absolute regularities in nature, true or false? The reason this question is still unanswered is that it is essentially a philosophical question; and one of the surest ways to lose sight of such a question, and of the evidence by which it may be answered, is to look for the complete answer in the results of a special science, such as quantum physics. But you may say that philosophers themselves have debated the question of determinism for thousands of years without coming to any conclusion. I agree that this statement is true of the history of philosophy up to fifty or sixty years ago. And it is with philosophy before that date that those who make the statement are most familiar. (Textbooks of philosophy are commonly many years behind the creative thought of the age in which they are written.) But in the last few decades much new light has been thrown upon the philosophical problem of determinism. The result has been overwhelmingly unfavorable to faith in absolute law. One could give a long list of important original thinkers of the present generation and of the one which just preceded it who have rejected determinism. Peirce, James, Dewey, Russell, Varisco, Bergson, Whitehead may serve as examples. Some philosophers, among them Russell, regard the issue as incapable of definite solution. But Russell (for example, in his *Science and Religion*) exhibits not the slightest knowledge of the principal reasons which have led to their conclusion the thinkers mentioned above. And this ignorance is characteristic of the deterministic writers who are still to be found.

There are at least three basic philosophical objections to determinism which do not depend on current physics: First, if determinism were true, then the concept of possibility, an indispensable category, could refer to nothing in the real world of nature and must be interpreted supernaturally or not at all; second, if determinism were true, then the concept of time, also indispensable, would become likewise empty of meaning; third, if determinism were true, then the concept of evolutionary change could not be taken as fundamental, but must be construed as a special case of a reality which in its broad features is changeless. As always in philosophy, these three objections are so closely linked together that they are really aspects of one organic insight. This insight reveals not only that determinism is incapable of proof — which nearly everyone now concedes — but that its opposite is very well capable of demonstration.

There are three views of what is meant by " possible." The first is that it is merely a name for our ignorance of what is actual. " Will it rain tomorrow? " " Possibly " — that is, we do not know that it will, and we do not know that it will not. If we did know which is to be, we would not speak of possibility, but simply of true and false, existent (past, present, or future) and non-existent.

The second view appears when we distinguish between possibilities within nature as it exists and possibilities involved in the fact that other natures are conceivable, that is, possible. On this view, the possible is that which is conceivably existent, but which nevertheless has never existed, at no time in the past could have existed, and never will exist. This is the supernatural view of possibility, for, according to it, the possible is not localizable within nature and the actual course of events, but belongs to no time or place and, like the medieval God, subsists purely in itself. (The view of logical positivism that possibility is essentially grammatical will be considered in a later chapter.)

The third view of possibility is the indeterministic one. According to this view the possible is what might be — and also might not be — in the future; or might have been, or might not have been, in the past, given the state of affairs in the still earlier past. Possibility is thus an element of indecision in reality with reference to the future of events. It may be settled today whether or not it is to rain tomorrow; but that it is to rain a century from now on this date, or precisely how much and at what instant it is to rain even tomorrow, may not be determined by the laws of nature. Within the range of this indetermination, various amounts and times of rain are possible. Such possibility is, according to indeterminism, a real or natural fact.[2]

Of these three doctrines of possibility only the third or indeterministic view is tenable. The first view is clearly false because it denies that any world other than this one is conceivable, whereas nothing is easier than to think of a world different in detail from the actual one. Any mathematician can, and frequently does, think of quantitative or geometrical systems not precisely exemplified in nature. For instance, Planck's constant, the number which measures the universal quantum of energy in nature, might mathematically have been any other of an infinity of numbers each just as readily conceivable as the one verified by experiment. If we ask, Why then has nature, so to say, adopted just the number Planck discovered? the only answer we can give is that she has done so because she has done so. For supposing we were to find a more general law from which Planck's constant could be deduced as a special case, this more general law would have to contain a constant also, and this, like all constants, would be mathematically arbitrary, so that the element of arbitrariness would not be eliminated. The truth is that this is, in a profound sense, a " funny world," simply full from end to end with things which, from the logical standpoint, are the merest oddities.

We can express this by saying that, if " chance " means the absence of any explanatory cause or reason why a thing should be precisely as it is and not otherwise, then it is scarcely to be denied that chance is a real aspect of things. This is true even if we grant determinism. Suppose I ask, Why is there precisely such a being as myself in the world? The determinist will say it is because previously there were just such beings as my parents. But why did they exist? Because of their parents. But now we may ask, Why was the whole series of past causes just what it has been? If the series is finite, then what started it? If infinite, still why was not every one of its members different, by virtue of its predecessors' having also been different? The determinist can give no cogent answer. He may say the question is foolish and that we can think only in terms of what actually has happened. But in fact nothing is easier than to think in terms of non-actual situations, as mythology shows.

The plain truth is that there is no conceivable cause or reason why the world is, in detail, what it is. In the literal sense, the world as a whole is a matter of chance. It happened because it happened; it is here because it is here. Thus the effort of the determinist to banish irrational existence is vain. Do what you will, it is an odd world from end to end, full of a stupendous variety of items *not a single one* of which could have been anticipated by the mere exercise of reason. The determinist believes that, given one segment of this basically irrational whole, all other segments follow in a manner which would be transparent to perfect reason. Thus for him there is no least chance within nature, though he must admit there is a colossal chance in the existence of nature as a whole. He conceives the world as a mathematical system the premises of which are arbitrary; but these premises once granted, an endless chain of consequences necessarily follows. But this analogy is plausible only because of several oversights. Modern mathematics has indeed shown that the choice of premises for a mathematical system falls outside of mathematical rationality, being a matter of " taste " or " convenience " or " elegance." But it does not fall outside of the real world, since choices are real events. Mathematical rationality is accordingly only one aspect of things, and it is the business of philosophy to show how other aspects are also real. The analogy of the world to a mathematical system suggests that the relation of premise to conclusion must be supplemented by the relation of personality to acts of choice if nature as a whole is to be understood. In short, the natural meaning of the mathematical analogy is theistic. Volition as well as reason is implied in the mixture of chance and order which is the world. " Let there be light." " Let there be non-Euclidean geometry." Why? There is no complete why. *Preference is ultimate.* It is presupposed in the purest of rational sciences. In philosophy, which tries to embrace the totality of ideas, it should not be merely presupposed but definitely included within the system itself. Mathematical systems are internally rational only because they omit the irrational as irrelevant to the purposes in hand.

Of course I know that the psychologist may analyze the personal motives leading a given mathematician to choose a given system. But the causes which he may allege to explain the choice are themselves arbitrary from the standpoint of reason. He is only leading one arbitrariness back to another, and so on. The need for preference is not excluded but expanded so as to include an infinite series.

In any case, the world cannot be strictly analogous to a

mathematical system; for such a system is built up of ideas or universals, whereas the world is built up of concrete individuals or events. Mathematical laws are laws about ideas, not about things.

Chance is inescapable. The only question is, Where is it to be located? Shall we suppose that the world as a whole is one vast throw of the dice, and yet within this whole all is the purest order? Or shall we not rather say that the whole is irrational, lacking " sufficient reason," because each part of it is devoid of such reason and incapable of furnishing it to any other part? Should not properties of the whole be magnified versions or superstages of the properties of parts? If the All has, in colossal fashion, an aspect of chance, then has not Each, in a humble and even minute way, its own share in this aspect? This is the indeterministic or naturalistic view of chance. It puts the irrational to work in every nook and cranny of the world, in every event whatsoever, and makes the cosmic irrationality the comprehensive upshot of innumerable little disorderlinesses. In short, it makes chance a cosmic variable on the irrefutable ground that the whole world in every detail is logically arbitrary.

From this standpoint the second view of possibility, which admits its reality but refuses to make room for it within the causal sequences of nature, is seen to be open to precisely the objections which humanists — rightly, I hold — have urged against religious supernaturalism. If God is simply " beyond " or outside of nature, then we know nothing of him and the very word " God " is meaningless. Similarly with chance, or the relation between actuality and unrealized possibilities. What " may be " but is not cannot be withheld from actuality by any " inviolable " and eternal laws, for then it would not really be a " may be." We must find room for open alternatives *within* nature, just as we must, if we are to be theists, find room for God there.

That there are open alternatives in nature we can also show from the relation of possibility to continuity. The real world is full of discontinuities (e.g., the quantum). But these discontinuities are measurable as greater or less because we can see them against a background of continuity, such as the continuity of space, time, color qualities. Now, that such continuities are broken in the particular way they are is a logically arbitrary fact. A continuity cannot imply any one discontinuity, for every continuum implies an infinity of different ways in which it *might* be disrupted. In fact, Peirce, as did Aristotle before him, cogently argues that it is in terms of these *possible* modes of division of an otherwise characterless, bare unity that the continuum must be defined. Continuity is real, a natural fact, hence possibility is real also. To say, as Spinoza did, that all possibilities are actualized is to say that continuities are disrupted in all possible ways; and this is a contradiction, for "all possible modes of cutting a continuum" is indistinguishable from the continuum as not disrupted at all.

"Continuous" is, as was suggested in the preceding chapter, the positive meaning of "universal"; hence it comes to the same thing as the foregoing to say that universals cannot imply their instances, so that if there are universals there are non-deterministic relations between them and their instances. The universal is essentially an *indecision* between its instances; to say universals are real is to say indecision is real. A universal is, in W. E. Johnson's words, a "determinable," not a "determinate." "Color" *may* be a red; it *may* be a green; it *need not* be either. Determinism finds no place for "may be's"; hence it must deny universals altogether. This is a perfect refutation of determinism, for if a law is not a universal, what is it? The reality of law means its non-absoluteness.

That universals imply indeterminism can be shown again

in this way. A universal is " one thing which is in many things." But if all things are integrated into a strict system, and each event implies all past and future events, then every-thing is logically implied by everything else, everything is part of the nature of everything, and hence nothing is more universal than any other thing, since all are absolutely uni-versal, logically contained everywhere. If every fragment of existence implies every other, then nothing is more important than anything else, or more fundamental, for everything is absolutely necessary to the system. Thus Spinoza's God is no more necessary to the world than is the most trivial detail of nature. This wrecks the Spinozistic system. The Spinozist can make no real distinction between God as the supreme cause and sole substance, and the least among the " modes " of substance.

A deterministic world also excludes purpose. For purposes are universals and hence are more or less indeterminate. Be-sides, if a purpose determined exactly what is to realize it, then it would be as definite, as full of detail, as its realization, and therefore it would be as good as the latter. If one had all the details of fruition, there would be nothing which one lacked and hence no distinction, such as purpose implies, between intent and its fulfillment. The claim of absolute idealism that it combines determinism and teleology is thus vitiated by self-contradiction.

The relation of determinism to the concept of time has al-ready been partly indicated. Suppose the future is precisely determined in its details by the present. Then to a mind which fully understood that present the entire future would be spread out like a map. But would the future to such a mind really be future? What is it that distinguishes the fu-ture both from the present and from the past? If we consult experience — " our only guide " — we find that future ex-periences are characterized by their lack of distinct detail. By way of memory, snatches of past experience may be lived through again in fairly complete detail. Present experience is a mass of more or less clear-cut details. But anticipations of the future are in terms of somewhat indefinite generalities. We face the future with hope or with fear, with resolution or with indecision. But one thing is common to all these attitudes: they concern outlines of the future only. A boy fears he will be scolded. But the details of the scolding, just how it will differ from previous experiences of the kind, he can predict only in a rough way, whereas an earlier instance of such tribulation may stand out quite individually in his memory. Or, a father may resolve to scold his son, and may even decide on a formula which he will use. But supposing, what is unlikely, that he actually does employ just that formula; still the tone of voice, the tempo, the circumstances will not all have been fixed in his resolution to nearly the extent that they may be fixed in memory afterward. Thus a man's present experience is much more definitely inclusive of his past than of his future adventures.

A man in part *is* a bundle of memories that are relatively detailed and of hopes and fears and plans that are relatively vague and general. He wants to " succeed " and fears " failure "; he plans to build a house, etc. But the successes or the failures, the execution or miscarriage of plans which he *remembers* have an individual and concrete character lacking to those which he anticipates. It is true that we forget details; however, psychoanalysis shows that this forgetting is not absolute, but rather a depressing of memories into the dimly conscious part of memory, the subconscious. (And in any case, human memory is not the only nor necessarily the most complete memory in the universe.) The future is in principle a rough blueprint; the past a photograph in full color. Past events, to the last item, are irrevocable, while the future, though it is sometimes spoken of as even in detail unalterably fixed in advance, is in no case actually revealed to us in this fixed character; and moreover, we are throughout our lives busily engaged in trying to decide what the future is to be as though it were *not* yet wholly fixed.

The question arises whether this uncertain and outline character of the future as we experience it is essential to time itself or whether it is merely a fact of human psychology. Granting that we are ignorant of the future, surely, many will say, this ignorance does not inhere in time itself. Indeed, we are ignorant also of the past. Memory, at least conscious memory, is fickle, and each man remembers chiefly his own past rather than that of other individuals. To be sure, an ideal memory might disclose *all* of the past; but would not an ideal anticipation equally disclose all of the future? The omniscience of God, as still conceived by many theologians, involves such a complete consciousness of past and future events. But then this consciousness, according to these same theologians, would not be in time at all. And that is just the point. The " not yet " can have meaning only for a mind not in full enjoyment of all details of what is to come. The future is that of which the full consciousness is lacking. But the past is not in this way constituted by deficient consciousness. I might remember with the utmost clearness my state of mind on my twentieth birthday, but this would not abolish the pastness of that state; for in it as remembered would be included the numerous uncertainties and outlines concerning things hoped, feared, and purposed, whereas now I know, and in detail, how a good many of these things have come out. But this distinction between past and present presupposes that I was once really uncertain. And if God can be uncertain and see the future as an outline only, then even his absolute memory would not destroy the distinction between past and present. But absolute memory combined with absolute anticipation, by removing all uncertainty, would abol ish both future and past, and thus would not really be memory or anticipation at all.

In sum, if determinism is true, then time, with its distinctions between past, present, and future, depends upon ignorance. In reality, or to an all-seeing mind, or in ultimate truth, everything is equally present and actual. On the other hand, if determinism is false, then time is real, for the seemingly " open " part of time, the future, really is open, i.e., really is future, and only the past, the seemingly fixed and unalterable, really is so. (Thus determinism read backwards is true — that is, the present does fully determine, in the sense of logically imply, the past.) Since all our knowledge is of a world of events, that is, of a world in time, this argument alone is enough to prove the falsity of determinism.[3] If time were unreal so would be everything we could mention, and " real " and " unreal " themselves would lose their meaning.

Of course the real openness of the future is not accurately measured by human uncertainties concerning it. All indeterminists agree that the future *could* be predicted with vastly greater precision than human science now makes possible. Nature has at least fairly definite habits, and these habits are imperfectly known to us; so much is universally admitted. The only question is whether the to-us-unknown definiteness is absolute or not. If time is as our analysis has shown it to be, then the definiteness cannot be absolute.

We must now consider the argument from evolution. This argument involves the perception that determinism and the evolution of the cosmos as a whole cannot both be true. Evolution means " change in the nature and habits of species." It is the idea of change or of time applied to *kinds* rather than to individuals only. Now the idea of change in the natures and habits of species becomes, if fully generalized, nothing less than the idea that all species whatsoever, and hence all habits, are in process of development. But the "laws of nature" are only the habits of the species of which nature is composed. Physics investigates the behavior of the most universally distributed species — electrons, photons, atoms, molecules, crystals. The laws of physics are the behavior patterns, the habits, of these species, no more and no less. Either these habits are absolutely fixed, static forevermore, or they are subject to change, however slight and imperceptible to us such change may be. Suppose, for the moment, they are thus subject to change. Then farewell to the dogma of immutable natural laws. This dogma has always been associated with determinism, and logically so, for an absolute law could change only by an inexplicable miracle; and on the other hand, a law which is subject to change could not be expected to hold rigidly and precisely even while it continues in force. The habits of a living being are subject to formation and suppression, and they are subject also to continual slight violations. Indeed, the idea of a habit is never, in everyday life at least, that of an absolutely inflexible rule. It is my habit to respond to a joke with a laugh; but how loud and long I shall laugh, and with just what expression and pattern of sounds, is not predictable from any practically available understanding of this habit, or of all my habits. And social "laws" are likewise both transitory and imperfectly enforced. An absolutely inflexible and unchangeable law, a more or less flexible and modifiable habit or custom or decree, these are the two conceptions that make sense. And in pure mathematics we do in fact find "laws" which are subject neither to exception nor to change. But in concrete nature we seem to find, on the contrary, modifiable species with only relatively fixed and precise habits of action. The determinist must, however, hold that *certain* natural species, the most universal ones studied by physics, are absolute in nature and behavior, and in so far equivalent to mathematical

ideals.   The arbitrariness of this assumption can escape only
an obstinately unphilosophical mind or a strongly prejudiced
one.

The foregoing argument may be attacked in several ways.
It may be said that evolution is a concept of biology and does
not apply to the "inorganic" world.   In reply we may remark that historically it was astronomy and not biology that
first suggested the evolutionary idea.   And it is in physics that
some of the best evidence for the developmental character of
apparently fixed species is found.   The chemical elements are
now known to have had a history; the very atoms are not indestructible, and it is hazardous to suppose electrons to be so.
Furthermore, the division between living and dead nature is
one of the chief points at issue between humanism and spiritualism, and there are no scientific facts which clearly establish
it.   Finally, the philosophical argument for cosmic evolu-
tionism stands on its own feet, whatever may be held concerning living and dead matter.   This argument is that the
only intelligible ground for supposing anything everlasting
is that its non-existence is unthinkable, at least if there is to
be any world at all.   Now there is no difficulty in conceiving
the non-existence of electrons, or the existence of a different
number of planets or of a world to which quantum mechanics
as we know it would not apply.   Therefore there can be no
evidence whatever that these features of nature have always
been or will always continue to be.   That which cannot conceivably be supported by evidence is to be supposed false,
unless its opposite is equally incapable of verification, in
which case both alternatives should be rejected as meaningless.   But the idea of a change in natural kinds has been
verified in numerous instances and is in principle always verifiable.   It ought therefore to be presumed universally true,
except as applied to those basic features of nature (or God)
without which no real world could even be imagined.   For

instance, though laws of nature (habits of natural kinds) may change, there must always be such habits, relatively rigid for a certain lapse of time, or we could not speak of " nature " at all. Thus the habit of producing creatures with habits is an everlasting habit of nature because it is one without which the very term " nature " is empty of meaning.

Some will attack this evolutionary argument for indeterminism by urging that even if laws change, there must be a law of the change of laws, and it will be the real, the ultimate law. But the answer is that whatever this law of the change of laws may be, it is either such that no other law is conceivable, or there are many conceivable laws of this kind. If many laws are conceivable, then again no one of them can have any reason to be eternal, and hence no one of them can be absolute (as determinism implies). But if only one law is conceivable, then this one must be involved in the mere idea of a " world " or of " existence." But it is clear that such a necessary law, while it would indeed be absolute and inviolable, could not be so in the sense required by determinism. For a deterministic law is one which defines in advance what the details of existence are to be; and it is clear to all modern logicians that from a general idea like existence or nature no particular details can possibly follow. For instance, as we have seen above, no definite *quantities* (" constants ") could be involved. For quantities are numbers, and one number is on general principles no more necessary than another, as any mathematician will admit. I conclude that determinism conflicts with any reasonable view of the role of evolution in the world, as it conflicts with any reasonable view of possibility or of time.

A fourth argument for indeterminism is found in Charles Peirce's theory of the categories. These categories are three — feeling-quality, relations of action-reaction, meaning. The relations among these categories involve a mixture of dependence and independence. There could be no relations of reaction without qualities, no qualities without relations, and neither without meanings (laws). Yet from a given pattern of relations no particular quality can be deduced, nor can a pattern be deduced from a quality. And no one has ever attempted to deduce a quality of sensation from any law. Thus the togetherness of qualities, relations, and meanings involves a factor of chance, of logical arbitrariness pervading all nature.

Still another argument, perhaps the strongest of all, for indeterminism is that those who have declared law to be absolute have failed in centuries of search to find any valid evidence that law, even relative, is real at all. The only type of evidence for its reality — other than our need to postulate it — which is now taken seriously by any competent thinker, is one which not only does not support the absolute interpretation but definitely opposes it. This evidence, set forth most elaborately by Whitehead, is that time is essentially an aesthetic-ethical unity of memory and anticipatory purpose.[4] This unity, being aesthetic, is a mixture of similarity and contrast, repetition and novelty, regularity and irregularity. (The aesthetic and ethical necessity of irregularity will be further discussed in the next chapter.)

Concerning quantum physics several considerations are relevant. The first is that while it is impossible that a natural science like physics should be able to settle a truly philosophical question in all its generality, such as the question whether, in all possible universes, law is absolute or relative, it is at least possible for a science to remove the misunderstandings of philosophical questions to which errors in the hypotheses of science itself have led. And perhaps it may show what is true of law in *this* universe we live in. Now determinism is partly due to erroneous inferences from modern physics in its Newtonian phase. The Newtonian laws were absolute in form, and they claimed to apply not only to the bodies of everyday experience but to the ultimate " particles " of which Newton supposed such bodies to be composed. We now know what Maxwell and Peirce long ago surmised, that the absoluteness of the laws can be explained in statistical terms as due to the enormous numbers of particles — only the *average* behavior of which matters — entering into the composition of all ordinary bodies. We also know that there are physical obstacles, apparently insuperable, which prevent us from applying absolute laws experimentally to the behavior of small particles (electrons, photons, and the like). This means that the strongest of all arguments for determinism — the only argument now used by any reputable philosopher — namely, its usefulness as a working hypothesis for science, has become questionable, since it now appears that further progress in applying law to electronic behavior has a definite limit — measured by the uncertainty principle — which can never be overcome. Consequently the younger physicists question even the usefulness of strict determinism.

There is a common misunderstanding of the statistical method of the new physics. As determinists often point out, it is not true that elements behaving in purely random fashion can yield in the aggregate statistical uniformities. From mere chance or randomness no order can arise, for there is no definite average of all possible modes of behavior. If the molecules in a vessel with a small opening are moving about " at random," it will take a long time for all the molecules to escape through the opening; but it is assumed that none of the molecules will develop sufficient force to burst the sides of the vessel. Insurance companies know how many men of a given age will die, but they assume that the general nature of men will not change. Otherwise one man might kill all the others or turn them all into immortal beings. Always there is a limitation upon what may happen. But this is not an argument for determinism, as it is often taken to be. For there is no necessity that the limitations to randomness should completely determine behavior, but only that they should keep it within bounds. And all indeterminists accept and insist upon the idea that there are such bounds to the irregularity of natural processes.

It may indeed be true that even the statistical laws could not be absolutely true if the behavior of individuals were in any degree indeterminate. The formulas of quantum mechanics are mathematically precise; if they are absolutely true, then there can hardly be anything uncontrolled or spontaneous going on in nature. But the strict truth of precise laws could never be verified. Also, as we have seen, no law — and the arguments apply to statistical laws as much as to any others — can be absolute if time, possibility, and evolution are real. Finally, quantum mechanics itself gives cogent positive evidence that the individual behavior is not fully determined. This is frequently overlooked; in fact it is commonly asserted that quantum physics only shows that determinism is unverifiable, and that therefore determinism is false only if one agrees with positivists that the unverifiable is false, or rather meaningless. But in the facts of quantum action there is direct and positive testimony to the reality of open alternatives.[5] If a light quantum approaches a prism under certain conditions, it will either penetrate the prism or be reflected from it. It thus has two and only two " degrees of freedom." But the determining cause includes the angle of the prism, and this has an infinity of possible degrees, in fact a continuity of them. There is thus a radical discrepancy between the mathematical form of the cause and that of the effect, unless one regards as the effect not the behavior of the individual photon, but the statistical behavior of a very large number of these. The action of the individual violates positively the form of causation in question; the only way to conceive (with or without verification) a common form in cause and effect is to take probability or statistical behavior as the ultimate causal reality. Probability is continuous, like the possible angles of the prism. Doubtless even the statistical behavior is not absolutely in conformity with our formulas; but approximation, as Peirce said, is the very substance of all science.

There are, as Jordan shows, other situations which involve the same necessity of taking probability as ultimate. And the general consideration is that the wave aspect of matter is now recognized to be its probability outline. This aspect is continuous. The particle aspect is the actuality of matter, and is discontinuous. But both aspects are equally necessary to describe the facts. This means that potentiality is part of what a thing objectively is. Continuity and possibility are inseparable, and the philosophic point of quantum mechanics is that actuality and the continuum of potentiality are inseparable. In this sense we return, as Wenzl says, to Aristotle.[6] (But it is not " matter " but " form " that explains potentiality. The continuity of form means an essential potency in forms themselves. The " return " is thus to Peirce, with his theory of continuity as the law of the possible.) [7]

Far from seeing in the unverifiability of strict determinism an intellectual predicament, we should see it as the removal of a predicament. For how else are continuity and discontinuity, possibility and actuality, to be put together? The old physics merely hoped that it could be done somehow; it had no real theory. If we could get round the uncertainty principle and re-establish determinism, it would only mean, as Heisenberg has remarked, that waves and particles, both necessary to physics, would become contradictory to each other. As it is, there is no contradiction. The waves are the particles in their " may be " character. The degrees of this " may be " are the degrees of likelihood of finding the particles in various places. The outline of these places has the form of a wave. This is, in principle, close to Peirce's view of reality held fifty years ago. But for determinism a " may be " is an item of our ignorance, since if we had adequate knowledge of causes we should simply see what *will* be. Thus the conflict between quantum mechanics and determinism is complete, as is the agreement between it and Peirce's Tychism.

But the reader may be asking of what human interest quantum uncertainty can be, since the very large numbers of quanta involved in the human body would render the statistical uniformity of its action as a whole very great indeed, just as the practical certainty of an eclipse is not jeopardized by the fact that each of the multitudinous electrons involved in the eclipse may, for all we know, deviate from any precise law. Some scientists, it is true, argue that the nervous system is so delicately balanced that even a few quanta can turn the scale for or against a given act, and hence that the individual uncertainty of these quanta may affect the body as a whole. But however this may be, we must not too lightly assume that human behavior is merely the outcome of the behavior of a large number of electrons acting in accordance with the same laws that govern the behavior of electrons in rocks or planets.

This assumption involves a philosophical and no mere scientific issue — and it settles this issue in a dubious fashion. After all, though a rock or planet may be approximately viewed as a mere crowd or swarm of particles, a bird or a dog or a man is something more and something different. An electron is an individual unit of reality, a rock is a crowd of such units; but an animal is itself a unit, a true individual, and no mere crowd or swarm. Indeed, the experience which each of us has of the unity and individuality of himself, or of " his " experiences as his, is the very basis of our idea of individuality. Whatever may or may not be a true unit of

being, a true " one," each of us is to himself, at least in his
momentary consciousness, such a unit. But being is essentially dynamic (a thing " is what it does ") ; and if a man
is a unit, then his action cannot be the mere composite of the
actions of the lesser units (electrons) composing him, but
must be a single expression of the man as a whole. On the
other hand, the man is in some sense really composed of
electrons as parts, and these too, being real units, must act as
such. The conclusion is that what the man does is partly dependent upon the general laws of electronic behavior and
partly upon himself as an additional unit of action (a human personality) ; and conversely, what the man's electrons
do is partly dependent upon themselves as having the general
character of electrons and partly upon the human being of
which they are parts. In other words, as some of the greatest
physicists now believe, the laws of electrons outside the body
do not apply without qualification to electrons within the
body, for a unit which is part of a larger unit loses some of
its independence, some of the nature which it has when it is
merely a member of a crowd of its equals. It is not simply
that the human being is partly free of the laws of quantum
mechanics, but that even in its law-abiding or regular aspects
human behavior could not be a mere consequence of general
physical laws. Neither the slavery nor the freedom, the
habits nor the power of creation beyond habits, of man
can be completely deduced from quantum mechanics (see
chap. 16) .

Yet though it is unphilosophical to look for the complete
indications of the determination or the indetermination of
our acts to mere physics, nevertheless the uncertainty principle is in one sense at least relevant to the question of human action. If the electrons are units of creative (not completely habit-bound) action, this is at least an illustration of
the thesis of recent philosophy that all action is free, from

its very nature as involving time and the passage from possibility to actuality. If electrons were held to be wholly unfree, then the philosophical arguments for freedom must be regarded as unsound, for these arguments are so general that nothing, whether man or electron, could be exempt from the spontaneity which they support. Thus, even if Jordan and Heisenberg and Bohr and others are mistaken in holding that quantum physics is a factual proof of indeterminism, at least it does not conflict with it, whereas Newtonian physics, taken literally — as it usually was taken — certainly did.

From a historical point of view it seems plain enough that determinism arose chiefly from a misunderstanding of the relation between mathematics and knowledge of reality, or between deductive and inductive reasoning. Deduction gives certainty, necessity, exactitude; induction gives probability, more or less irresistible tendencies, approximations. Since the certain and absolute knowledge derived from mathematics is flattering to our sense of power, it is natural that we should try to interpret our scientific discoveries in accordance with the mathematical ideal, especially since mathematics, being the simplest science, was the first to achieve a high technical development (Euclidean geometry). However, Plato long ago perceived that mathematical ideas are not literal descriptions of things, but unattainable limits, *ideals* to which things may approximate in varying degrees. As he said, we have an ideal of absolute equality; but between any two seemingly equal things in the real world sufficiently accurate measurement will always reveal some slight difference. (Or at least, no measurement can be accurate enough to prove there is not a difference.) Again, the straightest lines in nature are never absolutely straight. Generalizing, we may surmise that no pattern, no geometrical or quantitative law, is quite literally applicable to existence. We can only say that a certain abstract form is more nearly true of nature than any other form so far proposed. Since the logic by which we know nature is inductive, the logic of probability, we ought to expect that the logic according to which things really occur, the logic of events, is also of this type. And it is a fact that modern determinism arose in an age which did not adequately appreciate the inductive character of scientific method, the age of Descartes and Spinoza; and that the ancient determinists were the Stoics, the champions of deduction, whereas the Epicureans, who believed in chance and freedom, were the apostles of induction.

NOTES

1 See Peirce, *Papers*, Vol. VI, Book I A; E. Boutroux, *The Contingency of the Laws of Nature* (Open Court Publishing Co., 1916); E. G. Spaulding, *A World of Chance* (The Macmillan Co., 1936); Charles Hartshorne, " Contingency and the New Era in Metaphysics," *Journal of Philosophy*, XXIX, 421 ff., 457 ff.; Whitehead, *Adventures of Ideas*, Chap. XII.

2 On possibility see Peirce, *Papers*, VI. 364–68; Whitehead, *Adventures of Ideas*, p. 357.

3 On time in relation to indeterminism see Peirce, *Papers*, VI. 127–31, 147–49, 368; Whitehead, *Adventures of Ideas*, Chap. XII; D. H. Parker, *The Self and Nature* (Harvard University Press, 1917), pp. 134–54.

4 On the psychic explanation of causality see Peirce, *Papers*, VI. 147–57, 277; Whitehead, *Adventures of Ideas*, pp. 144–47, 165–73, 231–37, 259; Chap. XIII, secs. 3–5, 17, 18; D. H. Parker, *The Self and Nature*, Chaps. VI, X.

5 Pascual Jordan, *Anschauliche Quantumtheorie* (Berlin, J. Springer, 1936), Chap. V.

6 Aloys Wenzl, *Metaphysik der Physik von Heute* (Leipzig, F. Meiner, 1935); *Wissenschaft und Weltanschauung* (Leipzig, F. Meiner, 1936).

7 On continuity and possibility see Peirce, *Papers*, VI. 185–88. See also Frederick B. Fitch, " Physical Continuity," *Philosophy of Science*, III, 486–93.

X

INDETERMINISM IN PSYCHOLOGY AND ETHICS

AN ARGUMENT sometimes used in support of determinism is that psychology, especially psychoanalysis, has shown how even the most capricious action is traceable to causes or determining motives, conscious or unconscious. That this could be thought a cogent objection to indeterminacy only shows how little the indeterminist philosophy is understood. This philosophy does not assert that some events are uncaused, but rather that no events are either completely determined or completely undetermined by their causes. It asserts that regularity is never absolute but always relative or approximate. Thus psychoanalysis may show that unconscious motivation molds our every act. This only proves what every indeterminist grants, that all parts of nature are subject to habits, laws, causes. It does not prove in the least that such habits or laws are absolute, determining to the last decimal point what will occur. Perhaps unconscious malice causes a slip of my tongue. Does it also explain the exact second when this occurs, the tempo with which the words are uttered, the precise words used, the gestures and tone of voice, and also the precise number of occasions when my tongue does *not* slip? Psychoanalysis does not even attempt anything remotely approaching the accuracy required for a demonstration of determinism. And the looseness of thought character-istic of many determinists is revealed in their failing to note this extreme inexactitude of psychological determination as known or knowable by any available method.   In fact, to infer determinism from psychoanalysis is merely to fall into a much grosser form of the same error that is now known to have been involved in the deterministic inference from Newton's laws, the error of identifying real with absolute order.

Indeed, the very form of the uncertainty principle applies, as Bohr and Jordan have shown, to the mind. The real, for science, is the conceivably observable. Now, observation of electrons disturbs them essentially, so that a clean cut be-tween the electron and the recording instrument is impossible by the laws of nature. In psychology the situation is similar. It is manifest that all observation of subconscious motivation alters that motivation. This is the therapeutic essence of psychoanalysis. As for conscious motives, they too are modi-fied by close observation, whether by the subject or by an-other, who in any case could reach no absolutely precise perceptions of them. Finally, if for the conscious or sub-conscious motives you substitute the structure or behavior of the organism, you are not better off. The idea is fantastic that observational instruments capable of precise measure-ment of all the significant variables determining conduct could be applied without killing the organism long before they approached their goal. Physical determination is to life as position is to velocity; as we measure the one we render the other inaccessible. But the determinist is always a theologian or nothing; he unwittingly leaves to omniscience the observa-tions which alone could give meaning to his conceptions, never remarking that his implicit deterministic theology is the nonsense of a creator in a universe from which creativity is by definition excluded.

But after all, one might ask, is it conceivable that a man's act should not be fully determined by the strongest motive urging him to this act? This argument really begs the question. For what makes one motive stronger than another? Surely motives are not outside us, like mountains, each with its relative size, or like waterfalls, each with its relative strength or energy! The strongest motive for me is the one on which I concentrate my attention the most eagerly. And why, the determinist should ask, do you concentrate upon it? Must there not be a motive for this act of concentration? But we are now entering a vicious circle. A motive cannot move me until I attend to it; yet it is held I cannot attend to it until it has become a motive. It is clear that we must admit that the strength of the motive is partly dependent on me, and therefore it cannot be the case that I am wholly dependent on it. Besides, if by motive is meant purpose, it is strictly impossible that I should be determined fully by it, because a purpose is always more or less indefinite, always allows a slight choice of means and manner of realization. It will not do to suppose that the purpose plus other factors can determine the outcome. For the generality or indeterminateness of the purpose is essential to it and must have a function if the purpose has a function. This function can only be to connect the future determinateness, when it comes, to the present which lacks this determinateness, as a determinate to its determinable, a contingent particular to its universal.

Another fallacious argument is that action expresses character, and that therefore, in order to have done otherwise than he has done, a man must have had another character. But at the moment of action he had the character which he did have and therefore, it is urged, his act was unavoidable. In philosophical terms this argument is based on the doctrine that becoming is a consequence of being, that what a thing does follows from what it is. First a thing is something;

subsequently and as a consequence it acts in a certain way. But philosophers have now largely agreed to reject this doctrine.   It is really only an aspect of the neglect of time by earlier philosophy. We have no knowledge of " being " apart from becoming. A thing is what it is only by virtue of doing what it does; and so far is action from being a mere consequence of character that we can mean by " character " only certain, relatively regular aspects of conduct.   Only to the extent that there are such regularities or habits in a man's life can we ascribe character to him.   But to assume that the character is so definite that it will exactly determine action is only to assume that habits are absolute — which is just the point under debate.

Perhaps " character " should here mean rather a cross section of the man at a given moment of action?   Then, of course, if he had done otherwise he would have been, in cross section, a different man.   But there is no determinism in this situation if we suppose that the just *preceding* cross section left its successor partly undetermined — as the indeterminist believes, and as, according to him, the very meaning of time and succession implies.   For in that case the man of the moment before was free to become a different man than he did subsequently become, and thus to do a different thing than he did.

Determinists like to say that if a man were twice in the same situation and internal state he must act in the same fashion.   But it is inconceivable that such a repetition of all important factors should occur, since, among other reasons, the mere fact of repetition would itself consciously or subconsciously be important.   So the statement is meaningless. Determinists might, however, employ a similar argument to show that it is inconceivable that a man should have done otherwise in the given situation, since we cannot go back and try over again.   But the point is that we know certain things about the man's state in the case in question. We know that he was a being with a future and a past, controlling his conduct with reference to ideas, that is, universals. Upon analysis we find that futurity *means* incomplete definiteness, and that universals mean varieties of things which *can* be, though none must be. To say that there were available alternatives to what happened, and to say that the man acted with reference to a future and according to a plan, are two aspects of the same assertion.

It is often held that the freedom of the will, in the ethically important sense of this expression, has nothing to do with indeterminism.[1] What matters ethically, it is said, is not whether or no my action is inevitable, but whether or no it is determined from within, by my own nature, rather than from without — for instance through compulsion exerted upon me by other human beings. Self-determination, the ability to do what I choose, not the freedom of my choice from its conditions of heredity and environment, is proposed as the ethical meaning of freedom. It is further urged that praise and blame, reward and punishment, are quite appropriate to acts which though determined are not under external compulsion. Praise means, we are told, that the act is good in its intended results, and reward has the function of increasing the likelihood of similar desirable acts in the future, while blame and punishment have the functions of registering the badness of the will's choices and of deterring it from repeating them.

The deterministic view of freedom is also often expressed in this way: I am free if I can do what I wish to do, even though what I wish to do is fully determined by antecedent causes, including my own nature. But William James showed long ago that this is not satisfactory.[2] For when a man remorsefully wishes he had not performed a reprehensible action, he is really, according to determinism, wishing that the causes of the wishes that led to the act had been otherwise; and since these causes form an unbroken chain stretching into the past, what the man really wishes is that his heredity and environment, the heredity and environment of his ancestors, those, ultimately, of the animal progenitors of man, and the subanimal predecessors of those, and so on back through the infinite past, had all been different, in order that his wishing and his action might have been different. So this is the meaning of remorse: " Would that the whole creation, throughout all past time, had been otherwise "!

Not the criminal only, but he and all nature, or God, are at fault in the commission of every crime. Thus if we accept determinism the meaning of remorse vanishes into a cosmic cloud. It helps not at all to speak of self-determination, for even before the self was in its embryonic stage in the womb the action was already fully determined in every detail. Moreover, it is superficial to suppose that while one would object to the compulsion of others, one can have no objection to dependence upon one's own past actions. Who has not sometimes felt that his bondage to the habits formed through these actions constituted precisely the most humiliating and hampering restriction of all? And is there never anything alien and other about one's past self? The essence of ethical reform, and of mere growth even, involves precisely a distinction between the present self as *the* self, and the past as an erstwhile friend now become like a distant acquaintance, an awkward relative, or even an enemy.

The fact is that the self of the moment no more wishes to be wholly subservient to its own past character than to the character of anyone else; indeed, it would much prefer determination by a trusted friend than by a self it has outgrown or at least wishes to reform. It is ethically false in the highest degree to regard " self-love " as a relation of pure intimacy and spontaneous concord, and the love of others as wholly external and artificial. The self of the moment of action sees all the world, including its own past and future representatives, with varying degrees of sympathy, indifference, or hostility. To no one and to nothing distinct from its present reality does it wish to be completely subservient. How easy it would be to sell annuity policies, or to dissuade rash persons from yielding to self-destructive passions, if self-love were anything but a highly limited and fluctuating affair! But here as everywhere determinists have been unconscious absolutists, endowing with properties appropriate to nothing short of deity (if even to it) things so finite as human selfishness.

Only a self which is partially free, not only to do as it wishes, but to wish in partial independence of all the world and of all past history, is really a self. Otherwise it would be meaningless to ask what " it " wished; for the determination of the wish being fully provided by antecedent causes, localization of the agency in the present self would be arbitrary. The deeper meaning of the open future now becomes clear. The (partial) independence of each moment of time from all its predecessors is one with the possibility of distinct agents, real selves, acting in that moment. Unless each self is partially distinct and hence free, each self is causally indistinguishable not only from its past states, but from those of its ancestors, and thus all distinctness of self vanishes in one cosmic Activity, be this god, devil, or machine. So when Huxley asked if it would not be better to be selves fully determined, by God or nature, to do right, than selves free to do wrong, he was talking nonsense, since " fully determined selves " is a contradictory phrase. Similarly, when it is said that our feeling of being free may be an illusion due to ignorance of causes, it must be added that in that case our feeling of being selves is equally illusory. It is one difficulty in discussing determinism, or any other truly philosophical error, that a philosophically false position is not really conceivable, and hence those who defend it do so in words only, while in belief, so far as they have a coherent belief, they really agree with their opponents — since nothing else is possible. Naturally it is hard to get them to see the unsatisfactoriness of their position, for it is only in pretense that they have occupied it. Determinists persist, consciously or otherwise, in thinking that time is real, that persons are active and dynamically distinct from other, even their own previous, selves and that they often do one thing when *they* — not denizens of a nonexistent world in which all members of the infinite series of past causes were different, but they themselves — ought to have done another thing. Until determinists form the habit of refraining from such inconsistencies it is absurd to take their position very seriously. And surely such a habit will never be formed! For if all the beliefs which conflict with determinism were eliminated nothing of the attitudes by which men live would remain.

Determinists as a rule contend not only that their doctrine is compatible with ethical principles but also that it is required by them. For how, they ask, can we say that a man is " good " unless his nature is such as to determine him to perform good acts? And what is the use of encouragement or blame, reward or punishment, if acts cannot be controlled by causes? This reasoning consists in converting the need for a relative form of something into a need for the absolute form of that something. No one denies that human life would be a meaningless chaos without *considerable* fixity of habits and a *high* degree of dependence upon influences. Does it at all follow that the fixity and the dependence must be absolute, so that if we were wise enough we could say once and for all precisely how good or bad a man's future acts are to be and precisely how given influences would affect him? When did anyone ever attribute such absoluteness to human ethical judgments? Once more the determinist is revealed as a perverted absolutist. Having rejected the only rational absolute (the creativity of God, which is not in every sense devoid of relativity), he tries to make good his loss by ascribing absoluteness to such finite matters as the classification of men into good and bad, or the exercise of social- and self-control.

It may, however, be argued that if such ethical concepts cannot be absolute, still the nearer to absoluteness they come, the greater the ethical content of life. But even this would be going much too far. It is well known that repetition or uniformity is requisite to aesthetic design, but it by no means follows that novelty and variety should ideally be reduced to a minimum. And similarly, because personality involves some stability it by no means results that the less irregularity there is in its action the better. One might as well argue that since governmental interference with private conduct is essential to civilized life, private conduct should be abolished altogether and all action be parliamentary or dictatorial. Or that because in an engine air must be mingled with gasoline vapor, it would be wise to eliminate the gasoline entirely and allow the air to achieve absolute supremacy. Life is a blend of order and caprice, of pattern and its creative transcendence. These are all relative concepts, limiting each other, and in this mutual limitation contributing essentially to each others' significance. Control, prediction, classification of individuals are not the whole end of life. Nor are machine-made rugs, by virtue of their greater regularity, more satisfying than handmade ones. Would it not be a humorless and ugly world if (*per impossibile*) determinists were its creators?

Here one can discover an odd self-deception. Men who are enamored of scientific law, with its possibilities of prediction and control, extol the beauty of a universe pervaded by absolute order. But to what is the zest of scientific inquiry chiefly due? Without question, to the endless succession of surprises attending the progress of science. The last thing science predicts or reduces to law is its own future! And the one thing no enthusiastic scientist expects or desires is that the results of investigation will merely fulfill anticipations. Of course there is an absurdity in the very idea of precisely anticipating the future stages of science, since if we could anticipate what the future will know we should know it now, and future discovery would be impossible. This is merely a particularly clear illustration of the general principle that an absolutely predictable future would not be future. But it has one very important consequence. There are some who try to rout indeterminism by talking pretentiously about the need for social control through prediction according to laws of human behavior, e.g., according to the laws of Marxian materialism. But if future knowledge and scientific inventions cannot be accurately anticipated, then one of two things is true: either such knowledge will have no important effects upon social development, or, in so far as it has such effects, the development is unpredictable. The first alternative is manifestly false, and it is especially absurd on Marxian principles, since economic determinism is inextricably united with technological determinism, the influence of applied science upon human relations. The only tenable conclusion is that the future of man is, in principle, far from predictable in any absolute sense. This is, for all practical purposes, as certain as the multiplication table. Indeed, we may venture to predict this much of the human future, that it will never be predicted except in a very rough way.

Suppose, for the sake of argument, social prediction in the strict sense were possible. Then in so far as such prediction were made known to the members of the society concerned, it would itself become one of the social forces whose outcome is to be predicted. When an eclipse is foreseen, it is known that the act of predicting the eclipse will neither hasten nor retard its occurrence. But when human beings anticipate their own or one another's actions, this anticipation is likely to have some effect, however slight, on the actions anticipated. For instance, one of the most potent forces making for the election of a candidate is the belief that he will be elected. But in other cases prediction has the effect of arousing resistance sufficient to falsify the prediction. The truth is that prediction and choice can coexist in the same individual or group only if each is relative, limited by the other. The notion of absolute prediction is thus devoid of all human meaning.

There is of course a valuable stimulus to inquiry in the faith that the disorder in our hypotheses is unjust to nature; but this faith is not destroyed by indeterminism. Two quantities need not be equal because both are finite. I can believe that Plato's insight is greater than mine will ever be without believing that Plato was all-wise; and similarly the scientist can think that the regularity of nature is greater than our knowledge will ever fully grasp, and yet be convinced that even nature is not utterly regular. Nay, further; if there is a danger in mistaking the incompleteness or vagueness of our systems for real defects in nature, there is also a danger in mistaking for real aspects of nature the prim neatness and lifeless monotony which often appear in those systems. The quantum theory suggests that the universe is wilder than our dreams, as well as tamer. It extends our predictions in some ways as well as setting new limits to them in others. Could anything be more wholesome in science than the belief that there is no foolproof way of characterizing natural process, either by unlimited trust in the " reign of law " or by extravagant emphasis upon creation, novelty, or caprice? " Seek simplicity — and then mistrust it ": this saying of Whitehead is wise scientific methodology, and it perfectly fits the indeterministic philosophy held by that great thinker.

One more argument sometimes used by determinists is this: If the will is capricious, it cannot be free in the ethically significant sense; for the ethical will is the rational will, the will determined by principles, laws. There are two fatal objections to this argument. The first is that it is impossible that general principles, " reason," should indicate *in detail* what is to be done. It is a puritanical delusion to think that life can be reduced to rule. If " pure reason " were our only motive force, we could do nothing. Ethical reason tells me to be kind to my neighbor, to help him in his trials. Suppose his need is for a word of cheerful encouragement: can reason dictate the precise form of the joke or pat on the back or smile with which I meet this need? As little as poems can be written by learned professors of rhetoric who know all the rules of poetry but do not happen to possess poetic *impulses*.

The second reason why ethical free will cannot be deterministic is that, granting that the will should, at least in a measure, be determined by rules, these rules are not the laws of nature as discovered by science. As a rational being I am bound to accept the conclusion of a piece of reasoning which I perceive to be sound. Suppose I do accept it. Now I am determined by the reasoning, and I base my physical behavior upon its results. But that physical behavior is also determined by the laws of physics governing my molecules, is it not? Thus I am doubly determined. But how is it that the blind physical determination and the determination by reasoning lead to the same behavior? A fortunate miracle, it seems. Here are two sets of determining forces acting upon the same object. Surely each must somehow limit the other. Consequently, if determination by reason exists at all, then determinism in terms of physical laws cannot be absolute.

But, as we have seen, no form of determinism, nor all forms together, can be so, since the relativity of law is implied in the very meanings of possibility, time, evolution, plan, value, beauty, self — in short, in all our fundamental categories without exception.

Humanism, being the denial that there is a supreme creativity in the world, has in modern times frequently banished even lesser creativities in favor of a purely repetitious or deterministic world order. This is, in one sense, an unnecessary extreme; for why could there not be many creative agents but none supreme, divine? To this extent recent humanists, like Dewey and Santayana,[3] in renouncing determinism may be regarded as having returned to the sanity of Greek humanism — the Epicurean philosophy, which admitted irregularities in the motions of the atoms. Santayana, to be sure, denies that there is anything " spiritual " or exalted or psychological in this departure from strict order, and in *The Genteel Tradition at Bay* he derides those whose natures are so undisciplined that they think the values of personality depend upon arbitrary free will. But in the same essay he points out that arbitrary bias, departure from rational rules, is of the essence of individuality, and he derides Puritan moralists for overlooking this point! Dewey is more consistent here, holding always that values are essentially unique, irreducible to any absolute rule or pattern. But from another point of view, humanism weakens its case by admitting indeterminism. For this admission does not help humanism to answer the question, What is the ground of our trust in natural law? while it opens the way for a non-humanistic answer. Humanism never could explain absolute law — no doctrine could do this — but it is, if anything, even more apparent that humanism cannot explain relative law. The very moment we admit that individuals are to some extent free, it becomes a mystery what limits this freedom sufficiently to produce a reasonably orderly world. One may suppose that individuals limit one another, but not even human individuals, and still less others with which we are acquainted, possess the wisdom, power, and benevolence to account for the maintenance of world order by a combination of self-control and benevolent sway over others. There is, I feel confident, no rational explanation possible here except this, that just as order is promoted (for a brief period) within an animal body by the unitary drives which make the animal an individual, so the world as a whole is held together through common habits, preeminent over all local ones, by virtue of which the world is itself a living individual — in this case a deathless (though not an unchanging!) one. Theism is only the elaboration of this view.

Humanism, on the contrary, can give no reason for faith in law except the practical one that we have everything to gain by holding to it, and it can do nothing to render the fortunate existence of a world order intelligible. Thus humanism, which began by deifying law, ascribing absoluteness to it, upon closer analysis is revealed as the solvent of a rational faith in even a relative factor of order in nature. There is no paradox here. The point is that God is nature, envisaged as rationally and concretely as man can envisage her; therefore to fail to see God is always in some way to fail to achieve adequate understanding of nature, and there are many and more or less opposite ways in which to fall short of an adequate view of an object. Besides, to overlook any aspect of a thing is to overstate other aspects by failing to reckon with the relativity introduced into them by the omitted factors. Thus Dewey's renunciation of determinism and nineteenth century mechanism is a step in the right direction. For it means restoring to the picture of nature the factor of creative action, real possibility, and an open future, all of which determinists denied to her. But even Dewey's picture of nature is truncated and does not correspond to his real beliefs. For he is compelled to trust in the order of nature, and yet can give no intelligible theory as to the character and ground of this order. The real argument for God is just that every view which tries to deny him also denies some known aspect of nature or experience, or some practically indispensable belief. As fast as atheism is routed out of one such inadequacy it falls into another, and of course there is no precise table to be made out in advance of all the possible forms which this mutilation of experience and faith may take. And it is to be noted that not every doctrine that employs the word " God " can avail itself of the genuine theistic argument, but only those doctrines which really do contain in their conception of God the fullness of our apprehension of existence in its cosmic and eternal aspects.

The universality of order, and of creative freedom from order, are two expressions of the immanence of God, whose attributes are the supreme values of the cosmic variables.

NOTES

1 For the classic arguments for determinism in ethics see J. McT. Ellis McTaggart, *Some Dogmas of Religion* (Longmans, Green & Co., 1930) ; E. B. McGilvary, " Freedom and Necessity in Human Affairs," *International Journal of Ethics,* XLV, 379 ff.; Hume, *Treatise,* Book II, part iii, secs. 1 and 2.

2 On the ethical necessity for indeterminism see William James, " The Dilemma of Determinism," in *The Will to Believe* (Longmans, Green & Co., 1898) .

3 Cf. Santayana, *The Realm of Matter,* second book of *Realms of Being* (Charles Scribner's Sons, 1930) , pp. 110–11.

XI

MIND AND MATTER

IN THE preceding chapters we have considered the reasons for believing that all activity is creative. In this chapter I wish to discuss the question of whether all activity is also sentient and purposive. There are three ways of conceiving the matter: We may suppose that some activity — such as the behavior of a man — involves feeling and purpose, and some does not; we may suppose that no activity is sentient and purposive; we may suppose that all activity is so. The first is the view suggested by ordinary experience and common sense. The second is materialism in its extremest form, and is so plainly untrue that it is hardly necessary to discuss it.[1] As Whitehead says, a scientist imbued with the purpose of proving that there are no purposes is an interesting object of study. Rejecting the materialistic extreme, we have only to decide between the first or common-sense view, which may be called dualism, and the third view, which we may call panpsychism.

The first point to be made is that the dualism upon which the difficulty depends derives its support from common sense by virtue of the ignorance rather than of the understanding of the latter. That stones do not feel or make plans is common sense to the extent that our practical dealings with such entities furnish no evidence that they have these powers. We are able to use material things while looking upon them as unfeeling and aimless. Surely this is strange if they really are quite otherwise! And yet, according to science, common-sense knowledge of the inanimate things in nature is in all cases without exception extremely superficial — indeed, is always knowledge not of individual constituents of nature at all, but of crowds, swarms, aggregates, in which individual characteristics are lost in average effects or summations. The rock, for instance, is simply crystals, and these in turn are relatively loose organizations of atoms. The only individuals with which we have practical dealings are the living things of biology; and it is by no means common sense to deny feeling to most of these. Plants, indeed, may be so regarded, but a plant is also much less of a unit than an animal. The plant cells have more unity than the whole plant; and if we ask whether these cells possess feeling, we put a question with which common sense has nothing to do, since the very knowledge that cells exist is due to science, not to practical everyday experience.

An apparent common-sense basis for a relative, though not an absolute, materialism is the experience of the death of living things. A corpse is, I should agree, a dead thing; only I should point out that it contains a great many live things, and that *we do not know it contains anything else*. As an individual whole it is not alive, but all its parts may nonetheless be living — or at any rate sentient — individuals. Just so, a crowd is not necessarily a living individual because all its members have individual life. Antimaterialism asserts only that all the pronounced units of nature are living. A dead body has lost its life because it has lost its unity, because it has ceased to be a thing and become things.

The root of all materialism and dualism lies in the attempt to abstract completely from the value context implied in any possible mode of being interested in things, even that of

" merely " or " disinterestedly " observing them. This value
context is held to be subjective and irrelevant only because
valuation is thought of as typically selfish or non-sympathetic
toward the object contemplated. It is worth noting that the
original common sense of man was plainly committed to the
attitude of sympathy as basic. To primitive man tools were
obedient servants, more or less friendly gods, domestic animals; *mere* tools scarcely existed for him. They do not for
the young child, if recent investigations are trustworthy.

As for merely observed, unevaluated facts, modern aesthetics is revealing how far from " merely " perceptual our
simplest perceptions are — is showing, in fact, that " aesthetic experience " is in its very kernel precisely what ordinary perception reveals itself to be when not overshadowed
by practical and intellectual evaluations. It is showing, moreover, that this perception has a distinctly animistic semblance,
so that the aesthetic object seems to be immediately intuited
as alive and akin to ourselves. This phenomenon is far more
widely admitted among aestheticians than the particular
formulation of it known as *Einfühlung,* or empathy.

The most primitive and the most cultivated interpretations
of experience thus converge to suggest value as the key to the
relation of subject and object. In short, it is intellect, and
not common experience, which has produced materialistic
beliefs. Now what the intellect invents, the intellect may
also abandon, may discover to have been a mere confusion
of ill-defined terms divorced from the sole test of ultimate
meaning: experience. Abiding in the work of intellect is the
increased knowledge of the *habits* of our actual or potential
domestic animals, the organisms, simple, complex, in crowds
or swarms, forming our actual environment. This interpretation leaves physical science intact, explains primitive and
aesthetic experience, and is the only view which does not,
by implication at least, set limits, in advance of future sci-

entific discoveries, to the intelligibility of things, and thus "barricade the road of inquiry." It therefore deserves — as it is beginning to receive — very careful consideration.

But the question is whether or not science, which comes much closer than everyday experience to the individual constituents of inanimate nature, also indicates that some or all are insentient. Here we must be cautious. There are two difficulties. First, to say that a creature feels is not to say how it feels; and we have good reason to believe that some creatures feel very differently from human beings. The greater this difference, the harder it will be for us to understand the feeling or to see clearly that it is there. This difficulty is serious with the higher animals, more so with the lower, more so still with plant cells, molecules, or atoms — supposing, for the sake of argument, that these all feel. It is plain enough that atomic feelings must be vastly different from dog feelings, since the measure of this difference must be the gulf between atom structure and dog structure, between atomic activity and canine activity. If our imaginations were fully able to compass this gulf we should be as God, to whom all hearts, human or otherwise, are open. But difficulty of imagining is not in the least evidence of non-existence, so long as there is no definite contradiction in the meanings in question. Now since one man feels otherwise than another, and dogs feel otherwise than men, and since, as we shall see later, there is in the idea of feeling no definite reason for supposing that only animals with nervous systems feel, there can be no contradiction in the idea of feelings other than those of animals (unless this term has the very general sense of "organism," in which case the question at issue is merely whether or not molecules are animals).

The second difficulty in finding out by science whether there are insentient entities is that although science comes much closer than practical experience to the individuals in nature, it still does not quite reach them. Science knows that there are such individuals as atoms, but the measurable properties of atoms — even more, of electrons — which it knows are chiefly statistical averages. We cannot follow an atom or an electron from sunrise to sunset, observing its eccentricities and habits, and thus inscribe a chapter in its biography. If we did, who knows if the obstacles to imagining its feelings would not partly disappear?

For the two reasons given, it is out of the question that science, in its present state at least, can furnish any ground against the belief that all individuals feel. Can philosophy furnish such ground? Philosophy is, of course, the systematization of our most general conceptions. The philosophical criticism of determinism, as we have seen, is that if we assume determinism, a coherent system of general conceptions becomes impossible. We have now to consider the relation between a dualistic view of mind and matter and the possibility of philosophical systematization.

At first sight the analogy with the deterministic question appears to favor dualism. For we saw that order cannot be absolute but must be limited by and blended with disorder. Just so, may it not be that mind must be limited by and mixed with non-mind or matter? The analogy does not, however, stand analysis. Determinism insists that order is not a matter of degree but must be absolute, precise, perfect. Now panpsychism, the alternative to dualism, does not insist that " mind " has no degrees and must be present if at all in unlimited fashion. Quite the contrary, panpsychism insists always upon the graduated or relative character of mentality. It not only admits but emphasizes that a dog's mind is less of a mind than a man's, and that of a moron less than that of a genius. And it points out that this diminution of mentality need not stop at the dog, or the frog, or even the amoeba. Relatively and for many purposes we may say that the dog is mindless; still more that a protozoon, and even more emphatically that a molecule is mindless, unconscious, purposeless. But that such creatures are absolutely without the least degree of that which reaches a high degree in human awareness and purpose — this the panpsychist will not admit. And he further will not admit that the lower degrees of awareness are due to the dilution of mind by its mixture with increasing doses of another something, matter. He points out that when consciousness is lowered, as when one is falling asleep, there is no intrusion of a foreign element but simply the decrease in *vividness* of the aspects of awareness itself. The limit of this decrease in vividness is not matter but non-existence. The absolute opposite of infinite awareness is simply complete unawareness. What light is cast upon the zero point of mentality by calling it matter?

It may be said that when we lose consciousness we do not in fact cease to exist, since our bodily reality persists. Quite so, but this bodily reality consists, science shows, of cells, atoms, etc., and the question is precisely whether these units of existence are sentient or insentient. While we sleep our cells are busy enough; are they also aware? (Of course, too, it can perhaps not be proved that in sleep our own awareness falls to zero, since all that we know when we awake after " dreamless " sleep is that we do not remember having been aware, that is, having dreamed. It is at least plausible to hold that dreaming has all degrees only the highest of which are recalled distinctly, and that some degree is present in all sleep.)

It may be said that mind requires an environment upon which to act and a body with which to act, and that if these too were composed of mind we should have an infinite regress. But this argument forgets that action may be mutual. In society we see plainly enough that individuals can form environment for one another. Why should not the whole universe be a society, the environment of each member consisting of a portion or all of the totality of the remaining members? As for the body, it is simply a system of individuals of lower type than the one whose body it is. There is nothing in this idea to prove that these lower-type individuals are anything other than lower-type minds. Of course there may be a lowest-type individual, which as such could have no body, no system of still lower entities, belonging to it. This lowest individual would be a " disembodied soul," but there is nothing to prove it impossible, provided it be clearly seen that such a soul, so far from being a very superior kind of being, would be so utterly inferior that nothing was subservient to it — as my cells are to me — and that its most immediate action would be upon equals or superiors. It would be lord of nothing, the bottom of the cosmic social scale. Its " thoughts " would lack the complexity which awareness of a complex body can give. It would deal only with its external environment and could oppose to the complexities of this environment only its own simplicity. Its weakness, its almost complete slavery, follows. It would be a least-mind, a just barely sentient individual with the barest trace of creative initiative. The extremely orderly character of the inanimate physical world is due, according to panpsychism, partly to this meagerness of the lowest souls. (It cannot be wholly due to this cause, since — to mention only one reason — with sufficient lapse of time even slight forces unchecked could tear the universe to pieces. Nature can be maintained as an orderly system only if there is a highest soul creative of order. But this soul must be the extreme opposite of disembodied.)

If there is nothing in the ideas of body or environment which proves dualism, what other ideas may be urged in its support? There is the idea of " objects." If there are conscious subjects, there must be things for them to be conscious of, namely, objects. But since there are cases in which an object of awareness is itself mental in character, this argument is of doubtful force. Suppose the subject is conscious of its own feelings of pleasure and pain. Here the object as well as the subject *consists* of sentience. Is there any need that it should ever consist of anything else than sentience? One may argue that we never feel just our own feelings, but always some object in the environment as well. But this may only mean that besides our own feelings we always feel also some feelings of other individuals. In other words, the social character of feeling may be the meaning of the subject-object relation.

It is true enough that when we are conscious we are not usually conscious of what in the same sense is itself consciousness. Relatively, what we are conscious of is generally the unconscious. That is to say, a more or less thoughtless feeling is made the object of thoughtful attention. But this establishes no dualism of subject and object, mind and matter, but only of high and low degrees of awareness. Or, if you prefer, it is the contrast between mind as feeling and mind as meaning, or again, between mind as suffering and enjoying, and mind as the user of signs, especially language.

Another argument is the Aristotelian one that if there is form, there must be that which is formed; if there is order, there must be that which is subjected to this order. In this argument, form is held to be associated with mind (as intellect or reason), and matter with the mindless. But it is plain that feeling, as well as thought, belongs to mind, and that feeling is in very truth a more or less formless and passive stuff which reason has to discipline and mold into form and order. There is nothing whatever in Aristotelianism to justify the assumption that any " stuff " other than feeling is needed to explain the universe. This applies especially to the Aristotelian doctrine that matter is the principle of individuation. Feeling, socially interlocked with feeling, will do the trick (see chap. 14). Feeling is the "matter" of aesthetic, moral, and intellectual form-giving; and all form-giving as directly experienced is aesthetic, moral, or intellectual.

To see this more clearly, we have to consider the relation between sensation and feeling in experience. Our perceptions of the physical world are chiefly by contact-pressure and sight. It may appear to the reader that sensations of pressure and of color are not properly to be termed feelings. Still he will probably admit that they are like feelings in certain respects: they are not thoughts, not intellectual meanings, and yet they are elements of our experience. Even though the reader thinks colors really inhere in the physical objects which he sees, he will hesitate to assert that the qualities of pressure sensation are equally objective; and what will he do with sound qualities, smell and taste characteristics? The physicist has no need of these to describe his atoms and electrons, but the psychologist who admits the notion of awareness at all does need them to describe how one state of consciousness differs from another. Furthermore, the moments of most vivid sensation, say of color, are also those in which the whole of the experience exhibits itself as alive with feeling-tone, and with feeling so at one with sensation that the distinction between these allegedly distinct "elements" is revealed as a superficial one.[2]

The upshot of the line of reasoning indicated in these remarks is that the only material which is given in experience in contrast to form is feeling (and its dynamic contrasts and conflicts). Now in aesthetic experience the element of form is united with that of qualities of sensation or feeling into an indivisible whole, which is the aesthetic enjoyment. Here are all the essentials of existence and the means of their union into one reality. The panpsychist challenges his opponents to indicate any reason for admitting an additional factor of insentient matter to explain the world. Can the challenge be met?

Our argument for the reality of chance was based chiefly upon the temporal character of existence. Santayana has endeavored to show that this character also implies the existence of unconscious matter (see chap. 14). For, he says, if the past were in consciousness, it would be present, and then no temporal distinctions would be possible. Therefore the past must belong to unconsciousness or matter. But we saw in the last chapter that, given indeterminism (which Santayana is willing to grant, but makes no use of to explain time), consciousness of the past does not make the past indistinguishable from the present.

The truth seems to be rather that the idea of time is unintelligible unless panpsychism is true. For the only way in which we can conceive the unity of the different aspects of time — past, present, and future — is the way illustrated by our experiences of memory and anticipation. Without memory and anticipation " past " and " future " would be meaningless words; if nature does not remember and does not anticipate, we are forthwith at a loss to grasp how she has a past and a future.[3]

If the category of time favors panpsychism, that twin category of time — space — may seem to favor dualism. For though mind can be and is a process — that is, temporal — it has been held that mind is not and cannot be extended in space. Since *something*, however, is extended in space — according to our perceptual experience — there must be something besides mind, namely, matter. But careful observation leads to another conclusion. It may be plausibly denied that ideas have spatial extent; but feelings and sensations are another matter. Granted that the concept of a triangle is not triangular, the image of a triangle actually contains at least some rough approximation to a triangular ordering of its parts. And obviously if there were not a spatial pattern in some of our sensations, we should never have come to the idea of space at all. Even pains are vaguely large or small, here or there in the body. There are point-like pains, "shooting" pains, etc.

But you will say that these are metaphors, not literally meant. You will perhaps deny that the angle points of my image of a triangle are actually located in space in triangular relation to one another. If you mean that these points are not really out there where the triangular object I am looking at is, I agree; for I think that all sensations are located in the nervous system. But I should like to ask you what is meant by location. Is there any other meaning than this, that two things are in the same neighborhood if they act upon each other directly, that is, without first acting upon other things? If the fixed stars produced a more immediate effect on earth than on their nearest neighbors, would not astronomers say that the earth is their nearest neighbor? A thing is where it acts, but action is not upon empty space but upon things, so that "where it acts" can only mean those things upon which it acts. Space relations are between things, not between things and space. Space is the pattern of interaction between individuals, as time is the pattern of action or process within the same individual. This is all we know about space, and there is nothing in it to show that the individuals between which the action takes place must be other than sentient.

Of course some might argue that we cannot understand how one mind can act upon another directly and that matter is required to transmit influences from one mind to another. This brings us to the mind-body problem discussed in the next chapter.

In spite of its great philosophical advantages panpsychism has formidable opponents. It is incumbent upon the panpsychist to explain this fact. The following seem to be the principal factors favoring the persistence of dualism:

First, as has been pointed out, common sense has a dualistic bias. The recognition of psyches sufficiently below the higher-animal level to explain inorganic nature has no direct bearing upon practical life and therefore must appear far-fetched to practical unimaginative men. Moreover, the relation between philosophy and common sense is a delicate one. Nothing is more fatal to a philosophy than to be irreconcilable with the positive pronouncements of common sense in its proper sphere; and this leads some philosophers to an exaggerated anxiety to avoid positions which do not readily commend themselves to practical men. Morris Cohen says: " We can if we wish call the non-living a lower degree of life, and the non-conscious a lower degree of consciousness. But is anything gained by regarding our clothes or our household furniture as living and conscious beings? " [4]

Professor Cohen's choice of examples is significant. Tables and chairs and overcoats are not, as such, objects in whose nature, sentient or otherwise, we are interested, but means which we know how to bend to our purposes. This attitude of mere exploitation is the presupposition of materialism. But science shows that it is an attitude which is applied not to individuals but to very numerous aggregates. If a table were as individual as a horse or an electron, we should tend to put ourselves in its place and imagine its feelings, even in order to profit by predicting its behavior.

The case for panpsychism has been badly damaged in the eyes of many by its superficial similarity to the doctrine of " idealism " as founded by Berkeley, Kant, and Hegel. According to this idealism, physical things are not individuals in their own right, but are " ideas " in the minds of high-grade individuals, such as human beings or God. They are objects which exist only in or for subjects. (Panpsychism, on the contrary, holds that even the least of physical individuals is itself a subject of a low type, and that thus physical objects are only other subjects, quite as real as the subjects for which they are objects.) It was a bold measure for simplifying philosophy to propose to reduce all nature to the contents of higher-animal minds plus God, but the last fifty years have seen a general reaction against this simplification. It is as absurd as it is simple to say that when we think we perceive things, we really perceive only the states of our own minds, ideas, objects of consciousness.

This form of idealism is really a kind of humanism. If nature reduces to our ideas, then what can God, the most comprehensive unity of nature, be but the unity of the race mind? And further, since the conflict of nations makes it clear how far from a harmonious unity mankind is, the inevitable next step is to view the nation as the real God, more real than the highest God, even though theoretically subordinate to him. Thus how natural was the step from Berkeley to Hegel's exaltation of the state and the state-olatry of Gentile! The panpsychic form of idealism, from Leibniz to Whitehead, is, no less naturally, free of such a tendency; for this form of idealism in no sense reduces nature to man, and hence the higher unity it recognizes will not coincide with any merely human group.

Thus the absurdity of idealism has no bearing upon panpsychism, which fully admits the reality of the entities referred to in physics — makes them, in fact, real in the same sense as are the physicists who think about them. Panpsychism is quite free of all inclination to question the existence of atoms or electrons as individuals, in so far as scientific evidence supports that existence, but asks only, What are these individuals like? To the answer — They are as the physicist describes them and that is all that can be said — panpsychism replies that so far as all matters of detail are concerned this is correct, since philosophy has no jurisdiction over questions of detail, which belong entirely to the special sciences, but that there are some questions of principle which in the present state of the special sciences are likely to be forgotten.

At present, at any rate, physics describes the mere spatio-temporal outline of things, but says nothing about the qualitative stuff by which these outlines are filled in to constitute realities. In our experience this stuff is sensory quality or feeling; however, the scientific evidence is all against the notion that electrons and atoms outside the body have the sensory color quality which clothes them as objects of our perception. What quality can they have then? We may answer, something in principle analogous to such feeling-qualities, though in detail doubtless very different. This is the panpsychic answer. Another answer is that we can have no notion of what the quality of physical things may be. But then it becomes a problem how we can even talk about " quality " in an application in which the term is without the remotest basis in our knowledge. Again, even the spatio-temporal structure of things is not as yet adequately described by physics, since the flow of time from past to future and the necessary faith in law and order are not made intelligible by present physical theories. Philosophy has a right to point out that no way of making them intelligible other than the panpsychic way has ever been conceived.

When we look toward the distant future, it is not clear to what extent it will ever be worth while for physics to interest itself in the psychic individualities concerned in inorganic nature. The purpose of physics is primarily to predict the behavior of the observable aggregates of these individuals. If it is possible to describe the laws governing the phototropism of microorganisms without wondering how the creatures which turn toward or away from light feel about it, how much more must it be possible to say how still lower psyches change their spatial relations to other entities without including in the description any comments upon the feeling-tone involved. Or again, we need not say that an electron remembers a previous situation, but can content ourselves with noting that certain past causes have effects in its present behavior.

So long as comparative psychology can plausibly be conducted in merely behavioristic fashion, as simply the larger aspects of physiology, it cannot be astonishing if physics remains purely behavioristic, that is, not explicitly panpsychic. For panpsychism is the doctrine that comparative psychology as psychophysiology (and not just physiology, however broadly conceived) will ultimately include physics as its simplest branch. But the simpler the organism, the less important scientifically will it be to consider it from the psychological standpoint. Philosophically the importance is quite different, since in philosophy the aim is to understand the universal principles, however little can be done with these principles in application to certain detailed aspects of the world. Panpsychism represents just the point where this discrepancy between detailed control and general understanding is the widest. The curiosity which seeks to penetrate even where there is little opportunity to utilize is nowhere more requisite for appreciation of a philosophical doctrine. Yet it is never safe to prophesy the permanent inutility of any particular knowledge; and future discoveries in physiology, and even perhaps in the lowest branch of general physiology called physics, may be due to the consideration of the subject from the generalized psychophysiological viewpoint of panpsychism.[5]

The neglect of panpsychism has roots in some curious details of history. Until the late nineteenth century the only thinker of great power who might have put philosophy on the right track in the problem of matter was Leibniz. He was a panpsychist who *largely* (it is important to note that he did not do so entirely) avoided idealism in the Berkeleyan sense. But it was Berkeley who determined the development for one hundred and fifty years. There are many reasons for Berkeley's eminence. Leibniz, like Berkeley, but with more emphasis on the consequences, tried to combine panpsychism with determinism, and thus rendered his position fundamentally inconsistent. He was a mechanist but not a materialist; whereas mechanism and materialism are really two aspects of the same view — the view that the world is fundamentally dead, blind, uncreative, insentient. Then also, Leibniz accepted some of the main tenets of medieval theology, and it was this theology, with the strange novelties to which he tried to unite it, that attracted general attention, rather than the psychic doctrine of matter. One can see what in Leibniz's views interested his contemporaries by reading Voltaire's famous parody, *Candide*. The theology could not please the orthodox, for it was not orthodox; and it could not please anybody else, for the novelties were just radical enough to raise new difficulties and just superficial enough to leave most of the old difficulties intact. For instance, Leibniz accepted the absolute individualism of Aristotle's theory of substance. Like Berkeley, but again with more clarity concerning the appalling consequences, he made each individual a world to himself. The seventeenth century was not the age for a fundamental revision of theology, since the old doctrines still appeared to " work " in church and society. Today, when there is the choice of revision or collapse, and when all the sciences are revolutionary in spirit, is the long-awaited opportunity.

It is worth noting that in the nineteenth century the most widely read humanistic authors, Schopenhauer, Büchner, and Haeckel, were, in a manner, panpsychists. They held that every atom had a germ of psychic life. This should, if I am right, have led them to theism. That it did not do so is perhaps due chiefly to two circumstances. The first is that they held the absolutistic or superstitious view of natural law, believing that laws held strictly, but in a manner simply to be accepted without explanation or proof. (Schopenhauer had a fallacious proof derived from Kant.) Thus at one stroke they were prevented from seeing the role of creation in nature and from seeing the necessity for a positive ground of order. The other circumstance is that the atoms of nineteenth century physics gave so little support to the panpsychic hypothesis that the latter remained perforce an extremely abstract and uninspiring conception, not calculated to stimulate thought upon its consequences. Then, too, if such thinkers had become theists they would have had either to blink at the difficulties in the concept of God which had been standard since the thirteenth century, indeed since Augustine, or else to have hit upon a new conception. But only men primarily concerned with theology could have had energy for the second course, and only men lightly concerned with science and philosophy could have been satisfied with the first. So they fell into atheism.

Of course, Schopenhauer was biased by his reading of human experience as essentially pain and ennui, rather than as what it is in fact, a blend of pain, joy, ennui, and thrills of more or less pleasant excitement. The cosmic " will," which with him usurps the place of God, is accordingly a ground of suffering and hopeless defeat rather than a benevolent and omnipotent Providence. But he was in a measure justified here, since the relations of omnipotence and benevolence to the vast evils in the world are anything but intelligible in the old theology.

Schopenhauer, Haeckel, and Büchner were biased in another way. They denied that intelligence was essential to will. But this was because they took natural law for granted or established it upon an imaginary foundation, and, more fundamentally, because they did not see the problem of time.

Intelligence is feeling *plus memory and anticipation,* the whole unified by *purpose*. But time itself requires this unity of past and future, so that the lowest will processes cannot wholly lack a germinal intelligence and purpose. To be sure, Schopenhauer thought time was unreal. But that only makes his conception of will more incredible than ever; for how can there be real willing if nothing really happens?

Two writers who have enormously encouraged the denial of the psychic variables are G. E. Moore and R. B. Perry. These men have exploded the pretensions of " idealism," but in performing this great service have seemed to themselves and to many others to have weakened if not destroyed the case for panpsychism. This is an error. They have greatly strengthened that case.

Moore argues that when we have a sensation of blue, the blue of which we are aware must be distinguishable from our awareness. For unless awareness is in principle " of " something which is not just the awareness over again, we should never have any knowledge, even of an act of awareness. For in trying to be aware " of " that act, we would only set up another act which would be aware only of itself. An absolute solipsism of the momentary act of awareness would result.[6]

Since blue must be distinguishable from our awareness of it, there is no reason, Moore thinks, why it may not be distinguished from any and all awareness. Awareness is not itself blue; blue is not a function of awareness. This distinction is held to do two things for dualism: It shows that at least something, blueness, is non-psychic, and it seems to answer the otherwise embarrassing question of the quality to be ascribed to the physical object.

It does not appear, however, that societal realism has anything to fear from this argument. For the distinction between awareness and its object is fully preserved by the view of awareness as essentially sympathetic. Obviously there can be no sympathy merely between a feeling and that feeling itself. There must always be another feeling — and this means, in some sense or degree at least — another feeler or feeling subject. Only thus can all feeling be " feeling *of* feeling." The arguments for this sympathetic view do not conflict with Moore's real points.

The object, Moore urges, must be something other than a mere activity of the subject knowing it; hence it need not, he thinks, be an activity of any subject. Societal realism holds, on the other hand, that the object in being given to us does become a function of our awareness — without, however, thereby losing its status as real in another sense. After all, awareness has to adapt itself to the object; it must change when the latter changes. The awareness of blue must differ from the awareness of green, and this difference must be in the awareness as well as in the objects. On Moore's own showing awareness is nothing definite apart from its relation to the object. Hence changes in that relation are changes in awareness. So there must, in spite of everything, be something like a blueness of awareness as well as an awareness of blue.[7] The fallacy comes only when we assume, with Moore and some idealists, that a thing cannot become a real internal member of the system of our consciousness while at the same time continuing to be a member of another system in which it could exist apart from us. This assumption is simply the Aristotelian notion of mutually exclusive substances whose parts belong to no other wholes or which are *not* members one of another. The new logic of compound individuality shows that the contrary assumption is required if the world is to be understood.[8]

The question then arises: How much analogy must there be between two wholes if they are to have parts in common? Surely there must be some analogy, since to hold the relations of the parts in the whole completely external to the parts would be the Aristotelian doctrine over again, but regarding the parts as independent substances. In the experience of sympathy we have real distinction between two feelings, yet both belong to more or less analogous systems. In experiences that seem not to be sympathetic it will be found that, just to this extent, we are in the dark as to the kind of system to which the object belongs. If you do not admit that the object is really " in " the unity of consciousness, and that, apart from our experience, it can only be conceived as belonging to a more or less analogous unity, you will find that you do not know what it is in as part, nor how it can be a whole in which other things are parts. The unity of experience is flexible. Imagination can vary it indistinctly but nevertheless genuinely far beyond the specifically human type; but except for variations on this theme we have no notion of unity. The unity of a color is an arbitrary slice out of the sensation *Gestalt* of the moment, and this, a slice out of the complete *Gestalt*. Our business is to vary this *Gestalt,* not to dissolve it. People who follow Moore never do come out with an intelligible account of the unity of physical individuals as a synthesis of the aspects of time and space, of structure and quality. They never can find the key to the relatedness of things.

Moore rejects and refutes the theory of " internal relations," but, like Russell, with no suspicion of the importance of time in the matter. This causes him to commit at least one significant fallacy. He argues, in effect, that if relations enter so intimately into their terms as to modify their qualities, then no term can stay the same through changes in relations, and therefore to speak of " its " relations is meaningless; for in acquiring a relation the term ceases to be " it," since it changes its very nature.[9] But it is not true that qualitative change means absolute numerical change into a quite different thing, any more than a person becomes another person every time he becomes a slightly different person, that is, every moment of his life. Moore's arguments, like Russell's, may refute the old idealism; they have no bearing on the limited and temporalistic organic view now coming into fashion. This view admits the externality of the present to the past (indeterminism) and of concrete details to abstractions.[10]

But there is another point. Blueness and awareness are, in a sense, heterogeneous. Moore has a sound intuition here. But the man who has given a sharp rational formulation of the content of this intuition is a panpsychist, Charles Sanders Peirce. In Peirce's theory of the categories, experience has the three basic aspects of feeling-quality, reaction or conflict, and meaning. Now blueness is not primarily conflict or meaning, but feeling-quality, while " awareness " refers chiefly to meaning, the use of signs. All three categories are " psychic "; the " mind " is in all cases a unity of feeling, striving, and meaning. The doctrine of sympathy, which Peirce was one of the first to hold, is that all feeling feels other feeling, all reaction has an object which itself is reactive, and all meaning means other meaning, as well as reactions and feelings. Since the three categories exhaust experience, we could have no other predicates with which to clothe objects; and that we have objects at all is due entirely to the sympathetic duality or immanent sociality of experience.

Several commentators on Peirce, notably John Dewey,[11] have tried to purify Peirce's theory of feeling-quality from its psychic aspects by distinguishing between the merely formal meaning of " quality " as the simple intrinsic unity of a thing, its " monadic " property, and what they allege is the special case when this quality is a quality of feeling. But these commentators fail to see that they are merely ruining Peirce's first category altogether. First, they are saying that what explains the existence of red or blue is bare oneness;

whereas the whole point of Peirce's endeavor was to show how such feelings are the basis of logical unity, not the reverse. Peirce would never have had the slightest use for such an explanation of the concrete by the abstract — the " fallacy of misplaced concreteness," as Whitehead calls it. Second, these commentators are contradicting Peirce's category of universal "thirdness" or continuity as the essence of the universal. If they do not make " quality " bare oneness, they make it a bare word. Quality, as a universal, could for Peirce only be a continuum. A qualitative genus is a larger section of the continuum, a species a smaller slice of it. The word " quality " then refers to whatever is continuous with (through whatever range of intermediaries) such sensory or affective predicates as red or sweet or painful or the feeling-quality of a human consciousness as a whole. But this is also precisely the definition of the panpsychic extension of feeling to all things in so far as they are qualitative. That there seems to be a distinction between quality and feeling is due to the fact that " feeling" suggests the integration of the monadic category with the other two categories of reaction and meaning, whereas " quality " abstracts sharply from all relations. Since existence is an integration of the three categories, it is feeling that has the more adequate connotations. This is another reason why Peirce would not have been impressed with the antipsychic view of the categories.

The fact is that awareness is sometimes obviously blue in the sense in which awareness (or rather feeling) is sometimes obviously pleasant or agonized. Every artist at least knows this emotionally differential character of color. The direct object of awareness is *participated in* by awareness, and " colors " awareness (as feeling), so that its quality belongs for the time being to two systems, the object's and the mind's. Moore's arguments do not tell against this supposition at all, but only against the very different one that in order to become a predicate of the mind the blue must *cease* to be a predicate of the object. This would be a non-social view of awareness, the absolute negation of the root idea of spiritualism. In refuting this non-social idea Moore only serves the cause of true spiritualism.

That there is no difficulty in supposing the awareness of blue (as inclusive of feeling) to be itself blue is seen if we consider that the memory of pain is itself more or less painful, so that a predicate undoubtedly can qualify both awareness, the memory, and its object, the past pain.

Concerning R. B. Perry's famous "fallacy of argument from the egocentric predicament," somewhat similar remarks are to be made. The basis of panpsychism must not be that everything I know or think is something known or thought by me and hence dependent upon me. The argument is rather that everything I know or think is such that I can abstract from its relation to my system and still see the object as a member of some other system by virtue of which it exists as part of a real individual, and as such similar to and substantially almost identical with itself as part of my system. (This involves a mixture of internal and external relations. If the object is in the past, its entrance into my system makes no difference whatever to it.) Everything I know is sympathized with, participated in, by me and hence is akin to me.

This is emphatically not an argument from a predicament. For a predicament is an obstacle to some purpose. Now there are only two functions of knowledge. One is prediction, control, and increased consciousness of our own human experiences. From this point of view, positivism is the last word. The other function is participation in the experiences of others — and not merely of other human beings — through direct intuition or through imaginative representation on the basis of direct intuition. Experience can divide itself into more than one focus or self, and thus transcend "itself."

But to experience what an individual unit of reality would be like if it were *not* an individual experience or a part of one is obviously impossible. The notion that the function of rational experience could be to conceive itself dissolved into elements which are what they are, independent of all experience, is due to forgetting that we are seeking our own experiences, solely for their own sake, selfishly; or we are seeking the experiences of others for their sakes, altruistically; or we are blending these two in seeking to enjoy the experiences of others; or we are seeking nothing whatsoever of intrinsic interest.

The " truth " must appeal to us either as means (and in so far as it is *only* that we do not really seek it at all, since a *mere* means is nothing, like a hammer that was identical with the hammering which could be done with it) , or else truth appeals to us also as end. But the only conceivable end is experience. Thus to identify experience in its totality of varieties with reality in its totality of species is by no means to impoverish knowledge, or to " reduce " existence to some one of its known or conceivable aspects. Selfish possession and control of experience, unselfish sharing of experience — there is no third objective of thought. What seems to be so is mostly a subconscious or fanciful form of one of these two — as in aesthetic enjoyments of nature.

It is useless to propose verbal arguments that experience must be " of " something not itself. For the significance of this distinction is wholly traceable to the social character of awareness, the fact that our feelings and ideas are not given as simply ours but as at the same time partly independent of us. And the only glimmering we have of what other real things the feelings and strivings and thoughts can be referred to is our sense of the existence or possibility of other instances and types of feelers, strivers, and thinkers, including our own past and future selves. Any idea other than this differs from it exclusively in being less definite, as when we talk of "forces" or "causes" or "matter," none of which have any representatives in direct experience except through striving, feeling, or thought, with their types of integration into personality in its rudimentary or advanced manifestations. Physics seems very definite; but it only tells us how many reals there are in a given region, how their location changes, how some embrace others within them, and what observational experiences we can derive from them through acting in certain ways by will upon that group of reals which is our own body. None of this tells us what the reals are, but only *where, when,* how *many,* and with what predictable *effect upon us.*

Certain persons, indeed, tell us with a knowing air that the question of *what* things are is meaningless. But they are bluffing. It has a very clear meaning, which is: What other things are the things in question *like,* and in what *respects* of resemblance ? This again is shown by analysis to mean: What continuous variables connect the things with what other things, above all, with the properties of direct experience? These properties are qualitative and structural. Physics furnishes some of the variables by which molecules, etc., can be compared with ourselves, but by no means all that would be required for a logically adequate comparison.[12] Yet the new physics carries us definitely nearer to such comparison.

In the first place, the superiority of continuous to discontinuous variables is illustrated beautifully by the new physics. The quantum is of course a discontinuity, but it is wholly describable in terms of continuous space-time variables. It is a relative discontinuity, relative to a background of potential continuity. It is a question of degree, not of absolute difference in kind. Moreover, as a result of the relative discontinuity of quantum mechanics, the old seemingly absolute discontinuities in kind among electricity, radiation, and mat-

ter have been reduced also to relative discontinuities.   Thus
" our distinction between radiation and matter becomes one
of degree and not of kind." [13]   As several physicists have remarked, this substitution of difference of degree for differences of kind may be expected to take place also with respect
to matter and mind.   In fact, the evidence is accumulating
rapidly to support such a relativistic view.   J. B. S. Haldane,
Jordan, Bohr, Norbert Wiener, Russell, and many other
brilliant writers have pointed out the new evidences for the
possibility of assimilating the two concepts to common variables.   J. B. S. Haldane, for example, points out ways in which
an electron acts as if with regard to the outcome of its action,
and thus, behavioristically speaking, pursues an end; whereas
water in a barrel does not.   Nor does a falling apple: be
the ground hard or soft, near or far, it will leave the branch
at practically the same instant and fall in the same direction.[14]
This agrees with the conception of final causation as a variable of the whole scale of beings.   For this scale is of species
of individuals, and an apple is not an individual, nor is water
in a barrel; but an electron is another matter (in spite of the
" scrambling " of electrons in certain situations — individuality being in principle relative and subject to limitations) .

But the universality of final causes has further illustration
in physics.   The end of all existence is enjoyment, intensified
by contrast, harmonized by similarity, and enriched by the
realization of meanings.   (These are socially duplicated and
bound together in such a way that the simple name for the
end is "love," provided " beauty " be seen as included.)
This is not a hazardous speculation but an analysis of what
we all mean by " good." No one calls anything bad unless
he finds it to produce pain and suffering, or to lack contrast,
or to lack unity, or to lack meaning.   The analysis can be refined upon, but roughly it is ultimate.   Now the patterns of
behavior of quantum mechanics are much richer in their

synthesis of unity and contrast than the Newtonian patterns. The old motions were monotonously rectilinear; the new are wavilinear. The wave is one of the simplest types of aesthetic unity in variety. If light shot in straight lines across the breadth of the universe, for millions of light-years in one journey, what a monotonous journey this would be! But it pulsates in waves. Again, how bored an electron would become if it could move only in one orbit, or if it had to alter its orbit gradually. Instead it alters its position in jumps, and thus gets vivid contrast.

It is true that Kepler and others went astray by talking about circles as the most beautiful patterns. But their aesthetics was naïve, as any artist in the world could have told them. Rigid mathematical simplicity is a narrow intellectual type of beauty, befitting neither electrons, which are subintellectual, nor God, who is superintellectual.

While we psychists are scolded for enjoying the gifts of physics, that science continues to offer us new gifts so fast that we hardly have leisure to attend to the scoldings! If electrons feel — and they must do so, for feeling is one of the categories — then no doubt they delight in their existence.

One rather common objection to the notion that matter is low-grade mind is that it only means calling the same thing by another name. This objection is grossly untrue, however. First, continuous cosmic variables are logically quite distinguishable from a plurality of merely diverse local variables (see chap. 8). Second, mind is behavioristically different, not indeed from real matter as physics is beginning to disclose it, but from the non-teleological, non-mnemonic matter posited by those who think life is only a complex form of dead, insentient, non-purposive stuff or process. This is a special case of the first point. Third, " mind " is that with which at least some slight degree of imaginative sympathy, participation, is possible. To say that this statement is only verbal is to say that the social function, which is man's glory, drops to zero in some of his relations. The hope of rationalizing life lies in the possibility of exhibiting all human activities on a scale of sociality by which the relative value of each in terms of the only finally satisfying ideal — love — may be assessed and its interconnections interpreted. Those who cannot see the value of including *all* activities in this scheme, even though some of the values of sociability will be extremely low, can never have understood what generalization means in science. It is as though it were held to be unimportant in mathematics to include very small fractions in the number system. To literary-minded persons such objections may have weight, but not to anyone who has ever caught a glimpse of how scientific discovery looks from the inside.

NOTES

[1] For a defense of materialism as a methodological principle see Rudolf Carnap, *The Unity of Science* (London, Kegan Paul, Trench, Trubner & Co., 1934).

[2] See the author's *Philosophy and Psychology of Sensation.*

[3] On the psychic view of time see D. H. Parker, *The Self and Nature.*

[4] Morris R. Cohen, *Reason and Nature* (Harcourt, Brace & Co., 1931), p. 307.

[5] That the psychic is capable of scientific treatment is well shown by Donald Williams in his article, "Scientific Method and the Existence of Consciousness," *Psychological Review*, XLI, 461 ff.

[6] G. E. Moore, "The Refutation of Idealism," in *Philosophical Studies* (London, Kegan Paul, Trench, Trubner & Co., 1922).

[7] For a reply to Moore's contention that sense qualities are not psychic see C. J. Ducasse, "On the Attributes of Material Things," *Journal of Philosophy*, XXXI, 57 ff., and "Introspection, Mental Acts, and Sensa," *Mind*, XLV, N. S., 181 ff.

[8] On compound individuality see "The Grouping of Occasions," in Whitehead's *Adventures of Ideas*, p. 258.

[9] I owe this point to Miss Caroline Claiborne. See Moore, *Philosophical Studies*, pp. 276–309.

[10] On internal and external relations see Parker, *The Self and Nature*,

Chap. IX; Charles Hartshorne, "Four Principles of Method," *Monist*, XLIII, 43 ff., and *The Philosophy and Psychology of Sensation*, paragraphs 3, 4; Whitehead, *Adventures of Ideas*, pp. 251-55.

11 John Dewey, "Peirce's Theory of Quality," *Journal of Philosophy*, XXXIII, 707-8.

12 On the problem of the quality of physical things see Peirce, *Papers*, Vol. I, Book III; also VI. 132, 196-99, 203-6, 218-37, 264; and H. H. Price, *Perception* (London, Methuen & Co., 1932).

13 William Bragg, *The Universe of Light* (The Macmillan Co., 1934), p. 276.

14 J. B. S. Haldane, "Quantum Mechanics as a Basis for Philosophy," *Philosophy of Science*, I, 78.

XII

MIND AND BODY: ORGANIC SYMPATHY

THERE IS a certain story which has been told and retold in our books of science and philosophy and seems to epitomize our modern intellectual situation, so far as this results from the acceptance of dualism. This story is the account of what happens when a man perceives a physical object. A physical process outside the body acts upon the physical mechanism of the sense organs to induce a physical process in the nerve fibers, which in turn induces finally a physical process in the brain, whereupon — and with this "whereupon" the whole beautiful chain of intelligible sequences, ideally predictable from general physical laws, comes to an end — whereupon we must begin, *de novo,* with the admission that something perfectly non-physical, a sense perception, arises; whether we describe it as " produced by " the brain process, or merely as accompanying or running "parallel" to it is a question merely of choice of words. For in any case, the point is that the correlation of just such a perception with just such a brain process is considered a sheer mystery, irreducible to any more general law.

The doctrine of Spinoza and others that somatic process and consciousness are aspects of an identical substance is, as usually presented, a purely verbal account. We do not see the identity of the *particular* physiological process and the *particular* idea.   Scientifically we gain nothing save the formal admission that intelligibility implies a one-in-the-many — which is true, but not in itself the solution of our problem. Generically mind and body may be identical, but specifically there are differences.   Given the differences, why the specific correlations between the two series?

The double language theory advocated by Piéron, Ogden, Carnap, and others is open, in part, to the same objection. It throws light on particular occurrences only where the expression of an event in the two languages involves a common factor, such as time; and in order to extend that explanation to aspects of experience not yet covered by it, such as color qualities, it will be necessary to recognize further common factors the effect of which will be to reduce both languages to one in the sense to be explained later (see chap. 16) .

A primary rule of thought is that we should look for the answer to one question in the answer to another question, that we should make such solutions to problems as will be fruitful for other problems.   It is the universal rule of scientific induction that a hypothesis must explain more than one set of facts.   It is also a rule of philosophizing to systematize and solve problems by constant reference to other problems.   Now the mind-body relation is one problem. There is also the problem of the subject-object relation. There is, third, the general problem of causal order in nature. Traditionally these three problems have been too often dealt with in isolation from one another.   Moreover, there are still other related problems: the nature of time, the nature of individuality, the way in which one mind knows other minds.   These six problems are open to a single solution. The name for this solution is " organic sympathy."

We have already seen that the relation of subject-object is simply the direct instance of sympathy, in the generalized sense in which to sympathize is to feel, to struggle with, and to mean that which itself feels, struggles, and means. Thus we see immediately that at least two of our six problems have one solution. Experience has an object because it is immediately social.

But what is the " other " with which we immediately sympathize? Human minds, it may be pointed out, communicate only indirectly, through material means (barring a literal acceptance of " telepathy "). But this fact should set no very hard puzzle for societal realism. The same sort of reasoning which shows that we do not directly feel the feelings of others when we see their gestures or hear their voices shows that we do not directly intuit the objects outside our bodies which we see or hear or smell. In both cases we react to signals which are intermediaries between us and the object in which we are interested. In both cases, especially in the case of the physical object, science shows that we have only a superficial, scanty insight into the reality before us. Indeed, our sensation of an object may be almost wholly illusory if it is taken as a revelation of what is really there.

The situation is that the immediate cause of the sensation is not the object but the changes which it induces in the body. Now, how ought we to relate the " immediate cause " and the " immediate object " of an intuition? They have at least some properties in common. The intuition must conform to its object and the object's changes, and equally it must conform to its causal conditions and their fluctuations. The effect cannot alter the preceding cause; and the intuition should be at least relatively passive to its object. The possibility that these two relations are aspects of the same connection should surely be given a hearing. But in that case there can be little doubt which concept will throw most light on the other. The intuitive relation can itself be intuited; it is a moot question if the causal relation can, unless it *is* the intuitive relation.

So let us suppose that the intuitive relation, which we have held to be sympathetic in essence, is primarily a relation of sympathy with the causative processes in the body. It follows that the cells of the body or its molecules, or both, must be psychic in their manner and degree. Indeed, if causality in the mind-body instance is sympathetic, we should at once inquire if all causality may not be so explained and if the very idea of time does not involve the notion of a sympathetic bond between the moments of time.

We can now explain why men do not communicate with one another primarily by direct sympathy. Complex minds like ours derive their complex content from inferior minds through a relation of partial dependence upon them, i.e., upon the units composing their bodies. If we human beings reached one another directly, we should be dependent upon one another in the same drastic way in which we and our bodily parts are interdependent, and then indeed would human personalities lose their freedom and distinctness with respect to one another. But all this is thoroughly consistent with the idea that human minds do act directly upon their bodily servants, the cells, and vice versa (the advantage on our side being that *no one* individual in the body has nearly as much influence as our own personality upon the whole system). It is also consistent with the idea that low-grade minds, "disembodied spirits," act upon their equals directly and with the idea that men are cells in the body of God, yet are partially free with respect to him. It is only the combination of equality with complexity that makes indirectness necessary in the relations among men.

Moreover, it is not true that we have no direct experience of one complex mind acting upon another. For in memory we find the past self influencing the present self, and while both selves belong to the same "person" they are nevertheless distinguishable. This action of one individual upon another is of course in time rather than in space, but we also have experiences which to some extent illustrate the spatial instance of direct action. When a man struggles not to give way to a physical pain, there is a certain spatial contrast between himself as struggling subject and the pain as object down there in his body somewhere. Clearly, the pain is not a full-fledged individual. But the bodily cells concerned in it are individuals, though somewhat enslaved ones; and is there any interpretation which really fits our experience except this, that the pain is at one and the same time a part of ourselves, or we should not suffer it, and yet also in some way involves some other agency or agencies, some other feeler or feelers, or we should not have to struggle against it, since it would have no power opposed to our power? In other words, if just the one self were the feeler, there could be no understanding the difficulties of self-control. But if our feeling is sympathetic participation in cell-feelings — a sympathy from which we cannot escape because it is what makes us selves on the higher-animal level — then it is clear that a certain amount of conflict is inevitable. For sympathy without antipathy would mean the complete merging of selves, the destruction of individuality, just as antipathy without sympathy would mean the complete lack of influence or interaction among selves. That we do not distinctly feel the separate cells in the suffering part of the body means that we are finite selves whose superiority to subhuman selves is attained at a price. We include the lower selves and their feelings, but not without loss. Only deity could mean complete unqualified inclusion, the wholly distinct feeling of the feelings of lower-type individuals.

The alternative to this sympathetic view of the mind-body relation is simply to say that our feelings and our bodily parts are causally connected or are somehow involved in one reality, the psychophysical person. But nothing is explained by calling the relation causal, since, as we saw above, modern philosophy has totally failed to find any intelligible account of causality except the explanation of it in terms of the sympathetic rapport by which a panpsychic universe, and only such a universe, could be held together.   And " somehow involved " is not an explanation.

Of course, you might say that we have to start somewhere in explaining things, and that it is causality which must explain everything else without needing itself to be explained. But this implies that ideas are related to one another as a line and not as an organic, circular, self-returning system. Philosophy stands or falls with the possibility of finding mutual relations among fundamental ideas by which all of these ideas can be understood.   Panpsychism can furnish such a system; dualism cannot.

It is frequently asked whether sensation is " representative " or directly " presentative " of reality.   Social organicism holds that it is both: representative of objects outside the body, presentative of real cellular individuals within the body.   Of course it is a blurred presentation of the latter; but science knows, if it knows anything, that Leibniz was right about the indistinctness of all perception.   Unless it is a mere fairy tale that activity goes on in molecules at the rate of millions of movements per second, only a highly telescoped intuition of physical reality can be enjoyed by minds with a time threshold of a relatively large fraction of a second.

According to the view we have reached, the proposition that brain states flower into sensations means that brain cell feelings enter into a comprehensive superfeeling which is our sensation.   Or, to say that a thought issues in action of the body means that some aspect or feeling-tone of this thought is felt by brain cells, that this modification in their feeling is felt by motor nerves and ultimately by muscle cells, and that this change in muscle cell feeling involves a shift in the degree of interaction among certain parts of the cell, i.e., a change in the pattern of sympathetic interaction, that is, of spatial arrangement of muscle cells, thence also of bone cells and of the whole body, both in itself and, by virtue of similar social connections among things at the edge of the body and the outside world, in its relations to the environment (see chap. 15). Of course the boundaries of the body would not be absolutely sharp according to this view; in a faint degree the whole world is our body, but to a practically important extent only what is inside the skin has the bodily relation to us.

All the foregoing sounds complicated. But the body is not simple. The principle of social interaction is simple enough. Applied to the body, this principle may be called " organic sympathy," or " social organicism." [1] It enables us to admit the evidence of psychology that a sense quality is an effect of the object outside us upon our organism, and at the same time to explain how we know the world through sensation. For the body is a large fragment of reality in space-time with an elaborate pattern. If we experience this pattern in sensation, then the rest of the world can be causally inferred from this as sample and integral part of the larger whole. But since our awareness has feeling-tone, our intuitions cannot be regarded as direct knowledge of the bodily parts unless these also are affective in quality. And besides, what is the use of explaining the power of the body to determine our intuitions if we cannot explain how our intuitions control the body in purposive behavior? By granting that cells also have intuitions (of a humble sort), we make the same principle of explanation work both ways.

However, you may ask, does not physiology show that the mind depends upon a nervous system? I answer Physiology shows that the *human* mode of digestion depends on a stomach, liver, etc.; human oxygenation, on lungs; human motion, on muscles. Does it follow that all digestion, oxygenation, and animal locomotion depend on such organs? Certainly not. One-celled animals manage these operations without such parts. Similarly, human thought, feeling, striving depend on human nerves, all vertebrate mind depends on some sort of nervous system; but there is in these facts just exactly no evidence visible to my intelligence that all thought and feeling and mind whatever depend upon that type of organ. The nervous system is indisputably at least this: a means whereby many cells can act in concert with something like the unity of functions achieved, in a simpler manner, by a one-celled animal. The conclusion about mind is that a one-celled animal could not have a mind less dissimilar to the human mind than a cell is structurally and functionally dissimilar to the human body. But how dissimilar is this? Only a person with an ax to grind could deny that there is an appreciable analogy of functions between the two organisms. To hold that the concept of mind is probably incapable of sufficient variation to fit the remoteness of the analogy is to overlook the extreme scope, even the infinity, which we have seen is characteristic of the psychic variables. To use physiology as evidence against that scope is mere fallacy. For the physiological evidence proves only that *if* the psychic variables are narrow in the range of their values, then single cells — still more, molecules and atoms — cannot be psychic. Thus physiology leaves entirely open the question of the range of the psychic variables; or rather, it supports the belief in their catholicity, for the rough continuity connecting highest and lowest organisms suggests degrees and types of mind to correspond to these degrees and types of organization, like the degrees of other organic functions, such as oxygenation and sensitivity. Certainly no one can give even the feeblest evidence to prove that the simplest conceivable feeling must be more complicated than a single cell or a molecule, since these things — nay, even an electron (in its effective relations to other things) — are too complicated to be easily grasped by our complex minds! And it is very striking, after all, how simple feeling can be. A color sensation is much simpler than even a single nerve cell. The paradox is rather that such elaborate systems as ours should have feeling, with its simplicity, than that a simple entity, like an electron, should *enjoy* its almost incredibly lively career of rhythmic and not too rigidly rhythmic adventures. Let us have arguments from the dualists at this point, not expressions of esoteric insight into the allegedly vertebrate character of all feeling.

I have spoken of the function of mind as analogous to the function of digestion. What is the function of mind? It is to give the organism quality and unity as an individual, to make it a unit in time and space. Thus if there is no unit memory or anticipation, then the bodily system is not, as a unit, in time. For the past is memory or nothing intelligible; and the future is expectation and planning, or at least desire. In any case the lesser units, whatever the real individuals of the system are, would have to be minds. Physics furnishes no "principle of individuation"; it assumes one subconsciously. Only psychology can describe the individual as it is in itself.

A not uncommon form of realism (represented, for example, by G. E. Moore and H. H. Price [2]) attributes the sensory qualities, not to the body in which the sensation occurs, but to the extra-bodily source of the stimulus. In this way inorganic objects can, it is supposed, be endowed with quality without being conceived as psychic in ultimate constituents. For, according to this form of realism, sensory qualities are not psychic, or mind-dependent. In contrast to organic sympathy, which says the nerve cells individually feel the green or the sweetness, such a realistic view offers certain difficulties.

First, reality is dynamic; a thing is at least how and where it acts. But green, sweetness, and the like as qualities do not appear to act at all outside the body. The chains of cause and effect traced by physics are wholly intelligible to a blind man, and would be so to one who had no sense of taste. Not qualities but structures are found by physics to make a causal difference. True, qualities of some kind are necessary as signs to us of structure; but we possess such signs equally well on the hypothesis that qualities are within the organism, where they serve as signs of organic changes which by causal laws can be traced to patterns of change in the stimulus and its source. But no causal relationship is clarified by ascribing greenness to the molecular aggregate called " green jade." At best, it might be claimed that the greenness of the jade explained our sensation of green. But this is scarcely tenable, and if it were it would scarcely help. It is scarcely tenable because the proximate cause of our sensation is by all scientific testimony the physiological state, not the object. It would scarcely help, for if the *only* effect of greenness is to cause sensations of green, then it is clear that, dynamically speaking at least, green is a psychological or psychophysical, not a physical, property.

Second, if the immediate object of sense intuition is not the body but the source of the stimulus, then the mind-body relation is a mere mystery. Why does a certain bodily change imply a certain mental change? If the body is the object which the mind chiefly intuits, then of course a change in the object means a change in the intuition. A change in the optic nerve, for instance, means a change in visual sensation. Make the object of the intuition the green jade but not the optic nerve, and we have no ground in the intuition for inferring the physiological process at all. We can say it must be there as cause, but, the causal relation not being given in intuition, we have no basis for inferring its term. Thus we

give up intuition where we need it — to establish *causal* contact between the intuition and its immediate causes in the
body, and claim it where we cannot scientifically use it causally — with reference to the external object. And realists who
hold this doctrine usually emphasize the non-causal view of
the intuitive relation.

Thus, third, all information useful to science or common
life which can be supposed derivable from the proposition
that the intuited green is a property of the green jade is much
better derivable from the social-organic view of green. For
in either case no useful knowledge can be had without causality; and given causality, everything scientifically or practically applicable which could be inferred from the alleged
greenness of the jade follows inductively from the greenness
as a state of the body. This state being causally conditioned,
psychophysics and physics discover how. That is all there
is to it. Given a fragment of reality so elaborate as the human body is represented (in vision) and also intuited (in all
sensations) to be, and given the causal uniformity of reality,
knowledge of the rest of reality is a mere matter of inductive
inference. This is all the knowledge anyone actually uses
in living. The real shape of the object can be known quite
as securely from the shape of the sense datum, taken as direct
intuition of a pattern of organic process explicable only in
terms of a more or less similar pattern in the stimulus, as it
can from the sense datum taken as, under " normal " conditions, a direct intuition of the shape of the object. The
unavoidable uncertainty and vagueness introduced by the
concept of "normality" is precisely the uncertainty and
vagueness encountered in the other view.

It is to be noted that all the definiteness of the datum is
used by the causal organic view, and that it is no inconsistency
whatever that we do not know the physiological patterns
spoken of except on the assumption that seen or felt shapes

correspond closely to real shapes in the stimulus. For all induction consists in fitting theories to facts and checking by predictions, so that when Russell says that the physiologist observing another man's brain really sees (directly intuits) his own brain, he is not talking nonsense at all, as some have thought, but perfect sense. The physiologist has every right to adopt the *theory* that the shape of his visual image is roughly like the shape of the brain he is looking at, while at the same time holding that the shape he directly feels is only a shape in his own brain or nervous system (or whole body). The test of the theory that felt shapes in the body duplicate shapes outside the body does not lie in getting out of our bodies to intuit the external shapes. This is logically not required. The test is to ask: Assuming the intuited objects to be parts of a larger causal system, what view of that system enables us to predict further experiences? The answer is the view that intuited shapes in general echo shapes of outer objects. So overwhelmingly is this view verified that it is virtually a dead certainty. The image on the retina when a square object is seen will, when looked at by another person, look square. A large object will look large. So that the assumption that the body is a machine for echoing its surroundings consistently predicts what intuitions will be obtained.

Fourth, even if redness and sweetness are held to be in extra-bodily things, the case for panpsychism is not disposed of. For the emotional tone of these qualities, while subtle and delicate, is observable and intrinsic, and cannot be separated from mind in some sense. There is complete continuity between qualities obviously psychic, like pain or pleasure, and those less obviously so. The only result of putting sense qualities in external things would be to substitute an illogical, systematically confused panpsychism for a rational one.

Finally, what would be the qualities of the atoms and electrons and molecules and photons, etc.? Have they none? Are they colored? Or does the realist deny that these individuals inferred by science are real? In that case his realism is the most objectionable kind of subjectivism, for he is asserting that the most careful and completely objective effort man has made to distinguish realities results only in subjective devices, fictions, or what not.

Writers like G. E. Moore stress the adherence of common sense to the view that things are really colored, and the like. But in the first place, philosophers so forgetful of common sense as to accept a view wholly without *utility,* as we have seen Moore's view to be, are hardly good spokesmen for the practical philosophy of mankind which is common sense. In the second place, it is easily explained why the immediate object of visual or auditory intuition seems to common sense to be the extra-bodily object and not the changes in the nervous system and sense organ. For the object may be checked by senses other than the visual or auditory; it may be touched as well as seen and heard. It is no secret in genetic psychology how this interplay of senses contributes to our awareness of realities in space. The internal movements in eye, ear, nerve, and brain, on the other hand, are directly accessible ordinarily only by the particular mode of sensations they cause. Hence we do not easily think of them as objects of the sense intuition, but take them for granted as belonging to the body *with* which we know and as parts of ourselves as knowing, rather than as *what* we know. And this is pragmatically necessary, since it is the environment we have to manipulate, not the internal parts of the body. Moreover, it is perfectly true that what we *know* when we see is the seen object, while the body is only what we know it with, if " knowledge " has the pragmatically appropriate meaning of valid, overwhelmingly probable judgment. That the thing we directly *intuit* is not the seen object, but the body, is for common sense an altogether harmless assumption, since reliable knowledge, not blessed immediacy, is alone of practical import so far as extra-bodily things are concerned. And it is not the color quality upon which action is based, but structural properties and relations of likeness and difference in objects of which likeness and difference in color sensations are, within limits, overwhelmingly reliable signs. The cases in which we do act upon the sense qualities themselves are two: We may react aesthetically, but we do not then attribute the " warmth " of red or the " gaiety " of yellow to the objects; or we may interpret the emotions of others through the emotional tonality of a voice, for example, but then we do not attribute this tonality of the sound sensation to the person, but only believe that there is a resemblance and a causal relation between them. These modes of action are just as appropriate whether or not the sense qualities are outside of us. Thus the common-sense basis of Moore's theory is on all counts doubtful.

It is important to note that societism need not absolutely negate the externality of sense qualities. For since a thing is where it acts, and action, according to physics and metaphysics, is not completely localized but in some degree pervades the cosmic " field," the sensed color which is " in," that is, acts on, the mind and brain, acts also upon the sensed object. The question is whether this latter action is appreciable or significant. There seems no evidence that it is, though no less a writer than J. B. S. Haldane thinks it possible that the brain is in direct contact with the external object in perception through some process of outflowing into the extra-bodily field.[8] In this case organic sympathy and the Moore-Price view could be partly reconciled. Of course, by " acts on " the societist means " contributes to the feeling of." " Influence is always made possible by sympathy," is a way of describing sympathy (including antipathy as a special case) .

Again it may be that the molecules of the seen object themselves feel something like red or green and transmit this feeling to light photons which transmit it to the nerves. On the basis of the societal view there must be some truth in this supposition, but how much is problematic. For every feeler to which a feeling is transmitted adds its own individual emotional tone in this chain, so that the end of the chain may not much resemble the beginning.

Why is it so important to identify the relation of intuition to its primary object with the mind-body relation? Partly for reasons already given, and partly for two other reasons. These are ethical and religious. We can never understand the relations of power and knowledge to love unless we concentrate upon the mind-body instance of all three relations. And we shall never understand a God of love unless we conceive him as the all-sensitive mind of the world-body.[4] When we see a rock we seem to have knowledge but no sympathy and no direct power (merely by the seeing) . When we move the rock we have power but no sympathy. Nor does our power seem due, in cases of mere manipulation, to knowledge. Or again, a fond mother or sweetheart may love but not understand. Now this divorce of love from power and knowledge wrecks not only our cosmology but our ethics and our religion. Only in the mind-body relation is power also sensitiveness, is sympathy direct awareness, is awareness sympathetic power. This is the clue to the theory of values. By contrasting the degree to which we realize this relationship with the degree to which a supreme mind in a supreme organism would enjoy it, we can see what is good and what is potentially evil in man. He is not sensitive except over a small range; he has power indirectly, through this small range, over a very much larger range. The philosophy of power, the philosophy of knowledge, the philosophy of love, will each be clear only when they all coincide in relation to the supreme instance. Then and only then will it be intelligible and accurately definable how the limited and more or less indirect forms of the three variables can be separable and independent. Our integrity is to be won by aspiring toward the humanly unattainable ideal of such a complete interfusion of awareness, sensitiveness, and influence that power cannot fail to be responsible and open-eyed. And it is equally important to see clearly in what fashion we must always in principle fall short of this ideal unity and in what fashion we can in principle achieve it. The clue to both is in our double character as (1) directly, intuitively sensitive to bodily cells which are also sensitive to us, and (2) imaginatively sensitive to other animals and human beings.

The partly direct and partly indirect sympathy we have for nature as an individual infinitely sensitive to all its parts sets in clear light the minute extent of our own sympathy in the direct form of responsible (because responsive) and fully understanding (completely intuitive) power.

By despising the mind-body relationship or treating it inadequately as form in matter, philosophers and theologians have fallen into errors too numerous to list. The impassivity or non-sensitiveness of God is a good example. The inability to explain to atheists how God "causes" events is another.

But are we not told by some (e.g., Paul Elmer More or James Bissett Pratt) that all ethics and religion depend upon a dualism of spirit and flesh? Yes, indeed; and this is true. But the kind of dualism needed is fully provided by societism. For the cells and molecules in the body are so vastly inferior, as sympathetic creatures, to conscious imaginative human beings, not to mention the cosmic mind, that if we wish to call the latter spirits and the former non-spiritual beings we speak truth, provided we do not claim an absolutely infinite difference between the two types of being. More's point is surely Emerson's — " two laws discrete, not reconciled," one law for persons and one for things. Societism also denies a monism of laws. Molecules and cells have habits appropriate to their low level in the scale of beings; persons have ideals which require them to exert strong control over these habits, to struggle often mightily against them. There is no absolute pre-established harmony, but only a very rough and flexible one. The fineness of the harmony, or even its long endurance, depends partly on us as unitary persons or, if you like, as souls. There appears, then, to be no need to reject panpsychism in order to save the only dualism which is ethically valuable. A more extreme dualism leads to Puritan excesses and a morbid hatred of this beautiful world of organic life.

NOTES

[1] On organic sympathy see Whitehead, *Adventures of Ideas,* Chap. XI, paragraph 22; Chap. XIII, paragraphs 4, 6; Chap. XIV; Peirce, *Papers,* VI, 145–46, 158, 264–71, 272 ff.; Hartshorne, *The Philosophy and Psychology of Sensation,* paragraph 39.

[2] Cf. H. H. Price, *Perception;* G. E. Moore, " Some Judgments of Perception," *Philosophical Studies.*

[3] Cf. J. B. S. Haldane, " Quantum Mechanics as a Basis for Philosophy," *Philosophy of Science,* I, 78 ff.

[4] On the world as a mind-body or organism see Plato's *Timaeus* and W. P. Montague, *Belief Unbound: A Promethean Religion for the Modern World* (Yale University Press, 1930).

XIII

RUSSELL ON CAUSALITY

EVERY TYPE of philosophy confronts the embarrassing circumstance that numerous thinkers, seemingly able, defend sharply opposing philosophies. In view of this difficulty a certain amount of argument " against the man " is inevitable. In the following five chapters leading exponents of humanistic philosophies opposed to the new naturalism will be examined to see how far they succeed in justifying this opposition. We shall see that it is misunderstanding or lack of acquaintance rather than critical opposition with respect to the new doctrine which is chiefly found in these writers.

One of the most brilliant of all living humanists is Bertrand Russell. This writer never wearies of accusing religious philosophers of wishful thinking. Their fallacies, he says, " all tend in one direction." Agreeing that this charge has its degree of truth, I think it holds also, in a measure, against Russell. He reasons brilliantly and he is in some respects remarkably well informed; but where his reasoning fails to be cogent or his information is inadequate, his bias against religion seems in most cases to be the probable explanation.

Russell concedes that scientific induction rests on a principle of natural law which it does not prove but takes on faith.[1] He recognizes also that, apart from the difficulty of proving this principle, there is the disturbing consequence that it seems to render human choice illusory. Thus science is exposed to two main lines of attack upon its basic assumption. This situation, says Russell, is unfortunate. We apparently do not know whether science is true, and we apparently cannot have the "pleasant aspects" of science apart from the "unpleasant." Russell expresses the belief that no solution of either difficulty has been found and the hope that such a solution will be found. He does not add, " and may this solution prove not to involve a religious metaphysics " — but there is evidence that this is the sole condition upon which he is ready to give serious consideration to any proposed solution.

The problem of induction is one which philosophers who take mind as fundamental in the universe have always believed to be soluble by their hypothesis, and by no other. Law, they have held, implies a lawgiver; order, an orderer. We experience in our own purposes a way in which the future can be more or less determined in the present. Moreover, being anticipation and memory as *concerned with value*, purpose is a binding of the parts of time together, not merely anyhow but into an order or pattern. For value is essentially unity-in-variety, is essentially pattern, as the most elementary aesthetic analysis shows. Thus purpose is essentially an ordering of the parts of time, and is the only such ordering that direct experience discloses to us. To call for an explanation of our belief in order while scornfully rejecting the view that purposes are fundamental to nature is like asking for an answer to the question, What is the sum of seven and five? while insisting that it must not be twelve. The belief that nature is orderly is identical in implications with the belief that nature is teleological. "Man takes his law from nature, nature takes its law from reason, and reason takes its law from within itself," is the Chinese version of this universal commonsense view.

Recent philosophy has greatly refined and clarified this proposition. Whitehead has carried the analysis furthest.[2] Russell very properly considers the Whiteheadian theory.[3] But does he consider it carefully, as he certainly would if he were free from bias? Not at all. Like Santayana he rejects the conception of memory as real preservation of the past, but defends this rejection on the basis of some elementary misunderstandings.

The first misunderstanding is identification of memory with its distinctly conscious aspect, although the doctrine of degrees of consciousness which Whitehead adopts must be well known to Russell, since he wrote a book on Leibniz, who had developed the doctrine elaborately, and since it is also a doctrine widely popularized by Freud. It is only the dim background of memory that is identical in content with the past event itself.

The second misinterpretation lies in that Russell supposes Whitehead to be arguing that human memory alone is adequate to establish that connection between past and present which is required for causal laws. On the contrary, Whitehead insists that all order in the world depends upon the adequate preservation or "immortality" of the past which is effected only by the supreme mind, or God. The dimly conscious background of our memory is fully conscious in God; or in other words, this dim consciousness of our total past is the same thing as our dim consciousness of God. If we had not at least a dim awareness of the total past, we could not be said to have even a dim awareness of God's consciousness; and hence the whole theory is ruined if one considers, as does Russell, only the fully conscious elements of memory.

Russell is guilty of yet a third misinterpretation. If, he says, I recollect my past arrival in China, "it is a mere figure of speech to say that I am arriving in China over again." On the contrary, it is not a figure of speech but, according to

Whiteheadian principles, a mere self-contradiction to speak in this fashion. For what is preserved is not merely "arrival in China" but *the* arrival in China which took place in the past and which by being preserved does not take place "over again" but simply *continues* to have taken place when it did. To preserve the event is one thing; to enjoy a *second* event, *another* arrival in China, at a different time, with changed circumstances, is a wholly different thing. By confusing them so blithely Russell very clearly betrays his lack of desire to understand the doctrine whose contemporary importance he admits.

Russell makes the point that the past event as present in memory has certainly changed somehow, so that we still have the problem of law governing the *way* in which it changes. Assuredly. And Whitehead analyzes elaborately the principles of aesthetic congruence which determine this way. First of all, the mere pastness by which the preserved event differs from itself when it was simply present, i.e., not yet preserved, is shown to lie in the fact that when present the event contained anticipations of its immediate future which were incompletely definite, while as "preserved" the event is experienced together with the final definiteness of the events which in fact did subsequently take place and are also preserved. That is, each event adds to the definiteness of the world, as Russell correctly interprets Bergson — whose view is here similar to Whitehead's — as believing. Now in so far as anticipation is definite, the future is determined in the present. And in so far as anticipation is purposive, this determination will be according to a pattern, and hence scientific prediction will be possible. Human so-called anticipation is of course not sufficient, for both memory and foresight in man are partly intuitions of the real structure of time and partly precarious inferences. But even in us, what a man anticipates he will do can never wholly fail to color what in fact he does do, for as memory of his intention it will be a part of his new state of mind, while in God is the standard anticipation, which is identical with inexorable will. What God intends to do is what he *will* do, both senses of the word here coinciding.

We saw in chapter nine that the possibility of memory as preservation depends upon the incompleteness of the determination of the future in the present. From this it follows that not only is it unnecessary to accept the " unpleasant " doctrine of absolute determinism in order to have the pleasant doctrine of the reality of natural law, but rather it is actually necessary to give up the unpleasant doctrine if the pleasant one is to be justified. At one stroke the troublesome feature is eliminated and the desirable one established. And not only must there be some indefiniteness, some room for chance, in all predetermining order, but there must be wide variations in the degree of this disorderly factor; so that to say, as Russell does, that causality must be " applicable to human volitions as much as to anything else " [4] is wrong. For causality is a matter of degree, and there is no one degree which fits all cases. And it is precisely in such highly individual, complex beings as men and women that the highest degrees of originality, of possible departure from strict law, are to be expected. For while pattern is essential to value, irregularity, which is departure from the previously observed pattern, is also essential. Foresight and the sense of uncertainty are equally vital to value experiences, and the higher the being, the further do its enhanced powers of memory and foresight demand that its life depart from the monotony of strict order. Or, from another point of view, the higher the being, the greater the range of possibilities which it is able to appreciate and choose from; hence the wider the scope of its free action. To God even the laws of quantum mechanics are not valid forever, so that if the validity of induction means the possibil-

ity of quantitative predictions over infinite time, then indeed
is induction not justified. But what need have we for such
unlimited quantitative prediction?

There is another curious aspect of Russell's treatment of
induction. He holds that " the new philosophy " rightly renounces the " claim to a special philosophic method " or to
making " statements about the universe as a whole." But in
the next sentence he himself makes a statement affirming the
" piecemeal and higgledy-piggledy nature of the world "
(presumably " as a whole ").[5] Now obviously the validity
of induction rests, according to Russell's own account, upon
the possibility of making at least one statement about all
reality — that it is orderly — and this statement must set some
limit to the " piecemeal and higgledy-piggledy " character of
existence. No less obvious is it that the method by which
such a statement can be justified cannot be the usual method
of scientific induction, which presupposes the validity of induction. Thus it becomes perfectly clear what Russell is
about. He wants the pleasant aspect of humanism — its
" stark joy in the unflinching perception of our true place in
the world "[6] — as well as the advantage of a powerful weapon
against intrenched privilege and obscurantism. He wants
also to avoid the unpleasant aspect, the impossibility of knowing that science is true in its basic principles. The logical
positivists are less vulnerable, for they frankly admit the impossibility of " knowing " the truth of the principle of induction. There is only one choice today: either a theistic
metaphysics, or the renunciation even of scientific knowledge
as knowledge, as more than a hope which, to be sure, we cannot give up and yet remain rational beings, but which has
no other support than our desperate need for it.

In regard to the piecemeal-ness of the world, Russell repeatedly contrasts the old idealism, characterized by its notion
of an organic whole of reality such that everything implies

everything else, with the new view of things as externally related. But just as the idealists erred by lumping " everything " together in this blanket fashion, so Russell errs by asserting with equal lack of discrimination the external relatedness of everything. Both views are out of date, for a new view has arisen which assigns a definite and cosmic range to internal or organic relations, and an equally definite and also cosmic range to external relations, each type of relation having its own proper function. As Russell points out in discussing Bergson, events are external to their own predecessors. (It is an aspect of this externality that particulars are external to universals, concretes to abstracts.) But Russell refutes Bergson by taking advantage of Bergson's verbally unguarded rejection of all externality, whereas it is easy to rescue the Bergsonian view in its positive features by showing, as Peirce and Whitehead have done, that the significance of time lies precisely in the way in which it enables an organic whole to combine externality with interdependence, freedom with law, real possibilities with real existences.[7]

Russell gives no real consideration to the new view, in spite of the fact that his logical acuteness has led him to qualify his earlier doctrine of " logical atomism " to such an extent [8] that he really has no technical reason for rejecting this new version of an organic world, which is the only hope of establishing a ground of induction.

But there is still another questionable feature in Russell's discussion of causality. It is found, among other places, in his popularly written *Religion and Science*. This book discusses the problems of determinism, mind-body, and God with complete disregard of the new natural philosophy and the new Protestant theology. The cultural lag this disregard involves is not less real because the latest scientific data are respected. In discussing determinism Russell finds the scientific evidence inconclusive either way. Of philosophical arguments for indeterminism, he ignores those which have recently turned most thinkers, in all parts of the world, away from determinism. But he proposes one argument of his own which, if valid, would establish a kind of determinism. After all, he says, whatever is to happen, it must be true now that it is to happen. This is a method of arguing which Russell has contemptuously rejected when theologians have resorted to it. And it is at least no sounder here than in the ontological argument for God.

Russell's reasoning amounts to this: The definition of the future, or of truth as applied to the future, implies the existence in the present of determinate facts concerning future events. Of course no indeterminist will accept this definition as accurate. Nor need he. Instead of saying, Either it is now a fact that *a* will happen, or it is now a fact that *a* will not happen, he will put it this way: It is now a fact that one of the two, *a* or not-*a*, will happen, but which one it is to be is, as a matter of present fact, unsettled. By arbitrarily choosing the former expression, Russell has done no less than adopt a metaphysical position without any justification whatever. The partiality for absolute determinism which atheism has so generally shown, in the face of the fact that the evidences alleged for it are, on the most generous estimate, no stronger than the traditional arguments for God, and the further truth that without God neither absolute nor relative law (as Russell has admitted) has any intelligible ground whatsoever, shows how untrue it is that atheists differ from theists chiefly in the degree to which they base their views upon cautious and accurate inference from evidences.

On the problem of matter, Russell describes his position as "neutral monism." [9] Existence has certain fundamental common properties found in both mind and matter, and certain special properties peculiar to each of these two. Thus the difference between them is superficial. Common to both mind and matter are the property of possessing spatio-temporal structure and the property of possessing quality. Both mind and matter consist of events in interrelation and with intrinsic qualities. In so far as the interrelations are causal, it is probable, though by no means certain, that the structure of mental events is only a special extra-complicated case of physical structure. Here Russell agrees with Santayana. The laws of behavior are not psychological, have nothing to do with the peculiar properties of mind. Physics, without thinking about thoughts as such, should ideally be able to predict all our actions. Is this conviction due to prejudice? I incline so to interpret it. Russell is keen enough — had he not been prejudiced in favor of materialism — to have seen that he is here reasoning in a way which has got physics into trouble in the past. Because stars and other macroscopic inorganic objects behave in a certain almost infinitely monotonous, "lifeless" manner, it was supposed that of course atoms and electrons, being merely smaller planetary systems, would behave in the same fashion. Nothing further from the truth! Now we know that the behavior of large bodies is only a derivative effect of a fundamentally different type of behavior. The difference of scale makes a difference in the very type of law.

What about difference in degree of organization? A living macroscopic body is very different from a non-living one; why assume that this difference makes no difference to the type of law applying to the particles entering into it? Such an assumption is not merely rash; it is a guess in the less likely direction (see chap. 16). Why should not the very meaning of "inorganic" be that the whole is here determined by the laws of the parts, as these laws would operate if the parts were not in this whole; whereas in an organism, being in the whole would, on the contrary, make a difference to the parts? The point is that stars are apparently not individuals but collections, while a body is not a mere collection of individuals but is itself an individual in the fundamental sense in which an atom is so. This individuality is a datum, in a sense *the* datum, in the unity of our experience. And if a thing is what it does, then to be an individual and to act merely like a collection is a contradiction. Thus Russell is reasoning much less carefully than his ability would make possible if his unconscious or conscious desire to reach a certain conclusion had not persuaded him to be easily satisfied with reasoning leading to that conclusion.

It may be said that to declare that the body is organized does not mean that it is not a collection, but only that it is an organized collection. But the consciousness which we find ourselves to have is not merely an organization of elements attributable to our bodily parts; it is a unity, an integration of these elements, a *Gestalt quality* which implies partial suppression of the parts as they might exist outside this unity. Russell admits that mind and brain cells overlap in space and time, but denies that this space-time interpenetration means " logical interpenetration," i.e., partial loss of identity. But this denial only makes clear Russell's adherence to the absolutistic logic of Aristotelian substantialism. Entities exclude one another absolutely, or they are not different at all. That Russell thinks in this way is further shown by his contention that Bradley, in attempting to defend interpenetration, reduced it to an absurdity and thus revealed its untenability. For the fact is that Bradley employed the same absolutistic logic as Russell: either sheer plurality or sheer unity. Relative unity and plurality, distinctness as a matter of degree, is not really discussed by Bradley; nor is the contrast essential to this problem — that between past and future, determinate and indeterminate aspects of reality — drawn into his or Russell's discussion.

Would Russell suggest any criterion by which two events,

wholly identical in space-time distribution, could be distinguished as numerically diverse? And accordingly, if things are partially identical in their space-time relations, must we not say that they are partially identical in their individualities? If so, then brain electrons are not the same in their nature as electrons not in the brain, for some of that nature is the result of partial merging with the nature of the human mind.

The question then is whether the organization of parts does not involve unitary emergent properties which react on and modify the parts and serve to sustain or enhance the organization. "The body from the soul its form doth take, for soul is form, and doth the body make." Russell offers no good argument against the relative truth of this conclusion (which is doubtless far from the whole story, a poetic half-truth). Hence Russell's position that no events are mental in causal structure is unjustified.

Not all structure is known to be causal, according to Russell. For the direction of time is not yet satisfactorily statable in terms of physical law. That it can be given a very neat statement in terms of psychological law, he is not aware of, but Peirce,[10] Bergson, and Whitehead have elaborately developed this view. Moreover, there is no point in the hope that non-psychological laws may sometime prove capable of interpreting the direction of time, inasmuch as the very existence of law is left, on Russell's own showing, absolutely unaccounted for in terms of the idea of matter. Thus in claiming that causal structure is entirely non-psychic, Russell is rejecting the best clues we have to the structure of time, the only clue to the reality of order, the evidence furnished by the unity of consciousness against the view that the body is merely an organized collection, and finally, the evidence of purposive behavior that ideas are causal.

It is also clear that, in terms of structure, Russell's monism is mostly materialistic rather than neutral. In terms of quality it is quite the other way. Here only sheer agnosticism separates Russell from panpsychism. No neutral qualities are known to us, he holds, and no qualities of dead matter, but only the qualities of mental events which are located in the brain. Qualities of inorganic physical things are quite unknown to us. Now if all imaginable species of quality are mental — and Russell, like Santayana, mentions none that are not — how can we speak of a genus of qualities of which the mental are only one species? Surely one other species must be conceivable if the distinction between species and genus is to have any meaning. Russell avoids panpsychism here only by positing an absolutely unimaginable meaning for the word "quality," without considering the question of how the limits of the imaginable are to be transcended.

How different is Peirce's subtle treatment of the generalization from human sensory qualities to non-human! [11] The former exhibit, as Peirce pointed out, dimensions of continuity (such as those by which red shades into yellow through orange) which they do not exhaust. In this way specifically unimaginable qualities are shown to be generically imaginable.

In view of the fact that Russell's determination to arrive at a materialism (or neutralism — no matter, so it be a non-religious view) results in failure to find an intelligible doctrine of time, law, quality, one may recall a saying of Peirce: "Materialism is that mode of philosophizing which can be counted on to leave the world as unintelligible as it finds it." Which is more important, to understand the world or to avoid panpsychism?

In at least two passages Russell almost concedes that this is indeed the alternative. He says that his own view is closer to idealism than to materialism. And in discussing the old question of how mental events can be caused by physical events which are entirely different in nature, he says that since we have no knowledge of the quality of physical events, we need not assume that their quality is so different from that of mental events.[12] How much does this differ from saying that the difficulties which arise from the assumption that panpsychism is untrue may be met by pointing out that we do not know that it is untrue? For panpsychism it is which posits a systematic structural and qualitative analogy between the human mind and so-called physical things. Thus Russell's neutralism is in part a dogmatic materialism of law and an implicit idealism of quality. Nothing neutral is involved. And how unplausible it is, after all, to regard mental events as effects which are not in turn causes, purely passive factors which cannot react with other things! Russell declares, for instance, that the emotions produced by music are determined by purely physical causes. No one, he thinks, will deny this. Imagine William James or anyone who believes in the observably active role of attention failing to deny it! Imagine Bergson or anyone who believes that memory is not wholly controlled by brain states failing to point out that musical emotions are influenced by recollection!

In sum, Russell has not kept up with the march of ideas, yet he discusses problems before a wide public which thinks of him as an authority. He frequently substitutes wit for thoroughness in a manner at the same time delightful and disappointing. One is tempted to regard him as a *reductio ad absurdum* of the conception of an irreligious inquirer, a lover of truth who believes that the cosmic truths are quite as likely to be " unpleasant " as " pleasant."

NOTES

1 Russell, *Sceptical Essays* (W. W. Norton, 1928) , pp. 38–45.

2 Cf. Whitehead, *Symbolism, Its Meaning and Effect* (The Macmillan Co., 1927) .

3 Russell, *Sceptical Essays*, p. 42.

4 *Ibid.*, p. 42.

5 *Ibid.*, p. 71.

6 *Ibid.*, p. 35.

7 On time and relations see the author's discussion in the *Philosophical Review*, XLIV, 333 f.

8 For Russell's view of relations see *Contemporary British Philosophy*, F. S., edited by J. H. Muirhead (The Macmillan Co., 1924) , pp. 373 f.

9 Russell, *The Analysis of Matter* (Harcourt, Brace & Co., 1927) , Chaps. I, XXXVII.

10 On psychological law as the structure of time see Peirce, *Papers*, VI. 127–31, 147–54.

11 Peirce. *Papers*, I. 302–16, VI. 132, 196–98.

12 On the quality of material things see Russell, *The Analysis of Matter*, pp. 264, 388, 400.

XIV

SANTAYANA ON MATTER

PERHAPS Santayana's *Realm of Matter* is the greatest of recent expressions of emergent dualism, the view that life and mind have been evolved from mere matter. With much of this book the new naturalism can heartily agree. It renounces all pretense of establishing determinism, noting at least one of the chief reasons for denying this doctrine.[1] It demolishes Berkeleyan and absolutistic idealisms with cogent reasonings. It avoids old-fashioned atomism and, in so far, is not troubled by the new physics or the inherent contradictions of the idea of the absolute atom. It describes many positive properties of " matter " with matchless verbal felicity and identifiable truth. If its argument is seriously vulnerable, then probably dualism is vulnerable, for who has given greater powers to its defense? And, compared with Russell, the reasoning shows a higher degree of sympathetic understanding of the doctrines criticized. But although Santayana was writing in 1930, when the new naturalism was fairly launched on its career, it certainly cannot be claimed that he adequately understood the form which panpsychism — which he endeavored to show was only less indefensible than idealism — was beginning to take. Moreover, in his own position there are such basic incoherencies as even the charm of his rhetoric cannot persuade us to overlook.

Matter, as by Aristotle, is held to be that which is irreducible to essence, to definite quality. Moreover, change is also irreducible to essence. But change is, as it were, the essence of matter, or rather change and permanence are the two aspects of the nature of matter. There are patterns ("tropes") of change, and these patterns apart from matter are eternal, timeless essences. They are patterns of changing substance, not changing patterns. Now Santayana's two great problems are, what is the unity of the moments of time, and what is the direction from past to future? The unity (and direction) of time cannot lie in the essences of the moments, for these essences are timeless; it cannot lie in external relations between these essences, for then matter would be superfluous, whereas Santayana's most frequent argument for matter is that time requires it. Time is intelligible only as the unity of matter amid the series of its states and as a certain directional stress (many synonyms are used) in each of these states pointing one way toward a source and another way toward an outcome. But this unity, as we have seen, can have nothing to do with the essences of the states. What does it refer to then? The answer is plain: to the matter as bare matter, in abstraction from all intuitable and imaginable quality or relations. All Santayana's poetry cannot obviate this disastrous prose fact of his position. Surely to explain time by bare matter in its absolutely non-qualitative, non-intuitable aspect is like trying to make things clear by turning out the light. This is not less true because Aristotle — to whom frequent reference is made — fell into the same mistake. In fact, Santayana's book is the supreme current expression of Neo-Aristotelianism, supreme because not pedantic and literal-minded. It belongs fundamentally to the set of ideas to which there has been a radical alternative only since Peirce and Bergson.

It is convenient for this exposition that the contradictory

of Aristotelianism on this point is found in another great humanist, John Dewey. Dewey has recently suggested that qualities are not independent of their contexts in space and time.[2] The point, as I see it, is simple enough: the essence which we can abstract from the concrete is not quite so definite as the quality which we intuit in the concrete; for abstraction amounts to forgetting some aspects of an experience while trying to remember others, and this truncated memory is more or less vague — as, for instance, even the best color matching could only by a miracle be absolutely accurate. We say, " This is lemon yellow," but the phrase indicates only a roughly defined essence. No intuition of essence, as perfectly definite apart from the individual context in which it is at the moment intuited, can be had by human beings, and the whole of Santayana's *Realm of Essence* is founded on the notion of absolutes as unknowable as any God could be. The advantage of regarding essences as wholly definite only in the context in which they exist as qualities of individual things is that then no " matter " to individuate forms is required, individuality being merely the last touch of form. Of course there is still a distinction between form as structure, as relations, and form as simple qualities of feeling which are the stuff shaped into these forms (e.g., color in shapes). But this has nothing to do with any matter distinct from qualities and relations. As for the " possibility " Aristotle talked about, that lies in the more or less indefinite forms, the universals, and in individuals as embodying these by virtue of the openness of their future, the indefiniteness of anticipation.

Santayana's view involves the following result: If qualities can be at the same time perfectly definite and yet capable of appearing in various contexts, or of having being by themselves, then, since the realm of essence is wholly definite, existence adds only something *absolutely indefinite* to the already quite definite essence which receives existence. For even relations are essences and are already definite in the realm of essence. Hence absolutely indefinite matter is all that actuality adds to merely possible existence. What is the use or meaning of such addition?

Aristotle himself was less vulnerable. For his forms were not possibles, since they did not constitute a realm apart from existence. Aristotle was at least consistent in holding that the definite form was actuality, and only the matter potentiality, whereas Santayana holds in effect that the perfectly definite essence is potentially existent or not existent, while the intrinsically indefinite matter is also potentially formed in this way or that. An absolutely definite but merely possible entity is a contradiction; for if the thing is definitely all there, there is definitely nothing which it can lack, not even "existence." It is also interesting to reflect that the same paradox is involved in medieval Aristotelianism. The forms of possible existences antecede finite existence as part of the essence-existence of God, though by a mercifully veiled inconsistency this does not involve potency in the divine essence. Santayana is a medieval Aristotelian without the semblance of intelligibility which the divine mind gives both to the realm of essence and to the translation of portions of this realm into existent things. For how anything but a mind could select which essences are to be real, how blind matter, in itself without essence, a qualitative surd, could be differential with respect to qualities, none can conceive!

Santayana's all-explanatory yet completely unintelligible matter — just Locke's " I know not what " which underlies properties — is like God in the negative theology — " We know that he is but not what he is." Of course theologians did not adhere to this dictum in its full austerity, and similarly it does not appear that Santayana adheres always to his conception of matter as empty of predicates. But just as we may leave it to Roman Catholics to apologize for this proceeding in the one case, so those who favor materialism may be trusted to try to explain it in the other.

Considering how completely Santayana reverts to Greek and medieval doctrines concerning the relations of essence to mind and matter, one is reminded of William James' verdict concerning Santayana's philosophy — "dying Latinity." James knew, as scarce another man, that the modern world is irrevocably committed against any mere returns to the past. But Santayana has found little more to learn from modern thought (except some of Hume's doubts) than have the neo-scholastics. The whole drive of modern philosophy to relate concepts to percepts, thought to immediacy, not nominally or casually or merely in a general way, but at every step in philosophical reasoning, is sabotaged by Santayana, partly by iterated praise of Greek objectivity and partly by the argument that in any case we have to take a leap of faith beyond the circle of intuition. But modern philosophy is finding ways of transcending the field of immediate data exclusively in accordance with principles which can themselves be illustrated in immediacy.

Again, the gradual perfecting in modern philosophy of a non-Aristotelian theory of substance which is equally non-Spinozistic throws an interesting light on Santayana's defense of Aristotle against Spinoza. In general, current materialism seems to be a return to very old ways of thought, on the ground that more recent ways are less satisfactory, in neglect of the fact that there are some *very* recent ways which represent a higher synthesis of both the main types of preceding views, a reconciliation, at last, of Greek analytic genius with Christian insight and the modern sense for experience.

As an example, Santayana holds that teleology is out of the question because at best mental states cannot be supposed to operate in a vacuum, but only as imbedded in subconscious

bodily forces. But the new idealism is not interested in disembodied mind, even divine, and it is not interested in dis-
covering a teleological power which acts without the cooperation of other entities. Even God's power will be absolute
only in a sense which does not exclude a certain relativity
due to cooperation. Hence the fact that human purpose is
a very limited force, limited by the more or less rigid habits
of the bodily cells, not only does not in the least prove that it
is not a force at all, but also does not prove that the world as
a whole cannot be subject to a supreme purpose. This purpose naturally will not take the form of sheer tyranny, but
will involve tolerance of the habits and the freedom of all the
world-members.

There is one surprisingly dogmatic aspect of Santayana's
theory. This is his view of the future as no less real and
finished in all details than the past. There are four ways in
which Santayana might claim to know this. He might derive the definiteness of the future from some argument for
strict determinism. But he admits that the real arguments
are opposed to determinism. He might claim to have
revelation from omniscience. Needless to say he does not
do so. He might defend the fixity of the future on the basis
of the purely verbal argument, "What will be, will be."
This appears to be his position. We have seen the fallacious
character of the reasoning in our discussion of Russell's use
of it.

But Santayana has one more resource. It is commonly
admitted, he points out, that the past is definite, even though
in the perspective of consciousness ("sentimental time" —
what subtle snobbery in the use of such terms!) the past,
like the future, is more or less nebulous. Now if we distrust
consciousness in one direction, why not in the other? Why
not indeed — but that is not precisely the issue. For, as
Santayana virtually admits, it is not "like the future" that

the past is indefinite in consciousness, but decidedly in a different way and even to a different extent. Santayana scolds common sense for refusing to admit that what has not yet happened for us nevertheless is happening, " is present," in itself, i.e., in its place in the future, while yet it is good common sense to hold that past events still are in all details precisely as when they happened. If in one case we desert direct experience, why not in the other? But the fact is that in drawing this distinction between past and future, common sense is consistently abiding by experience and is not deserting it in one case any more than in the other. The principle of empiricism in philosophy (which Santayana here virtually rejects as sentimental, but which is merely the basis of intellectual integrity) involves the determination to abide by two rules. First, direct or perceptual experience is to be transcended only by imaginative experience. Second, this extension is to respect clues given in perceptual experience. Common sense observes both rules concerning past and future; Santayana, neither rule. The perceptual clue is that memory, retentive experience, is in principle more definite than premonition. Imaginative extension reveals that this difference persists through the widest conceivable variations of memory and foresight. For, as we have seen, even a perfect memory of the past would leave intact the distinction between past and present (and thus would be truly memory) only provided the remembered past did *not* contain a full anticipation of the present which now remembers it. Thus not only does the maximizing of memory not imply the maximizing in the same sense of anticipation, but it implies the opposite. Complete anticipation would render the future and the past both alike and equally present.

Santayana fails to see this, but common sense, in its implicit way, has never failed to see it. Santayana's conclusion that the past is definite is frankly taken from common sense without any notion of the basis of this common-sense conviction, while his attempt to construe the future in the same terms is in admitted defiance of common sense. And in both cases he lacks any precise technical reason, in terms of empirical evidence, for his contention.

But Santayana's position is worse than a groundless defiance of common sense. It renders time self-contradictory. All parts of time are in themselves equally present and actual, and all are contained somehow in every part, are equally defined in any now. This is exactly the collapse of time into eternity for which Santayana excoriates absolute idealism. He endeavors to rescue time from this collapse in two ways, partly by vague talk about the law of entropy (not explicitly referred to but the apparent gist of his metaphors) and partly by describing the conscious difference between past and future and suggesting that this reveals, by analogy, the nature of temporal flow in unconscious and non-purposive substances. Just what is left of the analogy, in abstraction from the conscious character of memory, foresight, hope, fear, desire, purpose, is the question, and I leave it to the reader to discover something definite in Santayana's discussion of "tensions," etc., in this connection. I can see only mirage, apart from the physical fact of entropy, which is rather a subject for scientific experts than for Santayana and concerning which (as the meaning of "time's arrow") perhaps not many would agree.

But might not Santayana rescue time by renouncing the definiteness of the future and retaining that of the past? This would certainly remove one contradiction. But it would still leave the other one, that neither matter by its blankness nor essence by its independence of relations can intelligibly constitute the unity-in-variety which is time. And moreover, if one rejects sentimental, i.e., experienced time, in favor of material, allegedly unconscious time and yet retains the asymmetry of conscious time while rejecting the symmetry of time as treated by physics (for by the uncertainty principle, the past, like the future, is not wholly definite to physical experiment), one is surely behaving in strange fashion. Mead is more consistent in holding that both past and future are as indefinite as the laws of nature and the data for inference existing in the present make them. But on that view, where, once more, is the asymmetry of time? And will common sense submit to the denial that past events have been in detail precisely what they have been, law or no law? And can one imagine Santayana accepting Mead's view which makes both past and future mere imperfect outlines inhering in, or constructible in, the present?

Materialists may take their choice. The gross possibilities have now all been tried. But none of them except the panpsychic view can make a clear appeal to the empirical principle. And, after all, Santayana insists upon the impossibility of directly intuiting matter or substance, so that his dogmatism is self-confessed. Scientific induction, he says, presupposes, does not prove, a real ordered world of substance. Direct intuition discloses no minute corner of such a world; animal faith merely posits it. And this is no accident in Santayana. For if direct intuition revealed causal, substantial activity, then it would follow — as Santayana is too keen not to see — that feelings and ideas are causal forces, and this would imply that all causality at least may be psychic. For immediacy is organic; you cannot pick out any datum in it which is unambiguously non-psychic, not of the nature of feeling. But in denying that consciousness is causal Santayana, like Russell, faces another nemesis of the materialist. For a man who can believe that the effect of a telegram could be explained without reference to the understanding of the telegram should be able to believe almost anything. It becomes too obvious how strong the will to believe must be.

Nor would it help to declare that even understanding or purpose are for behavioristic psychology material processes. For then it should be permissible to argue that all material processes should be considered psychic and purposive in so far as they show analogy to the human body, though different in degree and type of psychic character by whatever ways the behavior exhibited is different from ours. The whole battle would change its terms, but the question, Does *dead* matter exist? would retain much of its meaning and presumptively negative answer. It would still be true that by direct or imaginative experience we can construct no positive notion of time or law applicable to dead matter, i.e., matter that does not remember or anticipate.

There is one more point to consider: Santayana's criticism of panpsychism and pantheism. This criticism grants that panpsychism is a more scientific form of spiritualism than any other. But Santayana urges several difficulties. Feelings might grow out of past feelings — this he seems to grant — and in so far they might constitute time. But then he retracts this apparent admission. Relations themselves would for panpsychism have to be " mental, not natural." If, as I take it, this means that relations would have to be relational feelings rather than feelings in relation, the answer is to be found in Peirce's theory of " secondness " as dyadic reaction between unitary or monadic feelings, such reactions being by formal necessity irreducible to mere feelings-of-reaction, since the dyad is logically irreducible to the monad.[3] When we experience a sudden change of feeling or sensation, as when the enjoyment of music is interrupted by a jarring noise, or when the vivid expectation of experiencing one thing is disappointed by the experience of another, we are experiencing a dual *relation* of transition and shock between experiences. Is this relation any less " natural " because it is between psychic elements, and is it not also itself psychic, as much a character of experience as such as the feelings or sensations it connects?

Santayana's idea is apparently that relations between feelings must be external to feeling and to the psychic generally. For instance, if the relation between past and present feeling were felt in the latter, then the past feeling would have to be embraced in the present feeling and consequently could not be past. Even if memory were perfect, the factor common to present and past feeling could not be the latter as an event, but only its "dateless essence." Panpsychism, however, rejects dateless essences of individual events as self-contradictory. The essence of the individual is an individual essence, hence inseparable from its unique place in the context of space-time. The precise essence of the past event can be in the present only if the past event itself is there. And Bergson and Whitehead hold, and have explained very carefully, how memory is precisely the presence of the past, its "objective immortality." Santayana admits that memory seems to "bring the movement of events bodily within the circle of intuition," but holds this to be an illusion due to the fact that memory is imagery (which is present) plus knowledge with an external reference. But this reference to a beyond is a relation which is not, he holds, intuited, but is "faith." Thus time is not really given, and the external reference of knowledge is groundless so far as we can know. It too may be "illusion."

Santayana also holds that only matter can be in space. A good dose of Peirce's "law of mind" or Whitehead's geometry of feeling-of-feeling is the answer to this baseless contention. Space is known, even to a physicist, only as a pattern of interaction, and feelings are *given* as reactive. "My neighbor is he with whom I intimately react" is the basic idea of relative position in space, and there is nothing whatever in the idea to exclude feeling as the essence of the terms so related (see chap. 15).

Santayana argues also that even if relations of feelings could themselves be felt we should still have to face the fact that many real relations are not felt. The relation of the birth of a man's mind to its preceding causes cannot be experienced, nor can death be experienced. This, of course, only means that fully conscious human awareness does not constitute more than a fragment of the cosmic system. Panpsychism holds that minds overlap in their dimly conscious backgrounds, so that in fact a man dimly feels his parents as they were before his birth, and his embryonic cells felt the first stirrings of his feelings, while God feels all beginnings and endings clearly. How do Santayana's contentions upset this theory?

If I am not mistaken, no other attempt to show that panpsychism cannot be true is so ingenious as this one. But it fails. Santayana shows neither that dead matter can, nor that living feeling cannot, constitute the real substances in space-time.

This is peculiarly evident when he insists that there can be "no mental machinery," no mental causation, no teleology. For by his own admission we have no insight whatever into the way in which matter contains within itself the ground of pattern in the midst of change; even how the present has a future is described by Santayana chiefly by reference to mental events, whereas in purposive anticipation we find the present both constructive of the future and constructive of an order which the future shall embody. Santayana puts up a brave front, in which his genius shines clearly, but he shows that the case is hopeless. "Matter" is the asylum of ignorance, pure and simple, whose only useful function is to postpone for a more convenient occasion the specification of the type of psychic reality required in the given case. Aristotle had not the factual knowledge to achieve this specification except for the animals. We are *beginning* to get it only now.

Santayana's basic assumption amounts to the isolation, worthy of his genius, of the essence of materialism; the crucial denial of what spiritualism asserts, the *social* character of immediacy, the universal fact of feeling which is literally *of* feeling, direct, sympathetic contact of sentient individuals one with another. Santayana thinks the pure privacy or egoism of immediacy is self-evident and absolute. The panpsychist explores experience for evidence of immanent sociality and points to many more or less subtle phenomena which seem to prove it.

Concerning pantheism, Santayana concedes its superiority to supernatural theologies, but concludes that it is after all only an honorific way of referring to material nature. The habits of nature remain what they are even though we call them the habits of God. Moreover it is physics and not theology which tells us what the habits are. And since all existence is logically arbitrary, no reason can be given for the acts of nature even though they are regarded as acts of God. They remain as irrational as before.

All this is plausible. But it is inaccurate in many respects of which a few will be mentioned here. First of all, by calling the habits of nature the habits of God, we explain in the only way ever conceived why there are such habits, or, if you prefer, *how* there are such habits, guaranteeing order in the future as well as in the past. In short, our evidence for God becomes evidence for the validity of induction.

Again, the evidence of physics pointing to the eventual cessation of organized activities according to the law of entropy must, if pantheism is true, be taken to mean at most the eventual disappearance of the present type of organized activities, the life of God expressing itself simultaneously in the constructive creation, in ways not yet revealed to us, of other types. All *absolute* catastrophes, like the " heat-death " conceived as the last word and the whole story, are logically incompatible with pantheism and the pantheist will regard them only as highly interesting nightmares. But so will he regard many other plausible ideas, such as that life on this planet was the first appearance of sentient organisms in the world. Santayana says that most of nature is probably dead. Physics is already casting doubt on this proposition. The pantheist will say no atom or molecule, still less any electron, is dead, even though rocks (being mere swarms of the former) and porterhouse steaks be so. But the list of differences which pantheism makes is inexhaustible.

Santayana's reasoning is perhaps a little disingenuous. He blames supernaturalism for not taking nature seriously, and then he charges pantheism with futility because its divine acts are not favorable to man in the sense of a teleology naïvely expressive of tribal egoism. All man *should* want of God is that he should be intellectually and spiritually lovable and loving, that he should maintain a cosmos in which various types of individuals can enjoy themselves and one another with the degree of freedom, and therefore inevitably with partial conflict and evil, inseparable from individuality in each type; above all, that rational beings, not in the least necessarily man in particular, should come to exist and to express their powers. Atheists cannot have it both ways. If the worth and nobility of human existence are not destroyed by the denial of God, then nature is not, in its treatment of us, necessarily and self-evidently unworthy to be the body of a benevolent deity. But the fact is that atheists retain the full sense of human values only by a certain amount of inconsistency. They fail to take nature at its face value (e.g., they dream of "conquering death") in a manner that can be made consistent only on pantheistic grounds.

But Santayana argues that the cosmos cannot be an animate organism. How easily he satisfies himself of this! The cosmos, he says, neither reproduces its kind nor feeds itself. But according to the conception of the evolution of law, it does transform itself into a kind of offspring; and, anyway, what essential connection can analysis discover between animate unity and the production of other similar unity? The cosmos is the eternal organism, the only eternal one. Of course it does not reproduce. Similarly with the other requirement. Digestion is part of the traffic among parts of the cosmos whereby their interdependence and partial instability is expressed; and of course the universe has no external environment to deal with in this fashion. Plato long ago reasoned more carefully than Santayana on this point. The cosmic animal has plenty to do by way of organized activity without external action, for it has the most complex of all internal environments to maintain in ever changing adjustment. And what would be the end of this adjustment? Twofold: first, to keep its member-parts, its " cells " of all types, in a predominantly (though not possibly a completely) healthy and mutually helpful state; second (though this is only an aspect of the same thing) , to share sympathetically in the values thus realized. This is a fully intelligible end which implies no further purpose, and lack of digestion and reproduction is quite irrelevant to it.

Santayana does not point out, as complete fairness would require, that the men who have created the details and the outlines of our accurate knowledge of the physical world have in scarcely a single case looked upon the material world as the soulless, inexplicable mass of changing stuff Santayana describes it as being; nor does Santayana recognize that the habit of seeing in physical reality an ordering intelligence of infinite majesty and a universal life of inexhaustible variety and intensity has provided just the satisfying excitement that has made men neglect practical affairs, endure poverty and scorn, put aside man's natural preoccupation with himself and his fellows, and live for the contemplation of nature and the detection of her secrets — live " to add a new object, a page to science . . . for the proud sensation of not being useless on earth, of having detected another link in the creative power of God." [4] Santayana's materialism is essentially parasitic. It and all thought like it are made possible only by men who see much more definite greatness in nature than matter which, for no imaginable reason and with no imaginable guarantee of continuance, orders itself, and equally blindly sometimes flowers into living forms, forms valuable on their own account. The uninspiring, the fatal vagueness of this view is apparent.

Santayana is the foremost literary and poetic philosopher of our time. Unlike Plato, he is not also a scientific philosopher. For science is radical empiricism combined with radical logico-mathematical clarity. Santayana's pride is to be " mature and disillusioned," but science is born of love of the great cosmos, not of caution that casts a scornful eye on the presumed follies of others or on the errors of the past, still less on the errors of one's own time, seen against the background of a perverse return to earlier modes of thought. Only a real genius really animated by " malice " (to use one of Santayana's favorite expressions for his opponents) could have taken Bergson's theory of time and memory as the growth of feeling perpetually adding imperfectly anticipated feeling to itself, and have derived from this view the malice-appeasing corollary that while there is a feeling of change there can be no change of feeling.[5] It just doesn't follow. And even if the corollary did follow from Bergson's words, the words could easily be revised so that the implication of real process became unambiguous, as it is in Whitehead.

How long will the paradox of literary humanists calling for materialistic naturalism in the name of science, while the creative scientists and scientifically creative philosophers (like H. N. Russell, Jeans, Eddington, Einstein, Peirce,

Whitehead) call for the vision of God, be regarded with other than humor by mankind? Surely Santayana, for all his protests against mistaking poetry for science, is not an objective or a precise thinker in the highest degree, a Leibniz, a Peirce. His arguments are mostly in metaphors, he fails to realize that logical precision means either quantity or dimensional order, and consequently that such distinctions as those he makes between vital and non-vital substances, matter and essence, spirit and matter, being merely qualitative distinctions in terms of absolute, unquantified, unordered dichotomies, are prescientific as well as pre-Hegelian and pre-Leibnizian.

NOTES

1 Santayana, *The Realm of Matter*, pp. 110–11.

2 On the inseparability of qualities from their contexts see John Dewey, "Peirce's Theory of Quality," *Journal of Philosophy*, XXXIII, 287; Hartshorne, *Philosophy and Psychology of Sensation*, section 4.

3 On "secondness" or reactions among feelings see Peirce, *Papers*, I. 322–36.

4 Raffinesque, quoted in Donald Peattie's *Green Laurels* (Simon & Schuster, Inc., 1936) , p. 268.

5 For a nonmalicious view of Bergson's theory of memory by a very careful thinker see H. H. Price, " Memory-Knowledge," *Proceedings of the Aristotelian Society*, 1936.

XV

MEAD AND ALEXANDER ON TIME

GEORGE HERBERT MEAD was a great philosopher and certainly a humanist. Until his *Philosophy of the Act* has been published it will be too soon to pass judgment on his philosophy. But there are some aspects of his system which seem fairly well defined by his extant writings, and these aspects suggest the following criticisms. In his *Philosophy of the Present* Mead declares that each age creates its own past — not its own image of the past, for Mead seems to deny the validity of this distinction. The past *is* the best image we can construct on the basis of present experience in its past-pointing characteristics. The question then arises of how the past which we infer in this manner differs from the future which we may also infer. What is the direction of pastness? To this question Mead's writings seem to give only a cloudy answer. And in any case, it seems contradictory to assert that our efforts to know the past create the past we wish to know. In Mead's own discussion we can feel the unwished-for but really inescapable naïve meaning of past as the "irrevocable," the settled and done for, contrasted with the future, the unsettled, which can be more and more settled in this way or in that as it comes closer and closer to the present. Mead admits that an absolutely fixed past is possible only theistically, but he considers only the old type of theism according to which the future is fixed also, and he rightly objects that in that case past and future lose their distinctness and time is explained away, not explained. But then is this not also the result if we make both past and future unsettled? The point is to distinguish them, and both old theism and Mead's humanism seem, though in opposite ways, to confuse them together. Is it not striking that Mead's paradoxical view was expressly adopted under the conviction that the only alternative was the medieval or Roycean absolute (which Mead mistakenly supposed was also Whitehead's doctrine) ?

In theory of value Mead was a great thinker. But his view of the social nature of mind is dangerously unprotected against the conclusion that society is the only real locus of value. His sympathetic critic, Professor T. V. Smith, has warned against this danger.[1]

In any case, Mead's social psychology is compatible with organic sympathy, since the "mind" which, according to him, is generated by relations to other human organisms is mind as reflective consciousness, as understanding of "significant symbols," not mind as merely feeling and striving, and the embracing of these factors in a unity of awareness with its element of meaning as awareness "of" an environment. Or did Mead really think that *all* sense of meaning, including that involved in simple memory and desire and emotional attitudes, is due to "taking the role of the other" in the fashion which is achieved only by man? (That all life whatsoever is "social" in a broad sense Mead fully grants.)

Again, in *Movements of Thought in the Nineteenth Century*, Mead says that a physical object really is, in the perspective of the beholding organism, what it looks to be — colored, etc.[2] But the question between psychism and its critics concerns what the object is when *not* in the perspective of human perception, e.g., before animals existed on earth, or today when we are all asleep. Mead says the world is the totality of perspectives.[3] Then we must ask, What is the perspective that belongs individually to a molecule as a man's perceptions belong to the man? Does the molecule's perspective possess quality, and if so how can it lack feeling or sensation? Does it possess the past as real in the present, and then how can it lack memory? Is it subject to order, and then how can it lack some germ of purpose, i.e., of present pattern binding upon the future? Only if the *Philosophy of the Act* illuminates these questions will Mead's philosophy present a significant alternative to psychic naturalism.

Perhaps the most important of all recent efforts to interpret the world without resort to the cosmic psychic variables is that of S. Alexander in *Space, Time, and Deity*. Alexander's view is that the only cosmic principle is space-time or, as he expresses it, pure motion. If one asks, Motion of what? Alexander replies, in effect at least, that there need be nothing to move except bits of motion themselves. In other words change of position can take place even though there is nothing at any position except change of position. This frank assertion of a paradox seems to me more honest intellectually than Santayana's pretense to possess in the term " matter " a key to what it is that has locus and that changes.

Out of pure motion " emerge " certain special properties (" local variables " in our terminology) such as quality, life, mind. But there are no cosmic variables, except bare space-time or motion, by which these local variables may be described.

In cosmic terms this system differs from older materialisms in three ways. First, space is held to be essentially temporal. Second, " matter " is given up as a cosmic principle except in so far as it means simply what is spatio-temporal. (This of course is the only positive meaning it ever did have.) Third, really new, unpredictable qualities perpetually appear in the universe. (The quality now emerging is deity, nascent divinity.) Because of these differences Alexander greatly objects to being called a materialist. When this charge is brought, he points out with great earnestness that he has described time as " the mind of space." But if asked what this means, and whether or not, by virtue of time, space thinks or feels, he replies that his metaphor must not be taken too seriously. The psychist cannot but suspect that Alexander has an intuition of the cosmic range of memory and expectation as essential to time, but has not clarified this intuition.

So far as I know, Alexander's is the only carefully elaborated, honest attempt (unless we should except Nicolai Hartmann's) to work out a non-psychic metaphysics which the twentieth century has so far witnessed. By virtue of his thoroughness and honesty the following difficulties appear plainly enough. First, pure structure is made independent of qualities. For space-time is nothing definite except a changing pattern of relations. " Relations of what? " remains unanswered. Second, the fact that space-time does in fact produce qualities is not explained. Third, there is in the system no ground of order in change.

It is also interesting that Alexander, writing a third of a century after Boutroux and Peirce had exploded the pretensions of determinism, tried to combine the absoluteness of law in physics with the absolute unpredictability of emergent properties.[4] Both absolutes are groundless obstacles to any understanding of time. It is also interesting that Alexander's quasi-materialism was not deliberately chosen as an alternative to a temporalistic panpsychism, but as an alternative to absolute idealism and ordinary materialism.

Alexander's point that space is inconceivable apart from time is an improvement over older materialisms, yet a weakness. For it is easier to overlook the emptiness of the concept of non-psychic reality in a static than in a dynamic context.

That psychic reality is essentially dynamic is obvious, since thinking, feeling, striving, loving, hating, are all acts and since novelty and surprise are aesthetically valuable, and the very thought of their total absence is unbearable if we really strive to imagine it. But the blank notion of lifeless, insentient existence suggests no activity, for it suggests nothing definite, except, as Alexander says, the bare stuff of motion itself, and then it throws no light on what it is that moves. Becoming is a richer notion than being, and hence it reveals even more clearly the poverty of " matter " or of " non-psychic reality." If there is becoming, *something* must become which is not just a bit of becoming. Alexander's error is the universal one of all dualisms and materialisms, that of trying to explain the concrete by the abstract, " the fallacy of misplaced concreteness."

Alexander gives a very interesting argument for his rejection of quality as a cosmic variable.[5] He says that there is no " plan," or principle of variability, in quality similar to the plan of " humanity " as varied in Caucasian, Mongolian, and other races. He even doubts that there is any plan to color, and is confident that there is none uniting red and hard and sweet — all the sense qualities. Strangely, he says nothing about the continuity of colors, and of course nothing about the possibility that discontinuities among the different senses are due to the fact that human sense-feelings are not all possible feelings, but a restricted realization of these possibilities, even by comparison with other existent animals. Hence Alexander's conclusion that " quality " is only a collective name for red, sour, hard, etc., is hastily arrived at. Nor can it be justified, since no observation can prove the impossibility of qualities intermediate between red and sweet, or sweet and warm, or in general any discontinuity of this type. And the only plan of variability any universal can have is dimensionality, a continuous spread of values (admitting various discontinuous spreads as special cases).

Starting, as Alexander does, from motion as an ultimate, one cannot interpret quality and qualitative change. But if we start from the notion of qualitative changes as socially interlocked, sympathetically interacting with one another, motion becomes readily explicable.[6] For motion is change of relative position and position is determined by the principle: " My neighbor is he with whom I intimately interact " (Peirce). Hence motion is simply the changes in the degrees of interaction among qualitative changes. Furthermore, it is explicable why there should be such changes in interaction. For, given a certain feeling-quality in *A*, then the degree to which this quality is compatible with intimate relationship to a given quality in *B* is determined. To take an example on the human plane: If I am melancholy in such a settled way that it conflicts with my mood to be vividly aware of a cheerful neighbor, I shall tend to keep at a certain distance from cheerful persons and to seek out intimate relations with persons in a melancholy mood. But if I pass from this state to one of feeling cheerless in a restless, painful way that makes me wish to be " cheered up," I shall seek out the society of happy people. The aesthetic unity of contrasting feelings which is necessary if feeling is not to be indefinitely destroyed by boredom or intolerable discord thus implies that changes in feeling-quality should be accompanied by changes in degree of relationship to other feeling-qualities, that is, by motion. And it matters not how simple the feelings may be, how subhuman or superhuman, for this law of unity in contrast is perfectly general and implies no higher degree of complexity than an electron may enjoy. Thus there is no riddle in the fact that our human feelings may produce motions in the human brain and muscles, for the parts of these organs sympathize with our changing feelings to such a degree as to involve sharp changes in their internal qualities, and from this their motion follows necessarily. The reverse process is equally explicable. Motion in the brain particles necessarily involves changes in their qualities, hence, by sympathy, qualitative changes in us. It also involves shifts in our relative intimacy with different parts of the brain (shifts of attention), so that one can truly say that consciousness moves.

It is easy to see why it is that science deals with motion as the causative factor rather than with qualitative change. All motion involves qualitative changes, but these are usually inaccessible to us by ordinary practical or scientific means. Only with animals a great deal like ourselves can we rather easily infer something about the feelings involved in their "behavior." With inorganic bodies, which do not as wholes feel, since the feelings of their parts are not pooled into a single aesthetic pattern, we find it much easier to infer analogy to ourselves in terms of mere behavior than in terms of feeling-quality. And the behavioristic analogy serves our purposes. Why does it do so? How can we know the shapes of things whose feelings we do not know? How can we separate what in our sensations is due to motion in the environment from what is due to qualitative change? It seems almost a sufficient explanation to say that the aesthetic unity of the world is such that when we take the motions by themselves, we find them characterized by a very definite quantitative pattern. Doubtless the complete aesthetic pattern involves qualities also. But these qualities evidently change in such a way as to involve motions (changes in the relations between qualitative changes) which, considered in abstraction from the qualitative side, yield fairly definite patterns of their own, somewhat as the pattern of a poem is relatively independent of the meanings of its words. Thus the final proof of the atomic theory of matter was the proof that if there is a definite law of heat, heat must be a mode of motion, whatever else it may be. In other words, our sensations can be predicted if we suppose changes in them to be correlated with motional changes in the environment and in ourselves and if we suppose these changes to follow certain patterns. Not that it does not matter what qualities there may be in the environment, but that it does not matter to us whether or not we *know* these qualities. For we do know this about them, that they are such as to be compatible with the patterns of motion which explain our sensations, and this is all we need to know. We get the results of the qualities in terms of motions and of the qualities of our sensations, and that satisfies us.

But the fact is that we do not in reality know the precise motions in nature, nor even anything much like them. We know statistical patterns and certain *limits* of motions, but the course of behavior of an individual electron inside these limits escapes us. We have positive grounds for denying that this behavior follows an absolute law by which it could be precisely predicted; but if we really knew the individual behavior of an electron up to a given moment, it might well be that we should be able to make a fairly close estimate of what it would do next. But also we should have some sympathy for it as an individual. We should know how long it has endured a given energy-state, how likely it is, by the general tolerance of electrons for given types of monotony, that it is " tired " of this state and ready to " react " away from it to something affording the relief of novelty. But the wonderful fact is that this knowledge would not for practical purposes tell us anything we need to know unless we could simultaneously observe millions of electrons in this individual fashion; and we should then have to have superhuman intelligence to put the facts together into a significant story. For we live on the macroscopic plane, where individual particles are insignificant.

It seems to come to this, that motion is decisive because,

in abstraction from qualities, it yields the statistical patterns needed for our type of prediction and control of ourselves through control of the environment. The pattern of motions which is abstractable from the real but elusive changes of quality in the environment is continued into the body (not without some modifications no doubt, but to a significant extent), so that physiology is in a measure a mere complication of physics. But here motions and qualities begin to seem inseparable even for our knowledge. There is in a bright color a sense of exhilaration and in the sensation of black a "dead" quality which correspond to the fact that in one case the given part of the retina is stimulated, and in the other is merely left to its own internal energy or lack of it. And the cells or molecules concerned may be supposed to share (with appropriate qualifications) in such feelings of excitement or calm. Many other examples could be given (see the author's *The Philosophy and Psychology of Sensation*).

The facts on the whole seem entirely in agreement with the assumption that the ultimate or complete pattern of nature is a pattern in which qualities and motions are inseparable, but that the motion-patterns can be abstracted and, in statistical aspects, yield all the law we human beings can for most practical or scientific purposes desire; while, on the other hand, there is evidence that behind the statistical behavioristic laws there are patterns of individual behavior which could not be fully grasped apart from qualitative sympathy with the individuals. The study in which this double point of view enters even into scientific contexts is psychophysics. But here we must note the difficulty that quality, in the strict sense of the non-structural properties of things, seems inevitably to elude reason, for reason deals with patterns, structures. In the book mentioned above I have tried to deal with this question, essentially by pointing out that qualities are similar to one another, and that similarity is a relationship subject to exact — in fact, geometrical — patterns. Starting with one's own sense qualities as origin, such relationships might conceivably lead to an insight even into the qualities of microscopic entities. But the problem will hardly be adequately formulated in our generation, one reason being that the advanced psychophysical knowledge which would make such a formulation useful is not yet at hand.

It is quite different with internal properties of a structural character, such as memory or purpose or complexity of feeling. It should be possible to make rapid progress in ascertaining how long on the average an electron vividly remembers or how far ahead it effectively anticipates. Physics can in this regard pass easily into a branch of comparative psychology, hindered indeed only by the fact that we do not deal directly with individuals. This psychology of structural properties is the only kind that is generally admitted to be possible even for animals, nay even for human beings, if we believe the behaviorists.

Alexander is right in choosing continuous dimensions for his cosmic variables; but variables of feeling-quality and of thought and volition may be continuous as well as those of space and time, and for philosophy may be even more important. Of course we have to abstract from any one set of particular thoughts or feelings or strivings, just as we do from any one set of space-time patterns. But to abstract from a whole infinite dimension such as the variables of thought or feeling are, is precisely the indefensible process of explaining concreteness by the merely abstract, that which is not even potentially concrete. Space-time is potentially all that particular patterns of motion are concretely, but it is not even potentially concrete particularizations of quality or thinking. It requires these latter particularizations for the particular-

ization of its own dimensions, but the dimensions of qualitative particularization, for instance, are additional to the
physical dimensions. The opponents of psychism have yet
to explain what they take to be the relation of abstractions to
the concrete. Peirce and Whitehead and Bergson have explained this most carefully. For them, to generalize the results of experience is to generalize experience itself. The
variability of experience is itself experienced, by virtue of
the sociability and the flexibility or freedom of the latter.
Variability of a " reality " held to be distinguishable from
all experience is, on the other hand, experientially meaningless. " Pure motion " is unimaginable not relatively but
absolutely; it is a *contradiction* of the empirical variability
— which is irreducibly more than four-dimensional — upon
which the idea of motion and every idea must be based.
The totality of irreducible dimensions of the experienceable
variability of experience is the totality of irreducible dimensions of existence. The narrowness or provincial character
of human experience, both with respect to what is " below "
and what is " above " it, lies not in its dimensions, but in
the limits of the " slice " of values humanly realized along
these dimensions. If this statement is true, philosophical
understanding is possible; otherwise it is not possible.

NOTES

[1] Cf. T. V. Smith, *Beyond Conscience* (McGraw-Hill Book Co., 1934).

[2] Mead, *Movements of Thought in the Nineteenth Century* (University of Chicago Press, 1935), p. 414.

[3] *Ibid.*, p. 315.

[4] Alexander, *Space, Time, and Deity* (The Macmillan Co., 1920), I, 326 ff.

[5] *Ibid.*, II, 328.

[6] On space as a pattern of sympathetic interconnection see Whitehead, *Adventures of Ideas*, pp. 226, 258–60; and *Process and Reality* (The Macmillan Co., 1929), Part IV.

XVI

LOGICAL POSITIVISM AND THE METHOD
OF PHILOSOPHY

THE MOST recent important school of humanistic philosophy is " logical positivism," also called the " Viennese circle,"
of which the best known representatives are Moritz Schlick,
Rudolf Carnap, and Hans Reichenbach. By positivism is
meant the rejection as meaningless of metaphysical questions,
including the questions of theology, whether the answers
given to them are affirmative or negative. It is notable, however, that this school takes its examples of metaphysical and
theological doctrines chiefly from the past, or from reaction-
ary metaphysics of today. It discusses idealism in the old
sense, not panpsychism; supernaturalism, not naturalistic
theism; the strange Neo-Kierkegaardian obscurities of Heidegger, instead of the scientifically motivated systems of
Peirce, Whitehead, Stern, Wenzl, Montague. Consequently,
while the new positivism may have furnished the materials or
methods for refuting all metaphysics, the refutation itself can
hardly be said to have been achieved. Granting, as I believe
we must, that the new positivism is an immense improvement
upon all previous antimetaphysical philosophies — so much
so that there is justification for the doubts frequently expressed in the Viennese circle concerning the fairness of the
traditional term " positivism " for the new doctrine — we are

bound to balance this improvement against the equally thc oughgoing revisions in results and methods which recent metaphysics, in France, England, and America at least, believes it has effected.

It is dangerous to discuss the tenets of the Viennese circle unless one has mastered its new and elaborate symbolism and its subtle complexities of doctrine. But it is equally dangerous for positivists to discuss metaphysics without having mastered the likewise subtle and complicated novelties of the new metaphysics. Of course positivists deny the need for this mastery, since they claim to have refuted metaphysics in principle. But metaphysicians claim to have refuted positivism in principle.[1]

Again, positivism claims to have on its side the whole spirit and method of science. But Leibniz, Peirce, and Whitehead are high authorities on the philosophical bearings of science, and the new metaphysics is in considerable measure their creation. Sooner or later it will be necessary to meet the issue head on, and this means that knowledge of current metaphysics and of current antimetaphysics will have to be combined in the minds of at least a few students. The present chapter intends to be at most a first approximation thereto. I shall first discuss relatively non-technical issues, and then issues which will probably be unintelligible to readers not familiar with positivist writings. The chapter will close with some reflections of a general character.

Positivists are very sensitive to criticisms which confuse their position with older positivisms. But they have no scruples about dismissing most of what used to be called philosophy on the basis of arguments which clearly derive at least part of their force from dwelling upon errors which non-positivistic philosophy, in some countries at least, has largely outgrown.

Thus, for example, Carnap says: " Metaphysicians wish to

seek their object *behind* the objects of empirical science; they wish to inquire after the essence, the ultimate cause of things." [2] The truth is that metaphysics is seeking simply the most general features of phenomena and of things, that the word "essence" (as here used) is appropriate only to Hegelianism or still older philosophies, and that according to the new metaphysics there is no single ultimate cause, except in the sense of a cause exerting an influence maximal in strength and in extent through space and time. Such looseness as Carnap here permits himself in describing metaphysicians as a class would seem to him scarcely excusable if indulged in with reference to antimetaphysical philosophies. In all the examples of metaphysical concepts adduced by Carnap only Hegel, the older theology, and Heidegger are represented.[3]

Thus he urges against theistic philosophy that its procedure is to conceive God ostensibly in analogy to the human mind, but so to treat this analogy as to destroy its meaning, e.g., by denying that God has a body. This criticism is the very one that is made of the old theology by the new, so that it does not in the least tell against theism as such but only against one form of theistic doctrine. Again, Carnap says that theology involves the violation of the syntactical rule that existence is not a predicate, so that it is nonsense to say God exists. It ought to be, he says, " There is a God," and this implies the "elementary sentence," "X is a God," which Carnap thinks the theologian must reject. Now if " the universe " is a possible value of x, and if we omit the " a "—which has the untenable implication, refuted long ago in theology, that there could be more than one God — then the new theism can perfectly well state its thesis as, " the universe is divine," i.e., is the supremely integrated conscious organism.

But, asks the positivist, has this a meaning which might conceivably be verified? Does it imply any factual predictions? I think it implies an infinity of such predictions. It implies panpsychism, which, in conjunction with the facts of science, is an infinite class of predictions, none demonstrably incapable of verification, although perhaps none is adequately verifiable in the present state of knowledge. We shall return to this topic presently. Again, theism implies the falsity of determinism, which some high authorities think is also definitely refuted by quantum mechanics. It implies the eternal existence of finite minds of some kind in the universe; and this could be verified — if not for eternity, at least for greater and greater time spans — for example, by some evidence of human survival of death (which according to Schlick is a verifiable idea), or by the discovery of other inhabited planets. It implies also that there exists a complete memory of all past events, and that participation in this memory is possible to an indefinitely greater extent than that enjoyed by man, and that this could perhaps become known to us concretely in future life, or by some new kind of intuition. It implies (by reasoning which cannot be set forth here) the falsity of the idea of a single set of quantitative laws for all levels of reality such that human behavior, e.g., would be a mere matter of the laws of molecular, atomic, and radiation physics. It implies that the mind-body relation is one of sympathy, so that our cells feel somewhat as we do in states of pain or pleasure. It implies that love is the supreme good, not pleasure or knowledge or power, and that those who think otherwise will be disappointed. It does not, however, imply that there is no need for coercion, power, or resistance to injustice.

The idea of God is the integrated total of all predictions that can be made a priori. (How they can be made a priori will be considered presently.) To what extent these predictions can be confirmed empirically is not a matter for dogmatism, but for imagination. The more we have of imaginative power, the further we may be able to see into the future of science. It is clear that some assertions by definition *could not* be verified, as the assertion that there is something which is unknowable. But none of the predictions that I have mentioned are unverifiable in this verbally obvious sense; and I think it would be rash to conclude from any arguments yet advanced that they are really unverifiable.

Already more or less verified deductions from theism are the falsity of Newtonian atomism (which contradicts the view that the world is an organism) ; the dependence of space upon time (nothing, according to the new theism, is without some essential relation to time) ; the evolution of biological species and chemical species; the rhythmic character of all activity (corollary of panpsychism, aesthetic aspect) in contrast to the dull continuity of Newtonian motion; the falsity of the ethics of mere self-interest (refuted, for example, by the discovery of masochism, and in many other ways) ; the falsity of psychological atomism (*Gestalt* phenomena — God is the cosmos as *Gestalt,* and any absolute atomism contradicts theism) ; the falsity of Watson's vocal cord theory of thought (God has no organs of speech, yet he thinks) .

If such modes of verification were the only ones applicable in theology, it might be fair to describe theism as a rather wild speculation, meaningful perhaps but not probable. But there are two other approaches. One is through metaphysical arguments of a type to be explained below. The other is to consider the human values which belief in God makes possible. Such values would not show the truth of theism, but they might justify a more persistent search for evidence of its truth than positivists encourage us to make.

Curiously enough, while positivists accuse theists of wishful thinking, they do not believe that any very essential or necessarily permanent human wishes depend for their fulfillment upon the survival of theism.

According to Carnap, metaphysics is at best only an inadequate substitute for art. Mankind should learn to satisfy its intellectual interest through science and its need for emotional expression through art, and should abandon metaphysics as neither true science nor good art.[4] But will science and art together satisfy man's intellectual and emotional needs? In Part I we saw reasons for doubting that they could. A few points may be restated here.

On the intellectual side, positivism is unable — to mention one difficulty — to point to any feature of experience to which propositions about the future can refer. Prediction is a " wager," a practical necessity; but the predictability of future events is unknowable. That there are recurrent patterns in natural events cannot be known, though all scientific reasoning assumes that there are. Law, order as valid of the future (or even the past), cannot be given. And to infer it begs the question. This objection is decisive for anyone who believes that causal order is a *datum* which metaphysics can legitimately explicate and generalize.[5] Other failures of positivism to meet intellectual interests will be noticed later.

With reference to values in general the following hints must here suffice. Value is chiefly realized in social relations. These involve beliefs concerning the nature of one's friends and acquaintances. The beliefs involved in the consciousness of membership in a human community make possible values for which no artistic expression apart from such beliefs could be a substitute. Similarly, the belief that nature as a whole is a still more varied community of beings, all in some degree akin to man, but including at least one being vastly superior to him, has values for which also there can be no substitute. Life, from which art draws much of its inspiration, is at least mainly an affair of love — love of man for man, or man for woman, of human beings for the subhuman or the superhuman. Take away (*per impossibile*) the beliefs necessary to human companionship, and you take away one whole dimension of love — that among equals. Take away beliefs implied in the love for the subhuman (e.g., for the singing birds, which some Cartesians affected to regard as mere insentient machines), and you take away another whole dimension — love for what is much less than, though still akin to, oneself. Take away love for the superhuman, and the third grand dimension of life disappears or degenerates into the mild or more or less superstitious and dangerous form of hero-worship. In all three cases love is inseparable from belief. Only a panpsychic theism opens the whole range of being to love in the true sense of sympathy, dramatic participation, with the beliefs which this attitude involves.

Furthermore, the belief in a literal lovableness of nature as an integrated and in some sense perfect individual is the only possible means to clarity concerning all the modes of love. The perfect, as Plato said, is the measure of the imperfect. We can effect a systematic comparison of all loves in terms of the ways and degrees in which they fall short of perfect love.

Listening to Mozart may very well enable us to feel a supreme harmony, may make all existence as presented at the moment seem unified in something like a perfect love. But Mozart cannot enable us to *think* this harmony, nor to believe in it steadily and through this belief to interpret all science, ethics, and art. The race has had art for millenia, and for the same length of time has felt its insufficiency, apart from religious metaphysics.

But is this perhaps because science has been insufficiently advanced? In this explanation there is some truth. The scientific picture of nature has real though partial religious values. A sense of the intellectual beauty of the world order is one of the elements of a vivid belief in God, and science has immensely enriched this sense. Moreover, on one assumption, science may overcome much of its present deficiency as an intellectual basis for religious feeling. If panpsychism is true metaphysically, that is, of all cosmic epochs, then it is also true of the present state of nature, and it follows that science will tend more and more to reveal the fact. Even the psychic interpretation of the actual world-whole as the " consequent nature " of God must tend to be increasingly suggested by natural science. To this extent science may indeed take the place of metaphysics. But the latter will have at least anticipated this result — no mean consideration in view of the billions of individuals who will have lived and died in the meantime — and metaphysics will at all times add to the clarity and certainty of the psychic view and will give it what science could never impart: validity in principle for all cosmic epochs.

If, on the other hand, we suppose, as positivists doubtless generally do, that panpsychism will probably not be confirmed by science, then it is sophistry to regard science as capable of compensating mankind for the loss of metaphysics; and what science will fail to do here is precisely what art could not possibly do — give us the rational clarification of beliefs which are integral to the realization of the three main aspects of love, without which the range of love's forms has no clear interpretation. For the vision of perfect superhuman love, and of every member of the cosmic community as able in some measure to return this love and exemplify it, there can be no substitute. It is the only ideal that bears analysis to the end.

Positivism in ethics means above all finitism in ethics, the rejection of any ideal of perfection. With this ideal goes any clear meaning to the distinction between desire and the ethical will, the " is " of *de facto* interests, and the " ought " of right interests. Among animals there can only be a balance of power between competing desires, not an ethical judgment. This is true also of men except as they recognize an ideal desire above their desires. Think out explicitly what this ideal desire would be, and you have everything of God but the name. Of course the " ought " represents a *de facto* desire, the desire to desire as a being sympathetic with all desires would do, the interest in interesting ourselves in all interests. But precisely and only God could fully exemplify what we here strive toward. Ethics either formulates God as the ideal, or it leaves its basic concepts in an implicit, confused form. But if it formulates God, then nothing is gained by ignoring the relations of this idea to other problems and to the whole of knowledge. These relations are integral to the idea and their explication is necessary to its analysis.

Positivism holds ethics to be empty of theoretical meaning beyond that which is furnished by empirical social science. Similarly, psychologists have sometimes said that logic is a branch of psychology. This the new positivists rightly deny. But do not equally valid arguments oppose the assimilation of ethics to social science? Logic is not psychology, for psychology is one of many applications of logic. But equally truly ethics is not psychology or sociology or anthropology; for in psychologizing, man is either acting rightly or wrongly, and it behooves him to know this from the outset, i.e., it behooves him to apply an ethics. Moreover, even as reasoning about psychological problems is one form of reasoning, so is all reasoning only one form of conduct, of purposive behavior, for which ethics furnishes the general principles.

Again, ethics evaluates action in terms of a general idea of the good, and logic evaluates reasoning in terms of ideals of accurate and adequate knowledge. Peirce believed that aesthetics, ethics, and logic are the three normative sciences, sciences of ideals. And André Lalande and many other capable logicians admit the normative character of logic.[6]

The ideal of logic is perfect intellectual cooperation and

self-criticism; the ideal of ethics is perfect general cooperation and self-criticism. On sufficient analysis these ideals turn out to imply each other, and both imply the aesthetic ideal of harmony and intensity of feeling. Both imply also a super-human value for which omniscience and perfect love are two descriptions which differ only in emphasis. (The consequences of divorcing logic from consideration of the ideal of life and thought will be discussed at the end of this chapter.)

Logic is not a laboratory science, for its tests can be made in the armchair as well as anywhere. Ideal experiments, not real ones, are its observational sources. But, as Peirce said, the same is true of ethics or of aesthetics in their philosophical or most general aspects. Only imagination and power of analysis are required to teach us what general sorts of experiences will in principle satisfy, and what in principle will not.

Logic is a priori because it analyzes knowledge apart from the knowledge of particular things. But in the same way ethics analyzes value apart from particular embodiments. If everything, actual or possible, can be referred to logically or illogically, so can everything be evaluated rightly or wrongly. It is the merest confusion when people seek to establish the empirical nature of theory of value by pointing to the relativity and all too human character of *human* values; for this relativity is not only compatible with but a corollary of the notion of value as a universal, or cosmic variable. Beauty, for example, is — among other things — a mixture of similarity and contrast in the intuited environment, the limits of tolerance for similarity and for difference varying with the type of experiencing organism. It follows that there are as many kinds of beauty as there are intuiting organisms, and that no conceivable world or part of a world will be aesthetically neutral if any species of experiencing organism is there. Moreover, since any conceivable world is definable as the most inclusive organized whole, any conceivable world may have its own limits of tolerable unity and tolerable variety. Of course, beauty implies feeling also, but as we have repeatedly seen, feeling is an infinite variable, no more specifically human than time or space (see chap. 8). The same is true of desire or interest.

The neo-positivists insist that a scientific truth can always be stated in physical terms (doctrine of physicalism). Of course theistic naturalism can be so stated, for mind can indeed be viewed in terms of behavior, even the supreme mind. The behavior of the cosmos implied by theism involves, for instance, the indestructibility of order, but the perpetual slow change of the more general aspects of this order (" evolution of law ") so as to produce the indispensable values of contrast and novelty even from a cosmic standpoint. This proposition is as physical as it can possibly be. Whether or not it is empirically verifiable is a subtle question, and only the rash will dogmatize thereon. It seems to me that it is *imaginably* verifiable, though, as Poincaré says, it is not likely that man on this earth will verify it. Many other aspects of theism are behavioristic.

For the import of assertions referring to the psychic in its immediate, private aspect, the term " significance " has been proposed. This significance is not mere emotional connotation, for it admits of verification. The statement, " This pain is getting more severe," may represent what I know to be a fact, quite apart from any translation of the statement into behavioristic terms. We may call such facts "significant facts," and their verification " significant verification."

But positivists hold that since the aim of language in its scientific or intellectual aspect is to communicate, and only behavioristic import, " meaning," can be transmitted in verifiable form to others, the language of meaning must be taken as the sole scientific language and significant facts considered as equivalent to a certain class of meaningful facts, facts about the behavior of human organisms. Thus the psychic or significant language, in its intellectual import, is merely a part of the physical language of science.

Yet there are several curious features of this situation. Significant facts are not as such scientific facts, yet they are privately verifiable. Predictions about them can be made and tested. And since scientific testing is only a public consensus of private observations, it is clear that privacy does not mean non-existence. Furthermore, the language of significance is in a sense more rather than less inclusive than the language of meaning. That I feel pain is for positivism " equivalent " to my body's being in a certain state only by virtue of psychophysical laws which are purely empirical. The equivalence is not a priori or logical (" L-equivalence ") but a contingent scientific generalization (a " P-equivalence "). The conception of quite different psychophysical laws is meaningful though false. But panpsychism can show that significant facts involve internal social relations (see chaps. 12 and 15) which are adequate by any conceivable criterion to all facts of physical structure and behavior. For panpsychism, physical facts are only the relational aspect of psychic facts. Behavior is then an " L-consequence " not a mere " P-consequence " of feeling. The whole of nature is conceivable without residuum as an organism of social significance.[7] Thus the language of significance is sufficient to express all known facts. On the other hand, no situation is conceivable in which the physicalist language alone would suffice. Whether or not there can be *merely* private facts, there must be genuinely private ones if there are to be public facts or any meaning.

Positivists seem to feel that the only cognitive function of language is to communicate to others. But is communication to oneself wholly non-cognitive? You can define " non-cognitive " in this way, but then you must not say that non-cognitive is equivalent to emotive. For when I recollect or predict or compare my sensations and emotions, I may have the aim of accuracy, and I cannot but believe that I reach this aim to a greater or less degree; whereas the use of words to affect the emotions of others or induce a given emotional state in oneself treats accuracy as quite incidental.

If, as the new metaphysics holds, there is such a thing as immediate sharing of feeling, then the distinction between self-communication and communication to others is not absolute. It is true that direct sympathetic rapport is narrowly limited. We do not, in the main, share one another's significances by immediate intuition. But may we not share them indirectly by inference?

As Donald Williams says,[8] if we have the right to believe that the idea of probability can be successfully applied to experience, should we be wholly skeptical of there being probabilities governing the psychophysical correlation such that if my behavior is like yours my feelings may be presumed not very dissimilar? But if we can infer the significances of other men, why not — though less definitely — those of animals? And where can we draw the line? " Ideal experiments " show that there is no known phenomenon incompatible with the conception of the world as simply a system of interrelated facts of significance; whereas no ideal experiments can support the idea that the world is simply behavior.

The superior reach of the psychic language — which is only the infinity of the psychic variables (see chap. 8) — is also shown by consideration of the contrast between structures and qualities. Qualities, that is, monadic or unitary properties (Peirce), are given. But the physical language can refer directly only to structures, whereas panpsychism shows that we can conceive all structures as nothing but interrelations of feelings endowed with quality. Thus only the psychic language is adequate to both aspects. It is all very well to say language is the symbolization of relations, of structure. The lowest degree of complexity, that is, unity, is in as good formal standing as any higher degree. But only panpsychism can conceive all things as quality-in-structure, unity-in-diversity, and thus fulfill the formal requirements. Moreover, the question is a relational one in so far as it means, What are the relations of similarity and difference between the qualities of human feelings and those of other types of individuals? The assertion that quality is a merely private fact does not conflict with the necessity that all individuals in their private natures should possess it; and furthermore, " merely private " is equivalent to the absolute denial of immediate sympathetic sharing — a universal negative conflicting with certain subtle but persistent aspects of the given. (We shall later consider more fully the reply which positivism makes to the charge of neglecting qualities.)

The social-psychic language is the only unitary language in which all conceivable facts are statable. Physicalism is either merely a legitimate emphasis upon the public interconnections of things, or it is one of two forms of error — a monism which denies significant facts, or a dualism which makes the relations of meaning and significance totally unintelligible juxtapositions, and which implies that comparative psychology will meet with an absolute barrier in interpreting the simpler members of the scale of natural individuals. Panpsychism is the only monism which negates no facts and sets no absolute limits to the widening generalizations of science. Man (and God too) is a system of behavior as truly as is a molecule — this fact means that physics can be generalized to apply to all things. But a molecule has its privacies, its significances, as truly as (though more simply than) a man — this point means that comparative psychology, in whatever sense this term be admitted, applies also to the molecule.

The crucial question concerns the method of verification

used in metaphysics.[9] Positivists regard metaphysical propositions as pseudo-assertions incapable of empirical testing. But the idea of empirical test is not easy to define.[10] Positivists define it in such a way as to exclude the kind of evidence required for the most general truths. For knowledge of special truths, the kind sought in physics, sense data are all-important. For general knowledge the vaguer phenomena of emotion, more or less conscious memory, dim anticipation, aesthetic harmony and discord are more relevant. Philosophy has slowly and painfully overcome the opposite or sensationalist emphasis. Positivism represents a regression on this point as on a number of others.

Positivists see that sense data yield the particular facts of which physics is the systematization, and they are not disturbed by the failure of sense data to yield the general principles of physics, such as the principle that prediction is possible or that assertions may be true even though the events to which they refer have not taken place. Positivists are not disturbed because they know no one will give up faith in the possibility of reliable prediction merely because no evidence of this possibility is forthcoming. Similarly, very religious persons sometimes feel little interest in proofs for God, finding faith to be enough. But such persons are not entitled to deny the meaningfulness of the quest for evidence.

Hume's famous failure to find any causal bond between successive events is due to his failing to consult the character of the very data by which the idea of succession is made possible, that is, immediate memory and anticipation.[11] Concentrating on sense data and on the problem of causation in extra-bodily objects, he could find only a bare succession of states, like the series of numbers, or rather like that series deprived of its intelligibility. But he was manifestly looking in the wrong place. Sense data concern the body more immediately than the outside object, so that if they do reveal causality it must be primarily causal connections *within* the body which they exhibit, and for these connections we are not limited to sense data in the narrower sense but must consider also emotions, memories, thoughts, all experience whatsoever. When we do this, we discover that time is not a bare series connected by the blanket relation of "after," but an integration of states preserved in memory with those which have supervened upon them and, through anticipation, with those to come. The ways of this integration are describable adequately only in terms of concepts of value, of discord and harmony between feeling-tones. Psychoanalysis should make it more difficult today to make Hume's mistake over again.

If we do not make memory explain causality, then we shall have to presuppose causality to explain memory, with the double disadvantage that while memory is a datum, causal integration apart from memory is not, and that causality taken as independent of memory explains away memory by making it a mere present intuition of the effect of past events instead of the intuition of those events. Errors of human memory may seem to justify this interpretation, but only if we fail to distinguish between the element of direct intuition and the element of mediation or inference which of course is found in all mnemonic as in all other phases of experience.

In natural science verification is effected by attention to details of experience; in metaphysics, by attention to its generic traits, e.g., memory, anticipation, desire, vividness, discord. The aim of natural science is to generalize the details so as to arrive at the total system of details which distinguishes the actual world in this cosmic epoch, a giant detail in the eternal procession of world systems. The aim of metaphysics is to generalize the generic traits of human experience so as to arrive at the generic traits of all experience and so of all possible objects of experience, to discover the eternal characters of the cosmos not as apart from change, but as the abiding features of process itself.

Thus metaphysics is the generalization of phenomenology, with the object of relating us consciously to the outlines and the permanent aspects of existence, while physics is the specialization of phenomenology with the object of predicting the details of future experience. Carnap's reduction of the necessary experiential base of physics to the mere sensations of light and dark, or to mere touch sensations, exhibits this tendency toward specialization.[12] Positivism accepts the bias of science and regards features of experience which are not essential to detailed physical knowledge as mere psychological facts of no general importance. Thus the kind of difference which distinguishes memory from anticipation or aesthetic discord from harmony is set aside as a mere detail of human nature, whereas it is in principle characteristic of all experience and of all conceivable process. The possible variations on the theme of memory cover, as was pointed out in an earlier chapter, an infinite range. So far from being a detail of human psychology, memory is a far broader concept than any law of quantum mechanics, since the latter is not necessarily valid for the remote future or past, whereas it is only as remembered by someone that, in principle, " past " events can be conceived as such. Besides, there must be special features of memory due to the particular laws of quantum mechanics. Given other laws, types of memory other than those enjoyed by existing species of organisms would become possible. The generality or flexibility of the idea of memory is equal to any conceivable demand and is part of the unconscious basis of the generalized idea of time.

Scientific metaphysics is the search not for what is " behind," or the cause of, phenomena, but for the most general traits of phenomena as yielded by abstraction from all imaginably variable details of experience, and especially by attention to vague as well as distinct aspects. The most general phenomena in this sense are — to put the matter technically — the only possible trans-"syntactical" referents of the "all-words" or philosophical categories, such as relation, thing, change, actuality, which positivism holds should be restricted in principle to their syntactical meanings (meanings expressed by reference to the formal structure of language). The phenomenologies of Husserl and Peirce, and Whitehead's theory of feelings, are the classic developments of this topic. Carnap's *Der logische Aufbau der Welt* [13] might be contrasted to them as the nearest positivistic equivalent.

The attempt to discover the most general traits of phenomena, of what might conceivably be experienced, has also been made by Schlick in a recent article. One of Schlick's contentions was that a world which did not contain selves might conceivably be experienced.[14] But he employed the phenomenological method a little uncritically, since he did not distinguish sufficiently between experiences in which the self is not a prominent feature, or is indeed very slightly given, and those in which (perhaps) it is absent altogether. Moreover, he did not consider the possibility of setting up a continuous scale of selves more and more different from human selfhood, and running from a supremely complicated and unified self to very meager, infinitesimal selves. Finally, he did not consider what it is that constitutes the unity of experience if not selfhood of some kind, nor did he investigate the possible social, or multiple-self, rather than selfless character of "primitive experience." In short, Schlick was close to the evidence for panpsychism, and he did not really establish his notion of mindless realities; nor can a metaphysical position be established without consideration of all the chief philosophic categories and problems in relation to each question. Experience, perceptual or imaginary, is too full of vagueness for the simplicity of Schlick's resort to it.

Given a supersyntactical or phenomenological reference for categories, the rest is a matter of deduction from definitions which attempt to state the interrelations of categories exhibited in the phenomena. Metaphysical judgments from that point on are formally " analytic." The phenomenological inquiry, however, seems formally " synthetic." But it is not contingent or a posteriori in the sense of consisting of judgments whose contradictories are (a) empirically meaningful and (b) formally consistent. Metaphysical error avoids inconsistency only by combining in a syntactically correct way terms which are either totally undefined or else defined in such a way as to have no illustration in phenomena, and hence no meaning. The synthetic judgments of science are not of this character, since they may have both definable empirical meaning and formal consistency, and yet be false.

It might seem better to express the matter in another way. Perhaps we should say that metaphysics requires its own syntax, on the ground that general truths are formally different from all others; and perhaps metaphysical syntax could be so set up that metaphysical errors would always be formal contradictions and metaphysical truths formally analytic. But this is probably an absurd suggestion. For the aim of metaphysics is to arrive at supersyntactical general principles, principles applying to language only as a special case (God speaks no language) , and therefore it is inappropriate to look for the sufficient evidence of these principles in the rules of a language. Nevertheless, if by analytic we mean that meaningful consistency excludes error, then metaphysical truths are analytic as well as a priori. And if " syntax " includes an analysis of the idea of " verification," and so of " experience " as such, then its relations to metaphysics must be close indeed.

It is to be admitted that no one set of definitions of the

categories is uniquely right. There may be innumerable ways of stating the relations of the categories, all of which are correctly descriptive of generic phenomena. But there are also innumerable ways of stating these relations which falsify the phenomena. Very probably our generic observations are too indistinct to justify the confidence that we shall ever eliminate all falsifications, or that a perfectly true metaphysical system is even a meaningful idea (God might know generic factors perfectly without verbalization and, in so far, without system). But this is no fatal objection, since it does not imply that all systems are, so far as we can tell, equally bad.

It may be asked how we can distinguish generic from the higher grades of specific phenomena. The answer is that the hypothesis that a given trait of experience is generic will either conform to or conflict with the trait as given. No one will deny that he knows what is meant by a memory with other quantitative features than the human, such as longer or shorter span, greater or less vividness. These features are given as special cases. But if we try to generalize beyond memory altogether, we find ourselves in contradiction with the given. We find that we have left out not details of experience but experience itself. The very unity of time upon which induction is based vanishes, and we are left with a bare series whose connections belong to a type incapable of illustration, that is, a type which cannot be thought or else is thinkable only in some more or less unconscious way not compatible with the hypothesis.

The relations between formal consistency and meaning in metaphysics seem not without analogy to those found in mathematics. In order to prove formally the consistency of arithmetic we must go beyond the mere language of arithmetic; in order to prove the consistency of our wider language we need a still wider language. Always we stop with something not formally proved. This seems to be the point of " intuitionism " in mathematics, that sooner or later we have to rest upon evidence that is non-formal.

Mathematical meanings are in some sense generic, absolutely universal. The question is whether or not they exhaust the generic meanings. It seems that they do not. Mathematics selects from generic ideas those which can in principle, or in their finite aspects, be accurately diagramed in symbolic sets (Peirce). If one uses a, b, c to represent three values of a variable, the three letters are as literally and exactly " three " as the ideas intended, or as anything whatever. Thus complex mathematical symbols are themselves adequate, unambiguous samples of the general ideas which they mean. But other aspects of experience, no less generic than number, are incapable of symbolic embodiment of this neat and definite kind.[15] Not unnaturally, therefore, Hume and his contemporary followers regard the mathematical generalities as the only ones yielding knowledge. But Peirce, nothing if not a mathematician, and recognizing that only the formal or mathematical generic meanings can be perfectly clear and definite, yet admits the legitimacy of metaphysics as the " science of unclear thought," that is, thought which cannot be wholly clear nor perhaps wholly consistent, but which has degrees of clarity and consistency. By what reasoning is the legitimacy of this position to be disputed? If we cannot reach perfection of definiteness except in mathematics (and not in every sense there), is this any reason for failing to do the best we can elsewhere?

The fact that there are both distinct and indistinct generic phenomena is connected with the dual character of experience as involving both continuity and discontinuity — or at least the appearance of these. Mathematical symbols depend upon the sharp discontinuities, or at least abrupt contrasts, of sensory qualities (e.g., the black letters against the light background of paper). Of course continuity itself can be analyzed mathematically, but this means translating it into terms of discontinuity. And the problem is not simply one of stating what continuity as such is, but of marking out into distinct meanings what is really a many-dimensional continuum of differences. One of the dimensions of this continuum is that of vagueness-distinctness. Differences are not simply given or not given. They are given with all degrees of vividness. The notion of verification must be adjusted to this fact.[16] Also there is the question of whether, if some values of a continuous variable are given, the entire range of possible values is not thereby rendered conceivable (see chap. 8). We shall comment later upon the tendency of positivism to regard certain differences as not measurable by continuous variables, and so relative, but as absolute, sheer differences of kind (even if in kind of language) not of degree. This tendency is probably to be expected in a philosophy which tries to restrict a priori judgments to those possessing the same formal character as the judgments of mathematics.

An objection to metaphysics has been that if it is a priori it can convey nothing new but must consist of tautologous sentences. The sense in which this is true even of mathematics is perhaps not wholly clear. But in any case we can agree that metaphysics *of course* conveys " nothing new," if by that is meant that metaphysics can only make us more conscious of what we already know. How could it be otherwise, since it is self-evident (tautological) that *universal categories express what could never fail to be presented* in experience, even though not distinctly attended to? Only the degree of consciousness counts in philosophical insight. There is no such thing as complete human ignorance or perfect human understanding of any philosophical truth.

Perhaps the best way to summarize our account of metaphysical judgments is to say that they are formally synthetic but materially analytic, whereas the judgments of physics are both formally and materially synthetic. By "materially analytic" I mean that when the phenomena intended by the universal terms of the judgments are inspected, definitions grounded upon this inspection will yield the judgments formally. That some feathered bipeds sing does not follow from the experiences necessary to give meaning to "feathered," "biped," and "sing." But that the future is more or less indefinite is illustrated inevitably by any experience, however imaginatively varied, which exhibits a future — indeed, by any experience whatever. The older metaphysics or theology which talked about timeless experience, experience without past or future, had to admit that the reality so conceived could not be experienced or imagined by us. And the relation of this doctrine to phenomenology has been sufficiently clarified by its last great representative, F. H. Bradley, whose procedure is the reverse of an attempt to "save the phenomena," being rather a series of attempts to show that phenomena are self-contradictory and hence not wholly real. The contradictions arise of course from inaccurate definitions of generic data.

It is worth noting that metaphysical judgments are not the only ones that are materially analytic. Consider the statement: Orange is both red-like and yellow-like in a sense in which red is not yellow-like and yellow is not blue-like but in which purple is both red-like and blue-like, and lemon is both yellow-like and green-like, or in other words, orange is intermediate between yellow and red, purple between blue and red, lemon between yellow and green, in a sense in which yellow is not intermediate between red and orange, etc. If this statement is taken to refer not to physical but to psychic facts, not to meanings but to what we have called significances, then it is materially analytic, that is, it is seen to be true from inspection of the phenomena necessary to furnish the significance of the terms used. The intermediate status of orange with respect to yellow and red is intuited in a way which shows it to be forever impossible that this relationship of the three qualities could be contradicted by a situation which really embodied these qualities. But on the other hand, the relationship need not, for all that, be eternal, for in the past of the cosmos there may have been a time when these qualities had no relations whatever because at that time there were no such qualities. Metaphysical judgments are the only materially analytic ones which are positively applicable to all time and all space. They are the materially analytic or phenomenological judgments of the highest rank of generality, the ultimate descriptive (not inductive) generalizations.

It may be asked whether ordinary synthetic judgments are not really materially analytic, though not categorically general, judgments involving highly complex and obscure predicates, such as " feathered." An affirmative answer would not imply that particular facts are a priori. If there are feathered bipeds, perhaps it follows that some of them, under certain conditions, will sing; but that there are feathered bipeds subject to these conditions is in no sense analytic. Another question would be whether Euclidean geometry would not turn out to be materially analytic and categorically general as well. Have non-Euclidean geometries any phenomenal justification? I am content here to remark only that mathematical ideas are, as Plato seems to have been the first to see, not directly pictorial or imaginable. Lines and other geometrical ideas are not intuited except as ideal limits of intuition, in such a sense that even omniscience would have them as data only in a very special way. This question has been adequately dealt with by Reichenbach.[17]

Positivists cannot declare void the idea of generic intuitions on the basis of experience without danger of begging the question, especially since the evidence is all in favor of the view that in so far as they have made any effort to find such phenomena it has been with strong negative prejudices rather than with any real interest.   And certainly it is no refutation of the idea of generic phenomena that they are not specific, and hence that sentences about them are not verifiable in the same manner as specific sentences.   For instance, the demand that sentences be conceivably falsifiable is illegitimate with regard to generic sentences.   They could not be false; that is the point.   They describe experience in its non-variable aspects, or better, they identify the variables of which all possible experiences are values.   There is no alternative to them in so far as they outline the total system of alternatives.

A legitimate argument against generic insights is that claims to possess them have led to endless disagreement.   This, however, is not a conclusive objection.   (If it were, more would have been said in this chapter about the not inconsiderable disagreements among positivists!)   The argument does not even justify extreme pessimism concerning the possibility of a fair amount of agreement in the future.   For in the past metaphysics has been seriously handicapped — by religious bigotry, by antireligious bigotry, by the tendency of scientific men, or those impressed by their work, to overgeneralize scientific results so that they interfere with metaphysical principles, and by still other forces whose persistence unabated into the future is by no means inevitable.

Logical positivism holds that philosophical generalities so far as legitimate are adequately expressible " formally " or syntactically, that is, in terms of the properties of sentences and the rules of language; while general statements in the " material mode " (referring to the properties of things outside language) add nothing except rhetorical simplicity and the danger of ambiguity and " pseudo-questions." Thus possibility in its general or a priori aspect is held to be adequately expressed as the consistency of sentences asserting the states of affairs said to be possible.[18] There is, to be sure, material possibility as determined by the laws of physics, biology, and psychology, but innumerable things are syntactically possible which are materially impossible.

Contrasted to this view is that of Boutroux, Peirce, Bergson, and Whitehead, who hold that possibility is in all cases trans-syntactical, and that its non-syntactical aspect is found in the indecisiveness of the present with respect to its temporal successors, the aspect of the present as unfinished and in process of endless and unpredetermined completion or enrichment. When we say it is possible that s is p, we do not merely mean that the proposition "s is p" is self-consistent, nor necessarily that it is consistent with material laws now true of the world; but we mean that at least at some time in the past (when the very laws of nature may have been different) there was an event whose indecisiveness admitted of any one of the two events, sp, or s not-p, as its immediate or remote successor. Thus by giving up the baseless notions of absolute and immutable laws, material possibility can be broadened indefinitely, so that syntactical possibility turns out to be merely the linguistic parallel for the limiting case of material possibility without specification of any temporal or spatial locus, i.e., materially possible somewhere and at some time, no matter where or when. (Even a metaphysical impossibility like determinism can be treated as the unattainable limit of the series of possible indeterminisms.)

This is another aspect of the philosophical meaningfulness of the issue of determinism, since how the issue is settled makes all the difference in the relations between syntax and fact.

By neglecting the generic vagueness or indetermination of experience, the positivist is not only forced to admit a syntactical possibility which has no material reference, but he really loses any empirical basis even for the material possibility which he admits. For the laws of nature are based for him on no datum by which the causal bond as such is exhibited to inspection. He merely believes that references to the future can have truth without being able to point to a single illustration of such truth as a datum. This is essentially a nominalistic reading of experience, as several writers have pointed out. Positivists say both nominalism and realism are meaningless; but the fatal defects of nominalism are unmistakably present in positivism. If laws are not given, then one indispensable aspect of the reality of universals is not given, and if not given it is exactly as if non-existent. But the given generic vagueness of the experience of the future which justifies indeterminism also justifies a relative determinism. For experience is more or less definite, and this relative definiteness is found in the future as a datum of immediate purposive anticipation.

For positivists to say, as they often do, that it is impossible for the relative definiteness of the future to be a datum or for induction to be justified cognitively [19] is a species of negative dogmatism that seems inconsistent with the ethics of inquiry. How do they know that the future cannot be given? Is this an analytic judgment, and if so, how does it differ in form from the judgment which metaphysics opposes to it and which positivism condemns on principle? Of course the whole future cannot be given, the future in full detail, for then it would collapse into the present; and this is true analytically (in the material sense explained). But if the future were wholly ungiven, then how could it be thought? Hume overlooked the " impression" required for his " idea " here.

Positivists often say that both determinism and indeterminism are unverifiable, and hence meaningless. Now, as Peirce pointed out long ago, measurement cannot establish the exactitude of law, and as we have repeatedly seen, it is meaningless to talk of an experience of the precise details of what is going to happen. But it is not in the same absolute way meaningless to describe an experience to which the future would be given with the precise degree of partial determination applying to nature itself, so that nothing predictable from true laws would be unanticipated as part of the intuited or phenomenal future. Such an intuition would have as datum all that was in fact determined, and it would intuit that such was the case by fully experiencing the interconnections the fragmentary experience of which alone gives meaning to the distinction between the given and the real. More concretely, such an intuition would know the future as fixed by its own purposive determination, which would involve a partial acceptance and partial veto of all other determinations and which would leave complete definiteness for the future to provide (in becoming present). The conclusion is that determinism is indeed meaningless if by that we mean that it could not possibly be true, while indeterminism is meaningful and therefore either true or false, but, since its falsity is impossible. it can only be true. It is also arguable, as we saw in chapter nine, that physics has shown its truth for this cosmic epoch.

This result can be generalized to cover other philosophical problems. No experience could verify the existence of merely physical entities, entities not containing feelings, memories, or desires; but an experience might share sympathetically and immediately in the feelings of all other entities, and so verify the non-existence of dead matter and the truth of panpsychism. Hence the latter is capable of truth and incapable of falsity; therefore it is true. Again, it is not easy to see how science could verify the change of a law of nature, since we could always posit, even if we could not find, some deeper law as the real and unchanging pattern of events. But there is a more final difficulty in conceiving the verification of an unchanging law.   All time would have to be observed, and all time as equally definite with respect to the law.   But not only, as we have seen, must future events be experienced as more or less indefinite, but the indefiniteness must increase with remoteness in time, for uncertainties are cumulative.   The more the entities to which the law is to apply change, the less suitable must the law become to serve as the integration of these entities into one experience. Fully to elucidate this point would require an excursion into the aesthetics of habit.   But it must suffice here to say that every violation of a habit necessarily weakens the habit and is an impulse toward the formation of a new one, and that, contrary to Peirce's contention, habits cannot tend indefinitely to strengthen themselves but must rather lead after sufficient time to unendurable boredom and consequent revolt.   (Even Peirce admitted that monotony meant lapse from consciousness.)

The syntactical treatment of categories is applied by positivism to such questions as internal and external relations, realism and phenomenalism.   And in curious parallel to Kant's antinomies it is held that the material mode of speech cannot be safeguarded adequately against contradictory implications. Only by retreating to the syntactical formulation can we deal, for instance, with arguments by which relations can be made to seem both " internal " and " external " in the same instance.[20]   The careful distinctions by which metaphysics has finally succeeded in combining internal and external relations [21] without contradiction (involving, as usual, an indeterministic cosmology) are not considered in the discussion.   Consequently, the paradoxes which result are not to be ascribed to the material mode of speech, but to Carnap's use or misuse of it.

Again, Carnap argues that it is equally plausible, in the objective mode, to say that an object is a complex of atoms and that an object is a complex of sense data — once more an insoluble conflict of assertions. But the truth is that physics shows a thing to be literally a complex of atoms (or electrons and crystals), and nothing shows it to be a complex of sense data, except in whatever loose or figurative sense the indirect effects of a thing upon something else can be identified with the thing. The sense data are our evidence for the thing; but since when has it been said that a man *is* his photograph or the footprints or finger marks he leaves? (How easy, were this so, the arrest of a criminal would be!) Here again the objective interpretation is arbitrarily framed to produce the antinomy.

If human sense data were the totality of conceivable experiences of a thing, then indeed the thing would be that totality (or a part of it). But they are not. What about the sense data which other animals enjoy, or which conceivable animals, with other than human senses, *would* enjoy? What about the intuitions which a perfect mind might have of an electron, or which a molecule may have of its electrons?

The positivists admit that " thing " implies an infinity of possible sense data, so that quantitatively at least the thing transcends our experience. But there are also intensive quantities to consider. What about variations in degrees of distinctness among our intuitions? Or in time rate? Would not a really adequate intuition of an electron as infinitely transcend ours in the clarity with which it revealed *each* aspect of the electron as in the variety of aspects revealed? And would not the " specious present " of such an intuition have to be vastly shorter than ours? (In dreams we do approach slightly nearer to the time rate of electronic changes.)

When it is said that physicalism means the denial of the qualitative side of existence, positivists protest that by admitting the equivalence of sense-data-sentences and thing-sentences they are recognizing qualities as well as quantities.

Certainly they are including the qualities of sense data as enjoyed by human beings, that is, by all the evidence, qualities so far as relative to and dependent upon the human type of organism. While the structures of things are to be studied in generalized, de-anthropomorphized fashion, so that most of the details of real structures turn out to be rather radically different from the structures given in human experience, the qualities of things, on the contrary, so far as they are considered at all, are treated as simply the qualities we may directly enjoy. In view of the demonstrable possibility of non-human qualities, qualities specifically different from any we can distinctly intuit, but describable as values of the same variables, the infinite dimensions of quality as such, the positivist procedure seems careless in the extreme. Of course it can be said in defense of this procedure that there is no way to determine the particular non-human qualities of things, and that no predictions can be made through the supposition that they exist which cannot be made without this supposition. In so far as this is true — and its absolute truth is, I believe, indemonstrable — it is, as we saw in chapter fifteen, quite understandable from societal realism that this should be so. Yet if immediate sympathy is in some degree a datum, there is a sense in which the existence of non-anthropomorphic qualities in all things besides man is verifiable; for a sufficiently complete sympathetic intuition could intuit them all, whereas neither it nor any conceivable intuition could have as a datum the existence of things whose only qualities were in the perceptions of other (non-omniscient) individuals.

If the thing spoken of is another human being, then no one thinks that the collection or system of his own sense data of that human being *is* the latter. If every individual has an " inside," has feelings and the like, then all plausibility vanishes from the identification of " thing " with *human* feelings or sensations. Thus once more an allegedly meaningless philosophical issue turns out to be decisive for the relation between syntax and fact. Panpsychism removes whatever temptation there may otherwise be in the material mode of speech to admit one side of Carnap's antinomy. The dispute between ordinary realism and old-fashioned positivism, both stated in the material mode, is — as Carnap says — "idle," but only because, while the identification of the object with what we can directly enjoy of it falsifies the systematic implications of our experience, the assertion that the humanly non-intuited features of the object are not intuited at all, and are not of the nature of feelings, is meaningless. Panpsychic realism makes sense out of what is otherwise an assertion we can neither give up nor maintain.

Positivists have sometimes puzzled over the question of how the other person's experiences can be anything for me except possible experiences of mine. But, on the other hand, the other person's experience as such *could* not be mine. "If I were you," we say. "But then I would not be I," is the difficulty that interposes itself. However, if this is unqualifiedly true, it can only be because the Aristotelian conception of absolutely separate substances is correct as applied to persons. Whitehead holds that in some slight measure persons are one another. And this is in accordance with the principle of physics that a particle is not absolutely localized, but in some degree pervades all space. Most of such immanence of one thing in another is slight, but a more than slight immanence of one individual in another is conceivable in at least two cases. The bodily cells and the human mind are fused in immediate sympathy to a really effective degree which accounts for the mind-body relations. And God is conceived as precisely the only self which can *fully* participate in another's experience in all its vividness and detail.

It is necessary to this view that God should also be a datum for us, that we should directly participate in him. And if positivists do not know it, it might perhaps interest them to be told that the great theologians have asserted direct though faint intuition of God not only for mystics but for all men. Augustine's doctrine is notorious; but Aquinas can be shown to qualify rather than negate it. All talk of immanence is a quibble, indeed, if it be denied. Peirce asserted it.[22] Whitehead's theory of direct prehensions of one individual by another recognizes no exception with regard to God, whose control of the world is through the direct though more or less vague awareness which each occasion has of his envisagement of the future.

The notion of the direct awareness of God is the only explanation of the generic intuitions which metaphysics claims for man. In existential scope these intuitions are equivalent to omniscience, though in quality of clearness they are anything but equivalent to it. They tell us nothing whatever about details as such, and even as generalities they are at best obscure. But the range of objects to which they are relevant is identical with the range known by God.

In spite of the obscurity of metaphysical ideas, they can be given a certain definiteness by means of mathematical analysis. Peirce's definitions of feeling, reaction, and meaning in terms of the monad, the dyad, and the triad is one of the few great achievements of this kind. His generalization of the triad into the idea of universal continuity, not as excluding relative discontinuity but as excluding absolute discontinuity (all mere dichotomies), is particularly relevant to positivism. For a characteristic feature of positivism is its preference for unqualified dichotomies. Possibility is either physical or logical, and there are no transitions.[23] The widest physical possibilities are still infinitely narrower than logical possibilities. Or, the physical language is one thing and the psychic language is another, and the distinction is not one of degree.

Cognitive and emotive meanings are similarly separated, as are logic and ethics or truth and value. Or, nature contains things which themselves have sense data (perceiving organisms) and those of which sense data (or feelings) can only be had by other things. The distinction between feeling as private and behavior as public is absolute for positivists. Fusion of feeling among several individuals is not considered. Peirce regarded all such doctrines as belonging to a primitive stage of analysis.[24]

Reichenbach has wisely warned against too confident systematization of positivist doctrine at the present time, and for a Peircean, nothing shows the need for caution more than the dualisms referred to. Measuring the degree of a predicate generally if not always turns out to be more significant than asserting or denying it (unless the predicate is by definition limited to certain degrees). Positivists will of course deny that they are dualists in the Cartesian fashion. But I fear this means only that they have complicated the matter by some additional dyads, not that they have relativized the old ones by the introduction of continuity. Just as I do not believe mankind will be satisfied with the positivistic restatement of Hume's view of causality — his denial that the causal unity can be given — so I do not see any reason to think that the linguistic version of Cartesianism will permanently deter men from seeking the material intelligibility of the mind-matter relation where alone it can be found, and where alone the intelligibility of causality can be found, in the psychic variables, generalized sufficiently to admit of all values called for by actual or conceivable entities.

The positivist doctrine has been espoused by a number of leading physicists. In fact, both relativity theory and quantum mechanics are greatly indebted to the influence of Hume, Mach, and the Vienna circle upon such men as Einstein, Heisenberg, Bohr, and Jordan. Without this influence the new physical doctrines might not have arisen. But among physicists one finds three attitudes toward positivism. Planck is strongly antipositivistic. The younger physicists, however, seem almost completely resigned to positivism. But they interpret it in two ways. Philip Frank and a few others give their positivistic statements a strongly materialistic twist. Others, like Bohr and Pascual Jordan, arrive at a positivism which comes at times to the very verge of societal psychism. Let us compare the two views, as expressed by Frank [25] and Jordan. [26]

Frank says that the new physics is neither mechanistic nor organismic; it is mathematical. But so, he reminds us, was the old physics. Jordan, however, points out that organismic laws differ *in mathematical form* from mechanistic and that the best evidence suggests that all laws are of the former character, while the latter are always effects of statistical averaging or other disguises.

The statistical law and the uncertainty of events do not, Frank holds, " leave room " for free will, because if free will altered the probabilities of the case, it would *contradict* the statistical law. Jordan does use the " leave room " phrase, but he points out that what is uncertain is the *individual* (such as the electron) , that the organism is an individual, and for this reason it ought to be supposed to violate, that is, modify, the statistical laws, which, according to quantum mechanics, would apply to the parts of the organism if the latter were *not* parts of a unitary individual. Frank says nothing from beginning to end, I believe, about the individual as such. In other words, he never so much as discusses the principal problem, which Jordan never lost sight of. (The German quantum physicists have in general shown more philosophical grasp at this point than have most of their philosophical commentators or critics. They have seen all along that since quantum physics is the only physics that reaches individuals, it is the only physics that can throw light upon philosophical categories, all of which, as Aristotle was the first to state clearly, are concerned with the individual as such. Thus quantum mechanics is a generic and not a merely specific indication of how nature operates. Its principles, not its laws, are the basic discovery.)

Frank says that the impossibility of observing psychic states without altering them does not disprove psychological determinism, for the causal factors science should consider are the physical (behavioristic-structural) ones. Jordan says, first, that these too cannot be observed completely or anything like completely without being disturbed; and second, that the psychic states are not nothing, and that we should take their essential indeterminableness as one of the clues indicating the indeterminableness of organic behavior. Frank argues, however, that the psychic indeterminableness was known before quantum mechanics, and that consequently it is not made more significant by the latter. Jordan says that the problem is to unify scientific principles, that if psychology has long had a clue to the contingency of individual action as such, but has been deterred from accepting this clue by the prestige of a deterministic physics, then the passing of that physics opens the way to giving the psychic facts their due.

Frank says certain writers have found meanings for ethical "freedom" that have no connection with indeterminism. Jordan does not discuss this question. But he might have said that the Kantian and other versions of freedom that do not involve indeterminism have satisfied fewer and ever fewer philosophers, till today scarcely a single one of note still accepts them. The persistent favorable reference of positivists to the Spinozistic or Stoic view of freedom as necessity without external constraint is a fine example of how true it is that if you scratch an antimetaphysician you find an antiquated metaphysician underneath.

Frank admits that the concern of the new physics is with wholes, not mere parts in a "mosaic." But he holds that physics has always sought to relate things to larger and ever larger portions of their environment and that there is nothing new, except the size of the wholes which are considered, in the new physics. Jordan says that there has been a shift from differential to integral equations and that the principle of "no action at a distance" is now subject to limitations. Memory, e.g., is action over an interval of time and is probably in some degree universal in nature. It is not true that we have merely moved to the recognition of larger wholes. The point is, as Jordan shows, that some wholes are superficial (integral aspect negligible) and that there are many degrees of integration. This is just what an organismic view wants. No one wishes to regard an entire rock as a purposive individual. But Jordan holds that even a hydrogen atom is not quite a mere system of electrons. Frank says organicism would have a meaning only if things behaved analogously to animal and human organisms; if, for instance, a planet moved in a way to realize ends. But Jordan would presumably hold that a planet may be an unintegrated swarm, while its parts may, with some evidence, be regarded as purposive. What the purposes of electrons or atoms might be he does not consider, but the question is one of applied aesthetics, for organic "adaptation" is not the end but the means to enjoyment of the ultimate values of feeling, harmony, and sympathetic participation. Now the new physics provides, as we have seen, unity in contrast, order in the midst of chance, on the microscopic level where the old atomism denied it. Frank sees nothing teleological about chance; but the value of contrast *against* a pattern (thereby, to be sure, creating a new one) is as much an element of beauty as contrast *within* a pattern. Without chance there could be no value but only fearful cosmic boredom.

Finally, Frank says the issue is whether we shall return to a medieval view. Jordan says the issue is whether we give up all doctrines which are not purely empirical in their ultimate meaning. Besides, nothing is more hopelessly incompatible with medieval Aristotelianism than the notion of the human body as an organism whose parts are organisms, the latter endowed with their own " substantiality," freedom, form, etc. Aristotelian substantialism and a cell theory of substance are nearly at opposite poles. But there is no end to the unmedieval aspects of the new organicism. Whitehead and Peirce and Bergson are perhaps the most un-Aristotelian and unmedieval of current thinkers! The only reason this is overlooked is that in catholicity of interests these philosophers are indeed reminiscent of the thirteenth century, though surpassing it.

So much for the arguments of these two positivists. If positivism is not quite credible as the last word, there can, I hold, be no ambiguity as to the direction in which it should be extended. The entire galaxy of first-rate geniuses in quantum mechanics is, so far as I know, free of a single member interested in a materialistic transcendence of positivism. The only hints they give lead toward the notion of psychic cosmic variables and organic sympathy. Thus Jordan says the most general principles are the biological and psychological ones.[27] The age can choose. It may stultify metaphysical curiosity. Or it may adopt the general working program of psychic naturalism. These exhaust its " live options." The German quantum mechanicians want to make their principles fruitful over the widest possible range of facts and problems, not by applying the quantitative laws they have discovered to all things, but by conceiving of these laws as parts of a more complex system involving other equations but similar generic principles. If nature shows at certain points that her principle is to combine indeterminism, quantum discreteness, individuality, and organic or final causation, then if we find quantum phenomena in heredity — for instance, evidence of gene individuality — we should infer not that this is merely a complex statistical case of electronic quantum mechanics, but that there is need for a specifically distinct, though generically identical, bio-quantum mechanics which approximates to ordinary statistical quantum mechanics in limiting cases of degeneration or near deadness. This is the way scientific thought works, and not by doctrinaire monisms in regard to specific laws, nor doctrinaire dualisms in regard to generic types of law. Principles come first and should be as monistic as possible. Laws should be coherently interrelated, but no more reducible to one species than are biological kinds. The world is one and it is many; the many-ness involves a variety of groups or species, hence of laws, as well as a variety of individuals.

The terrified materialists (to paraphrase Santayana to suit the times) are afraid psychists may derive legitimate comfort from the new physics, just as once bishops knew all too well that atheists were bound to derive legitimate comfort (assuming the legitimacy of the Newtonian absolutes) from the old physics and biology.

But has not the time passed for settling such questions on the basis of reaction from religious superstition? Another set of superstitions has arisen. Russell says he believes the world "lacks unity, coherence, orderliness, and all the other things clergymen and governesses love." But dislike of the Victorianism of Russell's youth should not be the reason for our attitude toward the most beautiful physical theory that ever dawned upon the scientific mind.

Positivists sometimes allege that the persistence of metaphysics, even in admittedly able minds like Peirce or Whitehead, is to be explained psychologically rather than logically. They even suggest psychoanalysis. But what is it that explains the tendency of men trained chiefly in physics, mathematics, and logic to deny or depreciate the philosophic relevance of things other than physics, mathematics, and logic? And is it psychoanalysis or logic that is needed to justify the effort to make generalizations fruitful in as widely divergent applications as possible, even applications to ethics, aesthetics, and religion?

Such divergent application is one of the basic principles of all science. A generalization which is not helpful outside the field in which it arises is never entitled to much confidence. To explain facts other than those held in view in setting up a hypothesis is the chief mark of the probable truth of that hypothesis. Yet when physicists or philosophers try to gain new light from quantum principles for the understanding of biology or psychology or religion, there is a howl of disapproval at the very idea. If this disapproval is not at least as much an " emotive " or intellectually irrelevant reaction as anything of which Eddington or Jeans or Whitehead can be accused, I am much deceived. It seems to me sound logic to say that if there is no important bearing of quantum principles (as distinct from laws) upon biological and psychological problems, then quantum mechanics cannot, even in physics, be the basic truth it appears to be.

The widest possible use of the principle of divergent application is the application to " all time and all existence," that is, the metaphysical application. It is true that no observations of natural science can guarantee the truth of a hypothesis over the whole metaphysical range. But they can *discredit* generalizations alleged to cover this range if these happen to be false of actual nature. And conversely, while no metaphysics can decide what is true of the actual world in so far as this differs from alternative possible worlds, metaphysics can discredit propositions which are untrue both of the actual world and also of all possible worlds, that is, propositions which misuse the categories. The deterministic, materialistic, dualistic notions of Newtonian science, and much traditional metaphysics, were of this character. Metaphysics and physics have refuted them, the former as incapable of being true of any world, the latter as untrue of this one. The refutations are logically independent, but help to confirm one another.

To rule out this widest possible use of the principle of divergent applications is a pernicious limitation upon inquiry.

For philosophy to defend science against the laziness and perversity which continually threaten to restore primitive superstitions is a useful function. But philosophy should also counteract the laziness and perversity which continually threaten to turn the *de facto* scientific situation into a barrier to further progress.[28] Because science would not now know what to do with certain ideas — such as the evolution of law, panpsychism, non-human qualities, cosmic purpose — is excellent reason why scientists should neglect these ideas but a very insufficient reason for philosophers to adopt the same attitude. Positivism tends almost uniformly to encourage science in its exclusions and to rob philosophy of one of its main functions. The hard dualism between cognitive and emotive meaning is partly responsible for this tendency. Peirce held that the idea of God was more emotional than intellectual. But he did not commit the *non sequitur* of supposing that the idea was therefore not at all descriptive of the universe, but merely of the state of man's mind. If the universe is itself emotional in character — and some parts of it certainly are — the way for us to reflect this character is by paralleling the cosmic emotions in ourselves. The feeling that one's friend sincerely loves one is a feeling, but it can correspond to the actual state of the friend or not correspond; it can be true or false. And the properties of the friend which it aims to echo or duplicate, and in this sense " know," are things which could not be known adequately in any other way.

By dismissing theory of value from philosophy positivists help themselves to forget what the final aim of knowledge is. Conceptual knowledge, and intuitive and emotional knowledge, are ways of realizing the one supreme aim, participation in the activities of the universe more largely than can be done by either mere human perception or mere human thinking alone. By perception one enjoys the order of nature as revealed in the waves on a beach. By thought one participates in wave patterns that pervade even the stupidest and most inactive-seeming objects, and in rhythms that can be followed into the remote past and future. By both perception and thought one participates also in the life of a friend; and in this case in a more complete manner, including much more than bare spatio-temporal pattern. The whole relationship has a unity of intuitive and analytic elements which is closer to the ideal of understanding than is any of our present knowledge of inorganic nature. It is a maxim of the ethics of logic to apply this ideal to all our knowledge in order to remain sensitive to the totality of possible approaches.

As has been well said (by L. H. Myers) , discoursive knowledge is as distinctly human and all too human as anything else, since although it multiplies the items of knowledge and the power of accurate dealing with them one at a time, yet also, unless continually balanced by the resort to integral intuitions and concepts (note the word) capable of eliciting these, it tends to destroy the power of seeing life steadily and as a whole. Art will not altogether do this, nor mere art and mere science together, but only a science which sets before itself the final ideal of apprehension that is neither merely conceptual nor merely intuitive in the human way, and that in its maximal form could only be divine love. Science which does not orient itself in this manner commits what Whitehead calls the fallacy of misplaced concreteness, a one-sidedness useful if not carried too far or persisted in at any one stage too long, but calling always for the contrary tendency — much as asceticism and spontaneous enjoyment seem both necessary attitudes in the ethical life.

Positivists of today have begun inquiry likely to throw immensely valuable new light on the validity and nature of metaphysics. The new metaphysics has more to learn from them than from any other group of contemporary thinkers.

NOTES

[1] Cf. Whitehead, *Adventures of Ideas*, pp. 147–48, 159–65; Peirce, *Papers*, VI. 368.

[2] Rudolf Carnap, "On the Character of Philosophical Problems," *Philosophy of Science*, I, 5.

[3] Rudolf Carnap, "Die Ueberwindung der Metaphysik durch logische Analyse der Sprache," *Erkenntniss*, II, 219–41.

[4] *Ibid.*

[5] On the unsatisfactoriness of the positivistic account of natural law see E. J. Nelson, "Professor Reichenbach on Induction," *Journal of Philosophy*, XXXIII, 577–80; also Nelson, "The Inductive Argument for an External World," *Philosophy of Science*, III, 237–49 (especially 248 f.) ; and Whitehead, *loc. cit.* For the positivist view see Herbert Feigl, "The Logical Character of the Principle of Induction," *Philosophy of Science*, I, 20–29; Reichenbach, *Wahrscheinlichkeitslehre* (Leiden, A. W. Sijthoff, 1935) , paragraph 80.

[6] Peirce, *Papers*, Vol. I, Book IV; also II. 120, 196 ff.; Lalande, "Le formalisme et valeurs logiques." *Proceedings of the Seventh International Congress of Philosophy* (Oxford, 1930) , p. 127.

[7] Cf. Whitehead, *Process and Reality*, Parts III and IV; also *Adventures of Ideas*, Part III; Peirce, *Papers*, Vol. VI, Book I B, C.

[8] Cf. Donald C. Williams, "Scientific Method and the Existence of Consciousness," *Psychological Review*, XLI, 461 ff. For the positivist doctrine of physicalism see Carnap, *The Unity of Science* (London, Kegan Paul, Trench, Trubner & Co., 1934) .

[9] On the nature and method of metaphysics see S. Alexander, *Space, Time, and Deity*, I, 175 ff.; Whitehead, *Process and Reality*, chap. 1, and *The Function of Reason* (Yale University Press, 1929) , pp. 51 ff.; Peirce, *Papers*, Vol. I, Book II and VI. 1–6; Daniel J. Bronstein, "What is Logical Syntax?" *Analysis*,

III, 49; A. H. S. Coombe-Tennant, " Mr. Wisdom on Philosophical Analysis," *Mind*, XLV, 432–49; C. D. Broad, A. J. Porteous, Reginald Jackson, " Are There Synthetic A Priori Truths? " *Proceedings of the Aristotelian Society*, Supplementary Vol. XV, 102–53.

10 Cf. Gilbert Ryle, " Unverifiability-By-Me," *Analysis*, IV, 1–11.

11 On Hume's conception of temporal succession and causality see Whitehead, *Symbolism, Its Meaning and Effect*, pp. 30–48.

12 Carnap, " Testability and Meaning," *Philosophy of Science*, III, 419–71 (see pp. 469 f.) .

13 Carnap, *Der logische Aufbau der Welt* (Berlin-Schlachtensee, Welt-kreis-Verlag, 1928) .

14 M. Schlick, " Meaning and Verification," *Philosophical Review*, XLV, 339–69.

15 Cf. Donald C. Williams, " Analysis, Analytic Propositions, and Real Definitions," *Analysis*, III, 75 ff. Bergson's *Introduction to Metaphysics* (G. P. Putnam's Sons, 1912) , though an extreme and one-sided statement, is relevant here.

16 Cf. A. C. Benjamin, " The Concept of the Variable Given," *Journal of Philosophy*, XXXIII, 225–29.

17 Reichenbach, *Philosophie der Raum-Zeit-Lehre* (Berlin, Walter de Gruyter & Co., 1928) , paragraphs 9–11.

18 Cf. Carnap, *Die logische Syntax der Sprache* (Vienna, J. Springer, 1934) , paragraphs 69–70 and p. 230. Also Carnap, *Philosophy and Logical Syntax* (London, Kegan Paul, Trench, Trubner & Co., 1935) , pp. 68–74.

19 C. J. Ducasse tries to show that causality needs no metaphysical explanation, and quotes an interesting letter from Santayana which suggests that the only reason people ask for such an explanation is that they expect to find everywhere the sort of connection among events which is exhibited in purposive anticipation. All that these writers and others say leaves intact the two propositions: (a) the causal relation is intelligible if purpose is universal (and if there is a supreme purpose) ; and (b) it is not intelligible otherwise. See Ducasse, " Of the Spurious Mystery in Causal Connections," *Philosophical Review*, XXXIX, 398–403. See also Peirce, *Papers*, V. 93–107; L. S. Stebbing, *A Modern Introduction to Logic* (T. Y. Crowell C/., 1930) , pp. 402–19; Ralph M. Eaton, *General Logic* (Charles Scribner's Sons, 1931) , pp. 496, 534–42; A. Lalande, *Les théories de l'induction et de l'expérimentation* (Paris, Boivin & Cie., 1929) , pp. 249–63; Whitehead, *The Function of Reason*, p. 24.

20 Carnap, *op. cit.*, p. 231.

21 Cf., e.g., the chapter on "Relations " in Parker's *Self and Nature;* or Hartshorne, " Four Principles of Method," *Monist*, XLIII, 43–48.

22 *Papers*, VI. 162.

23 Cf. A. C. Benjamin, " Outlines of an Empirical Theory of Meaning," *Philosophy of Science*, III, 266.

24 On the limitations of dyadic thought see Peirce, *Papers*, I. 359–60.

25 Philip Frank, *Das Ende der mechanistischen Physik* (Vienna, Verlag Gerold & Co., 1935).

26 Pascual Jordan, *Anschauliche Quantumtheorie* (Berlin, J. Springer, 1936), chap. 5.

27 Cf. Whitehead, *Nature and Life* (University of Chicago Press, 1934, price $.50).

28 Cf. Whitehead, *The Function of Reason*, pp. 8, 28 ff.

XVII

CROCE, HEIDEGGER, AND HARTMANN

CONTEMPORARY philosophy, wherever it is most fertile and living,[1] appears to be characterized by one and the same dominant conviction. This conviction is that abstractions have exactly as much meaning as concrete perceptions and concretely identifiable human activities — scientific experiments, mathematical "operations," the conversation of friends — can give them; and that the sole function which words can perform is to intensify, control, and render publicly communicable, such perceptual or practical experiences. In America it is the pragmatists who have insisted that even the most abstract scientific ideas must finally be interpreted through those "concrete and familiar conceptions of everyday life" which express modes of human behavior and human purpose. This represented a profound transformation of traditional empiricism.

A somewhat similar reform of that vigorous branch of neo-empiricism which goes in Germany by the name of phenomenology has been undertaken by Martin Heidegger. True, phenomenology was from the outset a reform tending in the very direction we have been considering — the direction of ever greater concreteness of conception. Still, phenomenologists prior to Heidegger tended to interpret experience to a disappointing extent chiefly in terms of such traditional and relatively abstract conceptions as " consciousness," " object," " essence," " perception," and the like, to the neglect of the concreter ideas of *feeling, willing, valuing, loving, hating,* and their kin. As Professor Whitehead would phrase it, they have committed the " fallacy of misplaced concreteness "; that is to say, since by abstract we mean indeterminate in respects which a more concrete mode of representation would " fill in " or render determinate, they have tended to take as the most fundamental and all-explanatory ideas those which are the least determinate in their meaning. In other words they have sought to explain the definite by the indefinite. Thus bare " consciousness " or even " consciousness of " (Husserl's *Intentionalität*) conveys no conception of what is meant by " loving," but " loving " does convey some conception of " consciousness." It is at least not mathematically impossible that all consciousness should be — as many mystics and some philosophers have held — an activity of loving at least so far as to involve something like sympathy; and this, if true, is genuinely informative. But to say that all loving is a state of consciousness is either a mere tautology, or, if it means that love can be reduced to, or really understood in terms of, such abstractions as " contents of consciousness," then, as the phenomenologist Scheler, in his *Wesen und Formen der Sympathie,* has shown, it is false and commits the fallacy in question. It is easy to render concepts general by rendering them empty; but if there is no other possible mode of generalization, then philosophy, and all science with it, is likewise empty of meaning. Berkeley's attack upon " *abstract* general ideas " is worthy of perpetual renewal however changed the form of this attack must be.

Heidegger's program in *Sein und Zeit* [2] is the interpretation of the initially abstract, empty, and supposedly indefinable concept of " being " in terms of " phenomena," i.e., immediate appearances. The traditional doctrine of the emptiness

and the " not further analyzable " or self-evident character
of this concept is criticized, together with the doctrine of
logical definition — by genus and specific difference — upon
which in part it rests. The effect of this conception of being
is shown to have been simply the neglect of precisely the
fundamental philosophical problem, the problem of ontology.
Heidegger then points out that because phenomena are immediate, it does not follow that they or their characters, even
as immediate, are obvious. On the contrary, there is a quality
of obscurity in immediacy itself. Consciously we see what we
are prepared to see, and we are prepared to see for the most
part only what our inherited traditions assert to be there.
Thus Heidegger well shows how modern philosophy has been
led to see phenomena only as " data," as mere indifferently
registered termini of awareness (the latter conceived as an
aimless transparency of pure givenness) , and to interpret being in an equally negative fashion — all because of the over-
strained ideal of *absolute* knowledge which reigns in modern
philosophy from Descartes and Spinoza down to Husserl,
the founder of phenomenology.

But how, then, shall a more positive conception of being
be attained?

A universal category (such as being) cannot be clarified
by distinguishing between phenomena which do and those
which do not stand to it as instances, since the latter class is
null; but only, if at all, by specifying phenomena which are
peculiarly adequate illustrations of its meaning. Being appears in all things, but perhaps not equally clearly or with
equal fullness in all of them.

The search must be, then, for some *especially privileged*
instances of being. The test of the privileged instance is that
the less privileged can be seen to involve the same principles,
but in a " deficient " manner — that is, one infers, with less
clearness or intensity. Heidegger is here employing a mode

of analysis the logical principles of which he does not perhaps fully explain. One of these principles is that no concept can be so ultimate or "simple" as not to have a structure, that indeed structure itself is ultimate and all-pervasive. From this it follows that being is not a simple something at which we can only gape and stare, but an organic unity of aspects. As thus structural, being can be *explicated* or described by taking in turn phenomena in which now this, now that, structural aspect is peculiarly striking, though every aspect is inalienably present in some measure in every phenomenon. Heidegger is here developing a conception of cosmic variables without considering the geometrical and quantitative aspects of this conception (cf. Peirce's categories).

The starting point of the inquiry is human consciousness (*Dasein*); for that is the mode of being possessed by the *question* concerning being, and critical questioning examines first into its own ontological conditions. What are the phenomenal characters which constitute the being of consciousness? There is first of all the character of self-significance, illustrated by the fact that consciousness questions itself concerning its own being. Consciousness is "being that matters to itself as such" (*Sein das um es selbst geht*). Not a reflecting mirror but an active *concern* is its character as concretely given. And in the second place, it is essentially "being-in-a-world." The sense of an environment is not something additional to consciousness, to be justified by epistemological arguments, but one of its structural characters, to be recognized in a description of what is immediately observed.

In order to show how the "world" itself is phenomenon, Heidegger examines the manner in which things "in" the world are phenomena, and finds the ordinary conception of things as merely registered in consciousness, and of the latter as an indifferent mirror or stream, to be a "deficient" form of a more basic relationship which he calls *Zuhandenheit* and which involves an active and practical functioning of consciousness. Things are there first of all as *usable* in certain ways, and only by a sort of pseudo-purification from such practical reference can the illusion arise of their being merely " there." So *things in* the world. But the world itself is not just another usable thing. It is rather the total context of means-use-end, to which all particular use of means refers. The world is that unity of purposive significance whereby means contribute to ulterior ends; also whereby signs indicate things signified. Meaning, the more abstract (i.e., indeterminate) , is here explained by purpose, the more concrete, determinate conception. A subtle instance of the same principle of concrete interpretation is that of space. As what are " near " and " far " really given? As Heidegger reminds us, the person on the other side of the street to whom one calls out is " nearer " in the phenomenological sense, i.e., as appearance, than the pavement upon which one stands or the glasses on one's nose. The near is that with which consciousness is intimately concerned. The structure of consciousness, as being par excellence, is summed up in the term *Sorge*. Being is " concern," *for* itself as such, *about* things, and *for* other selves (for the *Sorge* is essentially social) , all in the unity of a single function. This function, the *Sorge,* can be articulated only by calling upon the most concrete phenomena possible, such as those of affective sensitivity and emotional attitude — especially fear and anxiety, including the fear of death — or such as phenomena of conscience, and many another not usually thought of prime importance for ontology. The whole analysis culminates in a perspective of consciousness as *Sorge* from the standpoint of its *temporal* structure.

The Heideggerian is prepared for the charge of unscientific extravagance which must in many minds be elicited by any philosophy of this type. For a principal consequence of the character of existence as *Sorge* is that the *Sorge* tends inevitably through practical obsessions to become obscured from itself. This is the phenomenon of *Verfall*. The remedy is found, according to Heidegger, in the consideration of such experiences as conscience, the foreboding of death, and the consciousness of time. But why not also in the consideration of aesthetic enjoyment, which also transcends the narrowly practical? When justice is done to the aesthetic aspect of experience, certain consequences, neglected by Heidegger, appear. If the *whole being* of consciousness, which is being itself, is *Sorge,* that is to say concern, rather than mirror-like reflection, then even the most apparently indifferent data of consciousness, the external sensory qualities themselves, must express the structure of the *Sorge* in their very essence. The fundamental aspects of irreducible sociality, emotional tone, and practicality characterizing the *Sorge* must be discoverable *in* the qualities revealed to the several senses. Only the barest hints of such a conception can be found elsewhere in contemporary philosophical literature — although ordinary speech, with its " gay colors," " kindly voice," " powers of darkness," and an infinity of other kindred expressions, reeks with them — yet no device is apparent whereby the negation of such a view can be rendered consistent with the type of philosophical conclusions we have been considering. In a very general way Heidegger doubtless conceives the matter so, and he emphasizes explicitly the essential role of affective sensitivity and emotional tone (*Befindlichkeit und Stimmung*) as the conditions of our being aware of phenomena at all. And if, in fact, consciousness is not registrative awareness to which a factor of " concern " has been added, but a concern of which registration (*pures Vorhandensein*) is merely the emptiest or vaguest possible conception, then correspondingly colors and sounds are not mere indifferent primary or secondary qualities to which concernful content (affective tonalities, " tertiary qualities ") becomes attached or " associated," but must rather *consist* of such affective or aesthetic tonalities.

This is Croce's famous doctrine of the " identity " of intuition with expression. According to Croce, the entire content of sense intuitions is feeling.[3] The notion of dead insentient matter is accordingly an illusion without foundation in sense experience. But is the human subject aware, in sensation, only of his *own* feelings? Croce seems to think so. But this is the Berkeleyan idealism so painfully outgrown by recent philosophy. Heidegger's view of the object as merely a means (if that is what he intends) is as plainly inadequate. Neither Croce nor Heidegger seems to see the possibility, opened up by physics and biology, of seeing in our sensory contact with reality the blurred sympathetic intuition of the feelings of other individuals, in the first instance the cells of our bodies. Perhaps the reason for neglecting this possibility is with both thinkers the tradition of subjective or anthropomorphic idealism in which both were brought up, together with the notion, encouraged by that tradition, of science as tending to an abstract and materialistic view of nature. Both writers regard mathematics as the enemy of philosophical understanding of experience in its concreteness. Yet Leibniz and Peirce have shown how mathematics can aid us in understanding the cosmic variables by which alone the concrete can be made intelligible.

Croce often expresses himself in vigorous opposition to supernatural theology, to " transcendence." But since he believes in a really changing world and is an idealist who does not believe in dead matter, it is far from clear that he has any very good reason for opposing panpsychism or the new temporalistic theism, with which he seems little acquainted. And it is clear enough that, outside of Italy anyway, most of those who reject this theism are equally unfavorable toward Croce's idealism. Thus Croce is rather the last creative representative of Hegelian humanism — which seems only mildly influential or relevant today — than an important determinant of the immediate future.

Those who believe in scientific method, or rigorous logic, in philosophy, will find Heidegger even less to their taste than Croce and as little convincing as almost any theologian you please. The positivists find him a congenial foil for their antimetaphysical arguments. Heidegger does, however, see the philosophical importance of the time problem. The reasons for Heidegger's atheism (which is not, so far as I know, explicitly asserted in his works) are as obscure as those for Croce's. Obscure also, to me at least, is either philosopher's conception of the world order, so clearly independent of man as that order seems to be. Both thinkers are aloof from recent work in science and live in countries where theology is largely authoritarian supernaturalism.

Nicolai Hartmann's writings (which have their value apart from the questions I wish here to discuss) show all the signs of the author's being one of those who have adopted humanism by a process of eliminating alternatives — except the alternative offered by the new philosophy of nature. Thus Hartmann is given to refuting idealism by arguments that do not touch the case for panpsychism. In his famous *Ethics* (Vol. III), he gives an elaborate discussion of free will and determinism in which he presupposes an old-fashioned view of strict causality without discussion of the cosmological difficulties which the past fifty years have discovered to be concealed in this view.

Hartmann opposes the indeterministic view of causality by an argument which seems a neat and clear case of begging the question. He holds that a non-existent state of affairs may be logically possible, yet denies that it can be *really* possible. For it is not really possible unless the series of past conditions is given; but if the series is given, the state of affairs is bound to take place. In other words, in becoming really possible, it becomes inevitable. But this is the question at issue. Do "conditions" determine unambiguously what is to happen, or do they limit the possibilities to a certain narrow range of open alternatives? This is what Hartmann's argument is supposed to decide, yet the answer is presupposed by the argument.

The idea that there are no open alternatives within the causal series of nature is precisely the supernatural view of possibility which we have learned to reject along with other supernaturalisms. "Logical possibility" which has no function in reality is the nominalistic view which belongs with determinism but which cannot be assumed in an argument against indeterminists, who of course believe that all possibility is real.

The acceptance of nominalism has serious consequences for philosophic method. Since, according to nominalism, logical possibility is functionless, the only evidence we can have concerning what is really possible must, if nominalism is true, be drawn from study of the actual course of nature, that is, from induction. Hence philosophy and natural science have no methodological distinction — except that we may expect philosophic inductions to be somewhat amateurish. And we shall find that Hartmann's reasonings illustrate this corollary.

Another consequence is that there may be philosophical ideas which can be formulated with entire logical consistency, but whose truth is unknowable because to know it we should have to possess complete knowledge of the actual universe. Apparently for Hartmann the idea of God is of this character. We shall never know if such a being exists, he affirms. Our interest here lies in this, that while Hartmann admits there may, for all we know, be a God, he apparently does believe that some conceptions of God are to be definitely rejected. He argues, for instance, that the assumption of an all-determining cosmic purpose is incompatible with the belief in the significance of human purpose. If the cosmic teleology takes care of everything, what can it matter how much or how little human teleology there may be? In fact, how can there be any place at all for human choice if all choices are made in advance by the deity? [4] Teleology thus means, says Hartmann, strict determinism of the worst kind. This objection is, I hold, unanswerable if traditional theology is in question. But the new theology denies radically the conception of purpose, human or divine, as absolute predetermination. And how absurd it would be to hold that a generous world mind must by the perfection of its generosity be compelled to deny the gift of freedom to the creatures who, as Hartmann shows, would not in its absence enjoy real existence. Of course love and all real superiority imply the opposite of such jealous tyranny, and hence the beneficent cosmic purpose asserted by religion must possess the flexibility required for the benefit of the creatures.

Hartmann further argues against theism that the more ideal purposes have less strength than the lower or blinder impulses and forces, and hence that the most perfect mind would have the least power. This is the extreme opposite to the foregoing objection, according to which the divine power would be uncomfortably great. But apart from this, the question is whether the principle that ideality and power vary inversely is really established. Inductively there may be a rough truth in it. The ground plan of the world studied by physics is, in some sense, stronger and more fundamental than the biological organisms and their purposive tendencies. But what is the power expressed in the ground plan? Looked upon as inherent in electrons and atoms, it is surely a low form of existence which nevertheless outlasts animal organisms indefinitely and in this sense at least is stronger than they. But there is one organism which may well outlast even electrons and atoms, and that is the universe. Cosmic change requires a cosmic, ever abiding subject. The ground plan of nature attaches to this subject, and not merely to electrons and atoms. The universe organizes itself into the basic types of particles, and this organization is hence presupposed by the so-called lowest level forces. Man is built out of pre-existent atoms; but in that unified whole which is nature, atoms themselves have had a genesis and may see an end. Thus the cosmic mind is not simply a precarious supercomplex like man, though much more complicated and even less stable, but rather a whole which evolves its own parts and, in the eternal aspect of its purpose, antedates each and every one of them.

Moreover, it is not possible to conceive a perfect intelligence or goodness except as so intimately united to the cosmos which it knows or loves that it also exercises the supreme power in that cosmos. On the other side, try to make clear the notion of a power great enough to maintain the cosmic order, and only a perfect and all-loving mind will suit the requirements. Thus it is in every way false to infer the supreme weakness of supreme goodness from the fact that human goodness is weaker than non-human forces. For though these forces individually are subhuman, the general fact that they exist and persist and do not hopelessly conflict with and destroy each other can only be due to a force in every respect superhuman.

In any case, the human mind as a whole is vastly more powerful as well as far more ideal than any other one individual entity in the bodily community, cell or molecule. Hence there is the possibility of a world mind which would literally be the supreme being in the world body. The fact may also be mentioned that the weakness of human ideals lies in their abstractness. Goodness is love; but human benevolence is love in the full sense only for a few intimates, while toward most men, and other living beings, only the second best of action in accordance with general principles of common utility is possible. Men who seem especially benevolent in the second sense may be actually inferior in the first. Thus ethical progress may be loss as well as gain. In knowledge also the great intellects may be inferior in concrete perceptiveness. Not thus is God's ideality to be reached, but only by maximizing the concrete aspect to the point where the abstract aspect becomes unnecessary (except to the extent that the future as such is abstract and can be known only so, even by God). Maximal love in the concrete sense is nonsense except as supreme power. Nor has Hartmann or anyone else attempted to show how it could be otherwise conceived. But Hartmann is not interested in the logical possibilities, for according to him not these but only induction from reality can show us real possibilities.

Against the idea of a personal God, Hartmann argues inductively that the larger wholes which are inclusive of human personalities, such as the family, the people, the state, humanity, are less rather than more personal than the individuals which they include. Hence we should infer that the most inclusive whole is the least personal of all. But he entirely overlooks the fact that there is no reason whatever to suppose that the universe is related to humanity as humanity is related to the individual man. It is the question at issue whether this is so. The family, the state, humanity, these are not individuals in high degree, but more or less loosely integrated composites. Is the universe less integrated than humanity, as humanity is less integrated than you or I? There is nothing in Hartmann's reasoning to show it. The human stomach is certainly less of an individual than the cells composing it; does it follow that the whole human organism is even less unified? The contrary is the case. The lack of individuality in the stomach is not so much lack of unity as lack of isolation, of radical functional boundaries. The stomach has unity, but only as a superficially bounded portion of an organism endowed with functional solidarity as a whole. The view Hartmann has to refute is that humanity is related to the universe somewhat as the stomach is to the body, or at least in a manner more analogous to that than to the way in which a person is related to the nation or race.

The vaunted categorial analysis of Hartmann, in this instance at least, is merely a rather uncritical form of induction. The obvious wholes larger than a man and inclusive of him are relatively impersonal — ergo, still larger wholes are even more so. How unlucky for this form of reasoning if the universe does not happen to have interposed between itself and the human being intermediate individualities apparent to our present knowledge!

Hartmann pays no heed to the infinite range inherent in the psychic variables as such. He rightly points out that personality as we know it implies the contrast of the " I " and the " you," as well as that between higher and lower, mind and body, and thinks that the world-whole could not have any other outside it to which it could be related in this way. But, with Scheler, whose theism he has especially in mind, he presupposes that the " you " must be outside the " I "; whereas the new philosophy shows that the coherence of the world implies that nothing is absolutely outside anything else, and particularly that the inferior individual need not be outside the superior in order to preserve its distinctness and independence. The distinctness is guaranteed by the inferiority; the independence by the supreme " patience " or passivity or tolerant sensitivity characterizing the supreme person above all others. To suppose that parts cannot have individuality is to contradict scientific facts of physics and biology; and worse, it is to make nonsense of the very idea of part. The stomach would not have even the slight distinctness which it has if it did not itself consist of parts in a more genuine sense. Being is power. If a being is divided, its power is divided. We know there are divisions of the human body; yet a man is one. We know there are divisions of the world, for all divisions of anything are divisions of the world also; but this is obviously compatible with the existence of a world unity at least as much superior to the unity of a man as the latter is to that of his stomach.

Like other contemporary humanists, Hartmann is forceful in his opposition to nineteenth century idealism and monism, or medieval supernaturalism; but he is moving about in worlds unrealized so far as the new naturalism is concerned.

In spite of his attacks upon various forms of theism, Hartmann says we shall never know whether or not there is some form of God. Here we may leave him to the positivists, who will wish to know how the absolute unknowability of something can itself be known or given any meaning.

NOTES

1 This discussion of Heidegger is taken, with a few alterations, from my review in the *Philosophical Review*, XXXVIII, 286–90, by permission.

2 Martin Heidegger, *Sein und Zeit*, in *Husserl's Jahrbuch für Philosophie und phänomenologische Forschung*, Vol. VIII.

3 Cf. Croce's article on " Aesthetics " in the *Encyclopedia Britannica*, fourteenth edition.

4 Nicolai Hartmann, *Ethik* (Berlin and Leipzig, W. de Gruyter & Co., 1926) , pp. 184–86, 601–3, 611–14, 740 ff.; chaps. 21c, 69e, 85.

CONCLUSION

THE HISTORIC ROLE OF HUMANISM

HUMANISM seems to be a mode of thought incident to a certain stage in the development of science. It arises after the downfall of primitive animism, which is the mythological form of man's fellowship with nature. The early Greek philosophers still possessed this fellowship and sought to render it intelligible. But the rise of critical logic (Socrates, and the skeptic, Epicurean, and empiricist schools), together with the decay of classical civilization, brought disillusionment. Nature became problematic rather than companionable, tragic and even ugly rather than an inspiration and the source of all joys. Man was driven back upon himself, his own hopes and fears, with no means of escaping his solitariness and despair except through the hypostatization of abstractions, through mystical communion with a One beyond all evil and change and uncertainty (Plotinus and Augustine). Mythical animistic communion with nature had been fanciful; but it did give some heed to the concrete phenomena of nature. But in scholastic theology the lingering sparks of animistic natural fellowship found in Plato (the world-soul as the mind whose body is nature) and in Aristotle (the souls of the heavenly bodies) were extinguished and the foundations laid for the modern view of the world as a vast lifeless machine, quite distinct from its mechanic-Creator, and in its general traits essentially alien also to man (except as its law-abiding character made it congenial to his intelligence). The final step was to drop the conceptions of creation and divine governance as superfluous, leaving man and the higher animals as the only creators of values and the only proper objects of imaginative sympathy. This was practically pure humanism, for the animals were seldom taken seriously into account. Man was left with what Robinson Jeffers calls an " incestuous " love for his own kind, and, for the rest, with a sense of the unintelligibility of existence.

It is worth emphasizing the point just made, that the isolation of matter from mind and purpose which has led to humanism is due to medieval religion as much as to modern science. It was religion which divided with a mighty gulf God from the world, this world from the next, eternity from time, the soul from the body, the spiritual from the sensuous and material. Humanism is the final version of this exaggerated dualism or otherworldliness. Abstract spiritualism has its correlate in abstract materialism, abstract teleology in an equally abstract mechanism or determinism. The problem is whether spirit can again be naturalized and made concrete as the only self-moving thing (Plato) and hence the indwelling principle of all activity. For the twentieth century was reserved the precious discovery that primitive animistic fancy, abstract mysticism, and abstract mechanism do not exhaust the possibilities, and that science itself may lead in the end to a corrected, trustworthy version of the ancient fellowship, the original " natural piety." Science shows that fanciful though he was primitive man vastly underestimated the variety of nature, its stupendous contrasts. But this means, not that the savage's mistake lay in peopling the world with beings realizable only through imaginative sympathy, but rather that he erred through the too narrow range and the too egoistic and wishful character of his sympathies. On the one hand, he failed to envisage the possibility of sentient creatures whose complexity, compared to that of man, would be almost infinitesimal. Instead, he endowed even relatively low-grade animals with consciousness equal or superior to his own. On the other hand, however wishfully he ascribed immortality and other merits to the gods, he did not do justice to the distinction between all merely superior and the supreme or cosmic individual. Also, in regard to the lesser beings, he did not understand the necessity for patient induction from observed facts; as in regard to the maximal being he did not grasp the need for exact analysis in terms of philosophical categories. He lacked critical science and critical metaphysics. He thought the forefathers knew, rather than that he must and could find out for himself.

When critical science and philosophy came, they destroyed the primitive view much more rapidly than they were able to elaborate a substitute. Some of the chief obstacles to this elaboration are now beginning to yield to scientific advance. Perhaps the most vital contribution of science has been to show that of the hierarchy of natural individuals only a small range is distinctly apparent to the senses, so that beliefs based simply and directly upon experience cannot possibly give much idea of the hierarchy as a whole. That, for example, plants are less unitary, less organic, than the parts (cells) composing them, even Aristotle was not able to guess. Only very indirect, extremely elaborate inferences from careful observations of a quantitative nature, and under maximally varied conditions, can penetrate the veil of pseudo-unities which the senses present (all that, to fulfill their biological functions, they need to do). Indeed, even science tends still to deal with the vast majority of individuals, such as molecules or cells, not as individuals, each with its own internal quality, but as bare terms of relations and as indifferent units of statistical behavior.

The real point of the scientific rejection of final causes lies in the fact just mentioned, that knowledge of the inner and individual aspects of microscopic changes is not essential to the formulation of statistical laws. A given electron may be about to "jump" from one orbit to another; and if we could participate in its inner life, we might know this because an anticipation of the jump might be involved in its momentary feeling. But what does it matter when the effects we wish to control are independent of the actions of any one electron? Not merely *final* causes of individual action but *any and all* causes of individual action are, in large measure, irrelevant to science. Only in biology and psychology, where definite individuals are isolated and their behavior followed perhaps from genesis to destruction, do individuality and purposiveness of action become themes for science. In psychology even quality must be considered; for somehow the qualities of our sensory and emotional experience belong to the nervous system, "physical" though that be. Moreover, science may in the future extend individual and qualitative treatment downward as well as statistical treatment upward, and meanwhile the only justifiable ideal of knowledge is the co-extensiveness of the two aspects. The human meaning of this ideal is the transience of humanism as the denial of sympathetic participation with the lowest and the highest levels of reality. Nature is dead machinery only to spectators who perceive as such neither her simplest individual parts nor herself as the most complex of individual wholes, but are aware of the subhuman and the superhuman only with such distortion or abstractness as practical egoism, limited imaginative generosity, and inadequate instruments of observation make inevitable. The ultimate ideal of knowledge and of action remains this: to deal with the world as the body of a God of love, whose generosity of interest is equal to all contrasts, however gigantic, between mind and mind, and to whom all individuals are numbered, each with its own life history and each with its own qualitative — enjoying and suffering, more or less elaborately remembering and anticipating, sensing and spontaneously reacting — natures.

Nevertheless, the day of humanism is not necessarily over. Science has perhaps a long road to travel before the outlines of a companionable nature can be made definite enough to convince men generally. There may always be souls too cautious to look beyond the obvious relationships of man to his fellows for the essential values of life. And the "incestuous" love of man for his fellows alone must be expected so long as our blindness or inaction in the face of major economic maladjustments and cruelties makes all other questions than these practical human ones seem trivial. Those who cherish the love of nature cannot hope to win to this love the men and women who are denied secure approach to the simplest necessities of natural existence. The dispossessed of this world cannot be blamed if they seek for the lovable, the truly good, either in a world that is yet to be, the human society of the future, or in a world "outside" the world, a wholly supernatural heaven. Nor will the dispossessors, busy defending their position, have much regard for what is beyond the human scene. For the time being, perhaps always, it is by its fruits of practical charity and justice that the inspiring vision of God as the mind of nature will be chiefly judged. But this vision at least encourages us to seek our spiritual solace through the realistic eyes of science and our part in the imitation of the cosmic sympathy through participation with those individuals whom we can really know, who are, in the first instance, our human fellows. And here we know it is not primarily any technical or intellectual difficulty that makes us fall so far short as we do of our ideal — that, for instance, makes us limit our cooperative understanding along class lines — but rather the ethical difficulty of over-

coming primitive passions and the will to power, or of renouncing the comfort of not knowing the cost to others of our
own privileges.

That men should have thought themselves entitled to this
willful ignorance is partly due to the separation of virtue from
knowledge, which in turn is connected with the failure to see
that both virtue and knowledge are aspects of love, in such
fashion that all knowledge involves at least a dim consciousness of sympathy for its object, while all virtue that is not at
least the will to understanding is really vice. There is but
one good, with many aspects — *deus est caritas* — and there is
some spark, however dim, of that good in all things, and in all
relationships of all things. A civilization which will take that
as its working hypothesis will do what Europe for twenty
centuries professed but never, even in its theoretical activities,
practiced. Does it not deserve a trial? The new philosophy
is the theoretical program for the trial.

INDEX

INDEX